George Ayliffe Poole

**The Life and Times of Saint Cyprian**

George Ayliffe Poole

**The Life and Times of Saint Cyprian**

ISBN/EAN: 9783337336424

Printed in Europe, USA, Canada, Australia, Japan

Cover: Foto ©Lupo / pixelio.de

More available books at **www.hansebooks.com**

# THE LIFE AND TIMES

OF

# SAINT CYPRIAN

BY

GEO. AYLIFFE POOLE, M.A.,
SOMETIME RECTOR OF WINWICK, NORTHAMPTONSHIRE.

*WITH A PREFATORY NOTICE OF THE AUTHOR*

GRIFFITH FARRAN OKEDEN & WELSH
NEWBERY HOUSE
CHARING CROSS ROAD LONDON
AND AT SYDNEY

*The rights of Translation and of Reproduction are reserved.*

# INTRODUCTORY MEMOIR OF THE AUTHOR.

THE present volume brings before us a chapter of Church History which finds fitting place after the volume on Tertullian. That writer, designated by Dean Milman, "the father of Latin Christianity," belongs to the beginning of the second century. St Cyprian is martyred in the middle of the third. The Church has grown immensely in numbers and influence. Several persecutions have taken place; that in which Cyprian was taken from the earth, namely, the persecution of Decius, was the fiercest there had yet been. There was a yet fiercer to come, that of Dioclesian, but it was the last. His successor made Christianity the national religion of the Empire.

And the days of Cyprian mark this further development, that Christian literature had greatly multiplied, and we are able to see more clearly the nature of Christian doctrine and practice. There is no need to expatiate on this subject here, as the volume before us supplies the information. It only remains for the Editor to offer a word concerning the author of the book before us, and so to render a tribute of respect to a pious and learned Churchman of our own stirring time.

George Ayliffe Poole was born in 1809, and educated at Emmanuel College, Cambridge, taking his degree in 1831. The same year he was ordained by Law, Bishop of Bath and Wells. After serving Curacies at Twickenham, St John's, Edinburgh, and St Chad's, Shrewsbury, he was presented to the incumbency of St James', Leeds, and held it until 1843, when he became incumbent of Welford, in Northamptonshire. In 1876, the Bishop of Peterborough preferred him to the rectory of Winwick, in the same county, and this he held till his death in 1883.

He was not only a well-read man, but possessed a refined taste and great skill in matters of art. The rise of æstheticism as part of the great Church movement of 1832 was not entirely happy in its results in early days. Gothic architecture came into vogue in place of the miserable "classical" style of the eighteenth century, and the principles of Gothic architecture were but imperfectly understood. It would be invidious to name Churches of that era, poor and ugly for the most part, which were nevertheless highly bepraised as being Gothic. Even the early works of Sir G. G. Scott were anything but happy, for Gothic architecture was a lost art which had to be slowly relearned. Mr G. A. Poole was much in advance of his time, and it has been said, and not untruly, that next to J. H. Parker and M. H. Bloxam, the revival of good Gothic architecture owes most to him. He was an exquisite painter in water colour, and when he would go about in his neighbourhood, as he loved to do, lecturing on the village churches, and endeavouring to kindle enthusiasm among his neighbours towards the history of their parishes, and the beautiful things which they possessed in their churches, it was always a delight to crowd round his drawings. He was the author of a History of England, which had a very large sale for a while, though it was almost the least satisfactory of his works. Pamphlets on "The Present State of Parties in the Church of England," and "The Admission of Lay Members to the Synods of the Church of Scotland," indicate his theological position—namely, that of a decided High Churchman of the earlier school, strongly opposed to Romanism. A story, 'Sir Raoul de Broch," was also his. But his best known works were "Churches, their Structure and Arrangement," "History and Architecture of Lincoln Cathedral," and a "Diocesan History of Peterborough," in the series of Diocesan Histories now publishing by S. P. C. K.

The book before us was first published in 1840, whilst he was incumbent of St James', Leeds, and is included in the present series, not only for its inherent value, which is very great, historically and theologically, but also because the name of one who did so much and such good work for his mother Church, and who was so revered and loved in his day, ought not to be left out of a series which aims at producing some of the best books in English theology.

W. B.

To the

MOST REVEREND FATHER IN GOD,

# WILLIAM,

LORD ARCHBISHOP OF CANTERBURY,
PRIMATE OF ALL ENGLAND AND METROPOLITAN,

THIS HISTORY
OF THE LIFE AND TIMES OF

# CYPRIAN,

ARCHBISHOP OF CARTHAGE, SAINT AND MARTYR,

IS

IN THESE DAYS OF UNGODLINESS AND INFIDELITY

AND OF

BITTER HOSTILITY AGAINST THE CHURCH,

WITH HIS GRACE'S PERMISSION,

MOST DUTIFULLY AND HUMBLY INSCRIBED.

MDCCCXL.

## AUTHOR'S PREFACE.

IF this volume at all answers the Author's design, there is one important consideration which the reader ought to carry with him during its perusal.

The work was undertaken with a desire to recommend that tone of religion, calm, reverential, implicit, self-sacrificing, and objective, which is well and conveniently called "CATHOLIC," to distinguish it from the bustling, irreverent, neological, self-seeking, and subjective character of the fashionable religion of the present day; and which was happily exemplified in St Cyprian, and generally, though indeed with glaring, and for our present purpose valuable exceptions, in the Church over which he presided.

Perhaps, too, something of the constitution and polity of the Church, as exemplified in the life and times of St Cyprian, and of the form and order of its several assemblies and offices, may be profitably contrasted with the impatience of rule and discipline, and the undervaluing of whatever is positive and ritual, which is characteristic of the loudest and most obtrusive party of religionists in the present day.

Now the spirit and form of the Anglican Church is eminently CATHOLIC, in the sense before mentioned. But we may contract a careless habit of judging our Church by its present members; and forgetting that she everywhere protests against their laxity and irreverence, we may lay that blame on the sorrowing mother, which ought to fall on the undutiful children. Or again, while we are studying the history of a particular Church and age, for the sake of the "*Catholic*" spirit which it embodies, we may be in danger of forgetting, that that spirit may animate very different forms: and so we may hastily condemn our own Church, because we, in our folly and pride, deem the various arrangements which she has made, in wisdom and in love, inconsistent with a primitive character, because they are not identical with a particular primitive form. This is a grievous error into which those are likely to fall, who are seeking to catholicise the present generation of the sons of the Church by a reference to the ecclesiastical records of any former age. But let us all remember (and the Author of this volume feels that the warning is necessary for himself, which he presses on others), that if, in pretence of a Catholic spirit, we touch but the hem of the garment of our own holy brother except with the deepest reverence and piety, we most unequivocally give the lie to our pretensions. There is no one thing which our Church can require, so long as she hath the grace of God with her, so wrong, so opposed to all Catholic form and spirit, as the unfilial judgment, or the imperfect obedience, of any of her sons.

LEEDS, *June* 20, 1840.

# CONTENTS.

### CHAPTER I.

Scantiness of strictly Personal Notices of Cyprian—Pontius his Panegyrist.—Questions of the Place of Cyprian's Birth,—Of his Age,—And of his Marriage.—His Profession and Condition as a Heathen—His Acquaintance with Cæcilius.—His Conversion.—His Use of the Scriptures.—His Baptism.—His own Account of the Spiritual Change effected in him at Baptism.—He adopts the name of Cæcilius . . . 17

### CHAPTER II.

St Cyprian's Writings while a Layman.—His Epistle to Donatus, on the Grace of God.—His Treatise on the Vanity of Idols.—The Death of Cæcilius;—Who appoints Cyprian the Guardian of his Family.—St Cyprian a Deacon.—Dionysius of Alexandria.—St Cyprian a Presbyter.—His Three Books of Testimonies against the Jews . . . . . . 31

### CHAPTER III.

Cyprian chosen Bishop.—His Attempt to Escape.—The part of the People in his Election.—The Constitution of the Church in the Cyprianic Age.—The State of Morals and of Discipline in Cyprian's Diocese, and the Acts and Writings which arose out of the Condition of the Church.—The Epistles of Cyprian.—The Case of Geminius Victor :—Commemoration of the Dead :—The Primitive Practice a Witness against Romish Errors.—The Case of the Player :—The State of the Stage in Cyprian's time.—The Case of the Rebellious Deacon.—The Case of the συνεισακτοί.—" Ancient Christianity " . 42

## CHAPTER IV.

Revolutions in the Roman State.—Their influence on the condition of the Church.—Edicts of Decius.—The Persecution commences.—Some retire from Carthage;—Among whom St Cyprian himself.—Cyprian's Reasons for retiring.—His care of the Church while absent.—His Letter to the Confessors.—The Insinuations of the Roman Clergy against Cyprian: and Cyprian's Answer to their Epistle.—The Progress of the Persecution.—The Sufferings of Mappalicus, and other Confessors and Martyrs . . . . . . 66

## CHAPTER V.

The Number of Apostates in the Decian Persecution.—The *Sacrificati*, *Thurificati*, and *Libellatici*.—The Discipline of the Lapsed.—Its Rigour,—And its occasional Relaxation.—The Privilege of the Martyrs:—Abused in this instance.—The Clergy chiefly in fault.—Cyprian's own Determination of the case of the Lapsed . . . . . . 84

## CHAPTER VI.

Cyprian's Return prevented by a Schism in his Church.—The Origin of the Schism.—Novatus:—His Character:—His Crimes.—He is cited to appear before Cyprian.—He escapes under cover of the Decian Persecution.—He makes a Party, and forsakes the Church.—He obtains the Ordination of Felicissimus:—It is questioned by whom.—The five Presbyters companions of Novatus in Schism.—Cyprian appoints Deputies to put his Regulations in force.—The Place which Voluntary Seceders hold, in respect of the Church.—Novatus goes to Rome.—Novatian:—His Character.—His secret Cabals:—Fostered by Novatus.—Election of Cornelius to the See of Rome.—His Character.—Novatian's Schismatical Ordination.—His Practices at Home and Abroad.—The Spread of of his Party.—Novatus returns to Carthage . . . 98

## CHAPTER VII.

Proceedings touching the Election of Cornelius, and the Schismatical Ordination of Novatian, at Carthage;—at Hadrumettium.—The Episcopate of Cornelius finally recognised.—Felicissimus and the five Presbyters Excommunicated.—St Cyprian's Letters to the Schismatical Confessors.—His Treatise *De Unitate Ecclesiæ.*—Letter of Dionysius of Alexandria to Novatian. A Synod at Carthage, and in Rome.—The return of the Schismatical Confessors.—Letters of Cornelius, the Confessors, and Cyprian.—Reflections on the Novatian Schism . . 118

## CHAPTER VIII.

A Review of St Cyprian's Tract *De Unitate Ecclesiæ* . 134

## CHAPTER IX.

A Schism at Carthage.—Its origin.—The Surreptitious Ordination of Fortunatus.—The Schismatics apply to Cornelius for his support:—They are at first repelled, but afterwards too favourably heard.—St Cyprian expostulates with Cornelius. —The extinction of Fortunatus's Party.—Maximus ordained by the Novatians in Carthage.—His Faction contemptible . 144

## CHAPTER X.

Persecution renewed on occasion of the Plague.—Cyprian's apologetic Letter to Demetrian.—His Epistle to the Thybaritani.— The Penitent Lapsed admitted to Communion, in anticipation of Persecution.—The Exhortation to Martyrdom.—St Cyprian's last Letter to St Cornelius.—Death of Cornelius.—Of Lucius. —How far Persecution a Test of Truth . . . 151

## CHAPTER XI.

The Plague rages at Carthage.—Cyprian's Tract *De Mortalitate.* —The Expectation of the Last Day in the Early Church:— Gibbon's use of it.—Cyprian's Opinion on the Time, Person, and Character of Antichrist . . . . . 178

## CHAPTER XII.

Weakness of the Roman Empire.—Numidian Christians carried captive by Barbarians.—Collections made in Carthage to redeem them.—Cyprian's Epistle to Cæcilius on the Mixed Cup.—His Doctrine applied to Half Communion, and other Errors in the present day . . . . . 193

## CHAPTER XIII.

Revolutions in the Roman Empire.—Questions of Fidus touching a Lapsed Bishop, and the Case of Infant Baptism.—The Case of Fortunianus:—Of Basilides and Martialis:—Of Marcianus of Arles.—The Insolence of Pupianus . . . . 213

## CHAPTER XIV.

The Question of the Baptism of Heretics, and the Controversy arising out of it.—Its origin in Asia Minor:—It is discussed in a Synod at Carthage.—Cyprian's Letter to the Bishops of Numidia.—The Character of Several Objections against his Rule.—A Synod of Seventy-two Bishops assembled at Carthage to determine the Question.—Cyprian's Account to Stephen of the Proceedings of the Synod.—Cyprian's Letter to Jubaianus 228

## CHAPTER XV.

Stephen, Bishop of Rome, interferes in the Controversy about the Baptism of Heretics.—Cyprian's Epistle to Pompeius.—The last Council assembled at Carthage to determine the Question; —St Cyprian's opening Address;—and several of the more remarkable Suffrages.—The unanimity of Council against the judgment of Stephen, and the Custom of Rome.—Irenæus and Victor.—Dionysius and Stephen . . . . 248

## CHAPTER XVI.

A General View of the Principles involved in the Controversy concerning the Baptism of Heretics . . . . 261

## CHAPTER XVII.

Valerian instigated by Macrianus to persecute the Church.—Death of Stephen:—and Election of Sixtus.—St Cyprian summoned before the Proconsul:—His Confession:—His Banishment:—His Vision.—Dionysius of Alexandria also Banished.—Cyprian recalled to Carthage by Galerius Maximus.—He retires for a short time when summoned to Utica.—He returns to Carthage, and is brought before the Proconsul.—His Examination,—Sentence,—and Death . . . . . 273

# The Life and Times of St Cyprian.

## CHAPTER I.

Scantiness of strictly Personal Notices of Cyprian.—Pontius his Panegyrist.—Questions of the Place of Cyprian's Birth,—Of his Age,—And of his Marriage.—His Profession and Condition as a Heathen.—His Acquaintance with Cæcilius.—His Conversion.—His use of the Scriptures.—His Baptism.—His own account of the Spiritual Change effected in him at Baptism.—He adopts the Name of Cæcilius.

THE personal history, even of great men, derives its charm not from the splendour and importance of those actions by which they were ennobled, but from the variety of incidents, in which the distinctive peculiarities of their character were displayed. The unity and expression of the whole, which are the sources of our gratification, result not from the greatness of the parts, but from their due proportion and subordination, and from a pervading tone, harmonising their very minuteness and variety: as the Mosaic must be wrought into an harmonious whole out of pieces infinitely small and diversified, or it will present, not a finished and striking tablet, but a cold and disjointed patchwork. Even in the lives of heroes and of statesmen, the reader is interested not only by the preparations for conflict, the bustle of the encounter, and the elation of success; but also, and perhaps still more intensely, by the lighter incidents: the child's question or the boy's exploit, a hasty expression of hope or disappointment or impatience, a liking or an antipathy, in short anything and everything which may serve to embody a marked trait of personal character, in the record of a trifling incident.

The charm, however, of these minute records, is to be referred to the more splendid incidents, and to the greatness of the whole subject. We are delighted to see one who is elevated to a dim and mysterious height above us, brought down to our level; identified with the man with whom his neighbours conversed, whom his associates admired, and whom his family loved. Hence it is impossible to throw the appropriate charm of biography over the history of a great man, if we possess but few characteristic anecdotes of his private life, and but few unstudied expressions of his personal feeling. With all our effort to keep the same person always in view, and always the centre of interest, we are still writing *History*, not *Biography;* and neither splendour of character nor importance of incident can supply the requisite material. They may elevate the pages in which they are recorded to the more exalted order of ethics or of history, and impart something of the interest appropriate to their new station; but they cannot invest them with the peculiar charm of the story of a life in its varied sameness, in its blended diversity of thoughts, of feeling, and of incident.

It is not inconceivable, that the very greatness of the part which a man has played, may have deprived us of these most valuable materials of his biography. While we are dazzled with splendid actions, we do not discern traits of character; and while we are proclaiming the deeds of high emprize which make the hero, we omit those little incidents which mark the man. Thus the means of gratifying it, are often in the inverse proportion of the interest with which we look for indications of the complexion of a mind, which has wrought revolutions in opinions or in empires.

These remarks preceding a life of St Cyprian are apologetic: for though he was the centre of most important ecclesiastical movements in his own day, and though scarce any single person has ever contributed more to give a colour to distant ages, so that we cannot repress a curiosity to know more of his individual mind and feelings, we are remarkably destitute of information on these points. His only professed biographer affords us almost no assistance; and while the public records of his Episcopate are a great part of the history of the Western Church in his day, the sources from which these are derived, though chiefly his own Epistles, are equally deficient in strictly personal notices. An account, therefore, of St Cyprian's life and times, stands in that middle ground between biography and history, which it is difficult to invest with the appropriate interest of either.

We have no records, and but very scanty intimations, of the incidents in the life of THASCIUS CYPRIAN before his conversion to Christianity, though it was doubtless varied by the political events of his day, and coloured with the peculiar energy of his character. Cyprian was not, indeed, without a contemporary biographer. Pontius, his Deacon, his companion in many of his labours and troubles, and, what is more, his affectionate friend and ardent admirer, sought consolation at the death of Cyprian in the pious task of enumerating his actions and recording his virtues. But Pontius was either ignorant of the specific charm of biography, or so conscious of the difficulties before mentioned in the particular case of St Cyprian, that he has not adventured to overcome them. We cannot help regretting, that one who had so full an opportunity of acquainting himself with Cyprian's former life and condition, did not think these subjects worthy of his attention. There is certainly more of the piety than of the judgment of a Christian biographer, in the resolution to commence the account of an illustrious convert with his spiritual birth; as if it was not interesting and profitable to know what a man was before his conversion, as well as what he then became: for surely an acquaintance with his former life and disposition is a necessary element in a comprehensive view even of his Christian character; and must form a part of our estimate of its importance, as illustrative of the grace of God. The world has recorded this judgment in its appreciation of the Confessions of St Augustine.

The expression of Pontius is worthy of remark, as giving at the very commencement of his work a clue to its real character. "Whence,"[1] says he, "shall I commence *his panegyric*, but from the dawn of his faith, and from his heavenly birth?" And in perfect harmony with this exordium, we find Pontius far more earnest in celebrating the praises, than laborious in relating the actions, of Cyprian: in eulogising, than in illustrating, his character. He professes, that not only his own eloquence, but even eloquence itself,[2] must fail to paint the virtues of his martyred Bishop in their true colours: he represents the seed-time, the harvest, the budding, and the pressing of the grape, the planting of the tree, and the ripening of the fruit,[3] as all crowded into the same season, in this illustrious convert: he prefers him far before Cornelius, who was baptised by Philip; and the very oppositions which Cyprian met at his entering on the Episcopate, he represents as providentially occurring, that they might reflect the greater honour on the holy Bishop by his conquest of them.[4]

Meanwhile we are left to collect as we can from other sources, all the most interesting particulars concerning Cyprian's former life. Where was he born, and when? What was

---

[1] Unde igitur incipiam? Unde exordium *bonorum ejus* aggrediar, nisi a principio fidei et nativitate cœlesti.

[2] St Augustine expresses the same thing by another strange conceit. Cujus reverendi Episcopi et venerandi Martyris laudibus nulla lingua sufficeret, nec si se ipse laudaret. Sermo cccxiii. vol. viii. p. 1258. Ed. Bassani, 1807.

[3] It is curious to find the modesty of Cyprian, and the admiration of Pontius, expressed under the same image. Exilis ingenii, says Cyprian, (Ep. i. p. 1.) angusta mediocritas tenues admodum fruges parit, nullis ad copiam fœcundi cespitis culminibus ingravescit.

[4] Quidam illi restiterunt, etiam ut vinceret. Pontius v.

his lineage and condition? Was he a married or a single man? And at what age did he embrace the faith of Christ? These are questions which Pontius will not answer for us, and some of which are still subjects of controversy: not of curious inquiry only, but actually of controversy, such are the interest and importance which they derive from Cyprian's character and position.

Where[1] Cyprian was born we have no means of discovering, and the time of his birth is equally uncertain.[2] A general notion seems to prevail, that he was already an old man before his conversion; but all the indirect evidence that I can find seems to lead to a different conclusion. His voluntary discipline while a Catechumen, which excited the admiration of Pontius, was more appropriate to one in the vigour of life than to an old man,[3] and all his actions and writings are replete with the energy of a mature manhood, not yet deprived of the fire of youth.

Such a life as induced some to invent the evidences of his noble descent is more honourable to Cyprian, than the most ancient and dignified pedigree could have been: yet there is a real elevation in rank and ancestral nobility, which harmonises well with whatever is great and good; it is only, therefore, for want of sufficient evidence, that I reject the notion of Baronius, founded on a passage of Gregory Nazianzen, that Cyprian was of noble birth, and of senatorial rank. Of the *personal* consideration, however, of Cyprian in the profession of oratory we have clearer evidence. Lactantius,

[1] Perhaps, however, we may obscurely collect, that he was not born at Carthage, the scene of his many labours, from this slight negative evidence. Speaking, during his temporary retreat, of his desire to revisit Carthage, he asks, "Where could my time be spent, either more delightfully or more profitably, than where it was the will of God that I should first believe, and continue to grow in the faith?" Ep. xxxvi. 49. It may be supposed, that if Carthage had been his birth-place, he would have added, Where can I better dwell? Where if I must suffer, can I better resign my soul to God, than where I first received it at his hands?

[2] Quando natus sit ignoramus. *August. Sermo.* cccx.

[3] Inter fidei suæ prima rudimenta, nihil aliud credidit Deo dignum, quam ut *continentiam* tueretur.

who prefers him above all those who had employed a cultivated mind in the defence of Christianity,[1] tells us of the distinction which he had gained as a master of Rhetoric: and Cyprian himself seems to refer to his own personal condition before his baptism, when he describes, in his Epistle to Donatus, the pomp of place, and the crowd of clients, by which a distinguished public character is surrounded. St Augustine mentions his wealth: and here again, his own account seems to infer as much; for all those allurements of pleasure and of sin which he represents as opposing the greatest obstacles to the reception of Christianity, and which he mentions in such a manner as scarce to admit a doubt that he was speaking from his own experience, are such as the rich only are acquainted with. Ease and luxury; vestments of gold and purple; the pomp and the projects, the passions and the pursuits, of the great and wealthy, had all combined to enslave the ardent mind of Cyprian, and to keep him still in the Egyptian bondage of heathenism and vice. Nor yet at the time that he wrote his Epistle to Donatus on occasion of their baptism, had he wholly ceased to relish the advantages of an honourable wealth. His rural retreat, which he evidently describes as it was then before his eyes, and filling his mind with images of beauty, was not unworthy of a Cicero or a Pliny; nor the use which he made of it of a Christian philosopher. "The season and the place," says he, "both alike invite us to serious conversation; the cool breezes that fan the face of the earth, gemmed with flowers, and this lovely arbour, excluding every obtrusive step and curious gaze, but admitting the free light and the whispering breeze through the hanging branches of the vine, invite us to the communion of Christian souls; and while we despise the pleasures of sense as an end, lead us gracefully and naturally to something higher."[2]

But the most honourable memorial of Cyprian's wealth, is the sale of his estates for the benefit of the poor, and the supply of their penury, out of his private fortune. To the Christian duty of almsgiving, it seems more than probable

---

[1] Lactantius, lib. v. p. 237. Ed. Cantab. 1685.   [2] See Ep. i. p. 1.

that he soon after sacrificed that rural retreat in which we have seen him delighting: for Pontius speaks of his "gardens," which were providentially restored to him in his last sufferings, though he had sold them long before for charitable uses. To these gardens he retired after his baptism, and from them he went to meet his martyrdom.

Opposite parties find an object in giving Cyprian a wife.[1] As the polemical importance of the question, whether he was married or no, is quite distinct from its biographical interest; and as there is no direct evidence of the fact, while all the presumptive evidence is against it; we may be excused in concluding, that Cyprian had no wife at the time of his conversion, and probably had never been married.

Such then, so far as we can collect, was Thascius Cyprian. His mind was matured both by years and study, but yet unchilled with the frosts of age. He had a soul ready to sacrifice wealth, interest, and ease to religion, and a sense of duty; and family he had none. He was of good repute for his successful practice of an honourable and lucrative profession; and he was rewarded by the possession of the fruits of his labour and reputation. The highest powers, unblessed from above, are unworthy of the office, for which Cyprian was designed; and by God's grace a more moderate share of talents and acquirements may adorn the highest station; but God does condescend to employ the talents of His creatures; and He had marked out Cyprian for His work, and by the ruling of His providence He had formed his mind, his character, and his circumstances accordingly.

It was surely providential, that Cyprian contracted an

---

[1] Milner goes yet farther, and gives his imaginary wife an imaginary character, in order to enhance as it seems to him the character of Cyprian. "In vain," says the *Historian*, (?) "his wife opposed his Christian spirit of liberality." In truth, the liberality of Cyprian would have been scarcely just, and altogether imprudent, if he had to provide for others, as well as himself. In the passage from the life of Cyprian by Pontius which has given rise to these misstatements, the biographer is speaking not of Cyprian and his wife, but of Job and his wife. The passage is given at page 25 of this volume.

intimacy, which soon ripened into no common affection, with Cæcilius, an aged Presbyter[1] of the Church of Carthage. This friendship with a Christian Priest was the means of Cyprian's conversion, which took place, as he himself informs us, at Carthage, and, as it seems most probable, very early in the year of grace 246. We may perhaps collect from St Jerome, that the book of Jonah was especially instrumental to his conversion. "Let us," says St Jerome, in his commentary on the third chapter of Jonah, "set before us the example of St Cyprian, who was before an advocate of idolatry, and had arrived at so great reputation as an orator, as to teach rhetoric in Carthage: but having heard this preaching of Jonah, was converted, and repented; and attained to such a height of virtue, as to preach Christ publicly, and to submit his neck to the sword for His sake."

Nor is this either the only or the strongest intimation that Cyprian, before his ordination, and even before his baptism, was freely permitted to study the holy Scriptures. Those who know how painfully the concession of the Scriptures to the laity in some countries has been extorted from the Church of Rome, and who have not escaped the vulgar error, that Rome really follows antiquity as she pretends, may wonder to find, that in Cyprian's days the Bible was not a sealed book even to Catechumens. We of the Anglican Church, following the principles of Catholic antiquity, encourage that godly custom, and use the practice of the ancient Church, not merely as an argument, but as an argument *a fortiori*. If the laity and new converts in Cyprian's time were encouraged in this custom, *much more* should they be now. For though it is impossible that the Church could then have provided so ample commentaries upon the Scriptures; and though Neophytes, fresh from the ranks of heathenism, could scarce be so well prepared for their interpretation, as all in Christian countries ought to be; and though, therefore, if it were true now to say with Rome, that more evil than good would arise from the reading of the Scriptures by the

---

[1] Cæcilius et ætate tunc, et honore Presbyter. PONTIUS.

laity,[1] it were much more true to have said so in the days of Cyprian: yet the use of the sacred volume was then fully indulged to the laity, and even to Catechumens. When only a Presbyter, we shall find Cyprian recommending to Quirinus, whom he calls his son, and who was probably therefore, and indeed almost certainly, a layman, a careful study of holy writ: and he himself, while only a Catechumen, read the Scriptures with constant and anxious attention; and bringing to bear upon them the strength and the resources of a powerful and cultivated mind, he profited greatly by their perusal; nor need we adopt the assertion of Pontius, at least in its literal sense, that the first approach of the divine light left in him no darkness at all, to shew that he was early prepared, as well in the knowledge of sacred things, as in the character of a Christian, for all the offices of the sacred Ministry. Even his earliest works, some of which were perhaps written while he was yet a layman, attest the progress which he had made in the true use of the Scriptures; and we have a beautiful picture of the practical account to which he turned these divine lessons, from the pencil of his affectionate biographer. "When he read of any who had received commendation from God, he would recommend the inquiry, Wherefore was it that God was well pleased with them? If Job, glorious in the testimony of God, was declared to be a true worshipper of God, and one to whom none other upon earth might be compared, he would exhort us to do that which Job also did;

---

[1] The Romanist adduces the unnumbered heresies which have arisen from the rash interpretation of the Scriptures by individuals: but let us only remember the fact, that almost every heresy has originated not from the laity, but from the clergy; and if we dared act upon *such* an indication of expediency, we may retort upon them their reasoning, and say, that if from the laity, then much more from the clergy, should the holy Scriptures be taken. But man is not wiser than God: and those Scriptures which were originally written as much to and for the laity as the clergy; some of which were actually addressed to individuals not clerical but lay, were surely adapted to the laity, and are not to be taken from them without impiety; as they cannot be without absurdity, except by those who would uphold a system contradicted by those inspired writings.

that while we follow the example of Job, we may receive the like testimony from God. Making light of the necessary expenses of his household, Job advanced to so great elevation of virtue, that he felt not the sacrifice which he made of temporal wealth, in the cause of piety. He was unbroken by penury and by grief: the persuasions of his wife could not move him; and he bore the afflictions of his own body unshaken. His manly virtue stood unmoved in its own place; and the deep root of his devotion remained firmly fixed. To no temptation of the devil did he yield, nor did he cease to thank God, in faith and gratitude, even in the midst of all his misfortunes. His house was ever open to the stranger. No widow was sent away unprovided; no blind man was undirected or unattended by him. He was a staff to the lame, and his hand was the protection of the poor and helpless. And so ought we to do, Cyprian was accustomed to say, if we would please God. And so would he run through all the records of the saints of old; and while he studied to imitate the best, he himself became worthy of imitation."

Cyprian has himself told us, in his Epistle to Donatus, some of the struggles which it cost him to leave the world, and to embrace the life of a Christian, cut off, as it then was, by external circumstances, from the secular employments and honours of the state, and from the pomp and revelries of a too luxurious wealth. We shall not be surprised to find, that some of the temptations which assailed the young convert were directed against his pride of reason. Like Nicodemus, he could not receive the mystery of a spiritual regeneration. "While," says he, "I was lying in darkness and in the shadow of death, and while I was tossed uncertain upon the waves of this tempestuous world, ignorant of what was my real life, and an alien from truth and light, I thought the method of salvation which was proposed to me strange and impossible. I could not believe that man should be born again; and being animated with a new life, put off, in the laver of regeneration, what he had before been; and though remaining the same in his whole natural and animal frame, become changed in his mind and affections." The favour of God, however, which had directed Cyprian to the good Cæcilius, did not desert him in these difficulties; and coming at last with faith and repentance to the Sacrament of Baptism, Cyprian received that grace of regeneration, at which his natural reason had stumbled.

All the regulations respecting the administering of Baptism in the Primitive Church, tended to invest that Sacrament with the highest reverence and interest; and none more so, perhaps, than the setting apart certain days, on which alone, except in extreme cases of danger, or other exigencies, it was administered. The custom of different Churches slightly varied in this matter, though the same spirit animated all. Easter, Pentecost, and the Epiphany, and in some places the festivals of saints, and the anniversary of the dedication of churches, were the times appointed for Baptism: and thus a double advantage was gained; the solemnity of the act and the reverence of the season reflected on each other associations of deeper and more intense devotion; the number of the baptised on each occasion was increased, in proportion to the infrequency of the ceremonial.[1] There must have been something singularly imposing in the crowd of Catechumens, distinguished not only by their white garments, but by the joyful alacrity, with which they hastened to the confession of their faith before the whole Church, and to the rite in which they were enrolled among the ranks, and assumed the duties and received the privileges of the Church militant in earth.

With respect to the custom of the African Church, Tertullian[2] mentions Easter and Pentecost only as the seasons of Baptism. But it is plain that such regulations must give place to circumstances, and as a Church increased greatly in numbers, the seasons of Baptism would be multiplied; every advantage being still retained, which was originally consulted

---

[1] The number of candidates for Baptism, under these regulations, was so great, that Deacons were sometimes permitted to administer that Sacrament at Easter, though at other times it was no part of their office; and we hear of three thousand persons baptised at Constantinople, on one of the greater Festivals.

[2] De Baptismo, xix. tom. i. p. 392. Opera, *Ed. Parisiis*, 1616.

in the restriction to one or a few of the greater festivals: and we learn from the history of the Vandalic persecution by Victor of Utica,[1] that the Epiphany, on which day it is supposed Christ was Himself baptised, was afterwards added to the seasons of Baptism by the African Churches.

Cyprian was probably baptised at Easter, in the year of grace 246. His own words will best describe the spiritual benefit which he received on this occasion: and as they are the words of one who was yet too young a Christian to innovate and invent; and as they appeal to the experience of his friend Donatus also, we may be sure that they express what was then taught and experienced to be the effects of the Sacrament of Baptism. "So entirely was I immersed in the deadly atmosphere of my former life, so enveloped in the habits and commission of sin, that I despaired of ever freeing myself, and began to look upon these things, and to love them, as a part of myself. But when the sulliage of my past iniquities was washed away by the waters of Baptism, the pure and serene light from above infused itself into my whole spirit: when my second birth of the Spirit had formed in me a new man, all at once what had been doubtful before, became certain; what had been shut, was opened; into the darkness light shined; that was easy, which before was difficult, and that only difficult, which before was impossible: and now I knew, that that was earthly and mortal, which had formerly included me in the bondage of sin; but that the Holy Spirit of God had animated me with a new and better nature."[2]

Thus does St Cyprian speak of the grace of Baptism, as a matter of his individual experience. In other parts of his works he treats of Baptism dogmatically; and says, again and again, that therein we receive the Spirit, have our sins remitted, and are born again. And nothing can more assuredly manifest the consent of the Church in this doctrine, than the way in which he makes these assertions. He does not go about *to prove them:* no, this was unnecessary, since they were confessed by all; nor were they in his day, nor till 1200 years

---

[1] Quoted from Bingham, Orig. Ecc. XI. vi. 7.   [2] Epist. i. p. 2.

after, a subject of controversy; but he assumes them as premises mutually agreed upon, from which to deduce the catholic doctrine on another subject.[1] In a word, in Cyprian's days, and long after, the doctrine of Baptismal regeneration was no more questioned in the Church, than the first axioms in Geometry are questioned in our Schools. If some pretended demonstration should involve the denial of the proposition that the whole is greater than a part, it would be rejected with contempt, without farther refutation: and so, if some new doctrine or custom should be clearly inconsistent with the doctrine of baptismal regeneration, that alone, in the eyes of the primitive Christians, would have branded it as false and heretical.

It was usual for the new convert to receive another name at Baptism: a custom fairly derived from the authority of our Saviour Himself, in giving new names to some of His earliest disciples; and one, too, which well enough harmonised with he solemn occasion of that new birth, wherein we put off he old man, and put on the new man, with all his attendant duties and privileges. And there was something of religion in the assuming a name which had been borne by some eminent saint or apostle; not, as the Council of Nice says, that there is any merit or fortune in the name itself, but that it may serve as a stimulus to emulate the character of him from whom it was derived. Cyprian, actuated by these motives, and by affection for his master in Christianity, took the name Cæcilius, from the venerable Presbyter who had first been his companion and friend, and afterwards his spiritual father. Henceforth then we speak not of Thascius, but of Cæcilius Cyprian, except when we find the Saint before a heathen tribunal: and we may perhaps look with some little interest even in this change of a pronomen, when we find here-

---

[1] "The argument of Cyprian and his adherents, against the validity of heretical Baptism, proceeds upon the assumption, that Christians are born again, and receive forgiveness of sins, and the Holy Ghost in Baptism." Bp. Bethell's *General view of the Doctrine of Regeneration in Baptism*, (Ed. 2) p. 117, note. See also p. 85, et seq.

after a proud professor, and a recusant of Cyprian's authority and fellowship, concentrating some portion of his malice and contempt in a recurrence to the old designation of Cyprian, calling him, "*Cyprian*, alias *Thascius*:"[1] while Cyprian retorts the opprobrium, whatever it may be, of such a designation, styling his uncourteous correspondent, "*Florentius*, alias *Pupianus*."

[1] For Cyprianus, the future Saint and Martyr, had already a name accounted of happy omen, as we collect from Augustine's panegyric: "He who rooteth up and planteth (Jer. i. 10), came unto him; and rooting out the old Cyprianus, and placing him on the true foundation, planted the new Cyprianus in himself, and caused the true Cyprianus to spring out of himself. For the Church saith to Christ, '*My beloved is a bundle of cypress*' (Cant. i. 15). At the same time then that he was made a Christian from Christ, he was also made *Cyprianus* from the true Cypress. For he became a sweet savour of Christ in every place; as the Apostle Paul saith of himself, who also was first as a persecutor a destroyer of the Church, and afterwards a builder of the Church as a preacher." Aug. Serm. cccxii. In Natali Cyp. Mart. vol. viii. p. 1257.

By some of the heathen, who ridiculed the application of his powers to the support of Christianity, this auspicious name of Cyprian was by a change of a single letter converted into one of opprobrious signification. "A doctis hujus seculi, quibus forte scripta ejus innotuerunt, derideri solet. Audivi ego quendam hominem sane sacrilegum, qui eum immutata una litera *Coprianum* vocaret; quasi quod elegans ingenium, et melioribus rebus aptum ad aniles fabulas contulisset." *Lact.* v. 1.

This playing upon names was not unusual either among the heathen or Christians. Thus the historian *Timæus* came to be called *Epitimæus*, the calumniator, for his malignant lies. St Jerome plays upon the name of Vigilantius: "Ais *Vigilantium*, qui κατ' ἀντίφρασιν hoc vocatur nomine, nam *Domitantius* rectius diceretur." And to return to an instance of better omen: Dionysius of Alexandria (in Eusebius) speaking of a martyr contemporary with Cyprian, says, "A native of Africa called *Macarius*, that is to say, *happy*, and who was *happy indeed*, since he possessed the favour of God, having been unmoved by the menaces of the judge, was burnt alive." *Ecc. Hist.* vi. 41.

## CHAPTER II.

St Cyprian's Writings while a Layman.—His Epistle to Donatus, on the Grace of God.—His Treatise on the Vanity of Idols.—The Death of Cæcilius;—who appoints Cyprian the Guardian of his Family.—St Cyprian a Deacon.—Dionysius of Alexandria.—St Cyprian a Presbyter.—His Three Books of Testimonies against the Jews.

St Cyprian's active mind sought occupation in his altered state, in recording the mercy of God in his conversion; and in displaying to his former associates in pagan wickedness and superstition, the vanity and folly of the religion which he had left.

The first-fruit of his conversion seems to have been his Epistle to Donatus, on the grace of God; the subject of which sufficiently indicates its date. Donatus was a companion of Cyprian as a catechumen, and also at baptism; and the more ingenious and learned of the two friends under the form of a familiar Epistle, arising out of certain past conversations, addresses to the other an appropriate exposition of the importance of Christianity in general, and especially of its initiatory rite, together with an exposure of the vanity and wickedness of the world, from which true religion is the only safe refuge. These important topics are rendered yet more interesting by many personal allusions; and the whole Epistle has a tinge of individual feeling, which gives it much of the warmth and brilliancy, which are only found where the highest matters are treated by those who have themselves felt their importance. But the singular interest of St Augustine's *Confessions* has so entirely cast all other works of this character into the shade, that I shall be excused for treating Cyprian's Letter to Donatus rather as an historical document than as an interesting literary production; and for having made use of it for the hints which it suggests of its author's former life and character, instead of presenting to the reader a connected view of the work itself.

Of his treatise, *On the vanity of Idols*, which seems also to have been written about this time, and while he was yet a layman, I must, however, speak more at length: although in this class of writing also St Augustine has surpassed all others, before or since his days. Indeed St Augustine's work *De Civitate Dei*, surpasses all other writings, *adversus gentes*, in learning and general importance, as much as his *Confessions* surpasses all other religious autobiographies.

There is a singular interest attached to the writings of the early Christians, addressed to the heathen, whose society and superstitions they had lately deserted. Whether such works appealed to the heathen by way of apology or of instruction, they must be such as a pagan could understand and appreciate; such as might, if possible, interest him: and yet they must be imbued with a spirit of religion, seeking higher objects than any which this world contains. Accordingly, they present Christian literature to our view in a transition state, so to speak; freed from the living death of the heathen, and casting off the garment spotted with the flesh; but not yet soaring into the purer empyrean of Christian mysteries, nor opening its seraph wings to the full blaze of day.

Works of this kind were often, perhaps generally, undertaken by late converts, or by those whose profession did not lead them into the depths of theology: and such persons were on some accounts the best suited to such an undertaking. They were themselves somewhat in the same moral condition with the works which they had to produce. Neophytes, and fresh from the memory, even from the love of paganism; or still living in the busy pursuits of the world; their zeal and their courage would be ardent and aspiring; while their arguments might be expected, if any might, to find a way to the hearts of those for whom they wrote, whose opinions were so fresh upon their minds; on whose prejudices they could make so direct an attack; whose language they could so readily assume.

It would not unfrequently happen, that the very persons who, as Christians, thus stepped forth in defence of the Church, had before been its direct opponents, as the avowed advocates of paganism. It was the most appropriate method such persons could take to manifest the sincerity of their faith and repentance, and to promote the service of God, to exert their earliest energies as Christians in the demolition of the temple which they had before assisted in propping, or in the construction of outworks to that sanctuary which they had endeavoured to demolish. We learn from St Jerome, that Cyprian himself, when a heathen, had been a defender of pagan idolatries. If the words of St Jerome imply that he had engaged his pen in their cause, the unhallowed work of his ignorance is lost: of his palinode I subjoin the following sketch.

It opens with a general reference of the deities, temples, and images of the heathen to their acknowledged origin in a desire to maintain the memory and reverence of kings, and other benefactors of the several nations; and descending to particulars, he mentions Castor and Pollux, Æsculapius, Saturn, and Mars, as illustrating his assertion; shewing, moreover, that the Moors still worshipped their kings, without veiling their practice under any other form.

Hence arose the variety of deities and the different character of their worship in various countries: and hence, too, the whole system of idolatry was exposed to manifest objections and ridicule; as for instance: Wherefore is it that the gods, who were formerly so prolific, have long ceased to multiply their kind; as if Jupiter were too old to be a father, and Juno had lost the privilege of bearing children? Wherefore is it that the gods who are powerful enough to assist Rome, have not an equal power to defend other nations? As for the origin of the gods, Romulus owed his apotheosis to the perjury of Proculus. Even courtesans were deified: and vices and diseases had their patron deities. Viduus, whose part it was to dissolve the connexion between the soul and the body, is banished from the city on account of the terrors of his office: and Venus the Bald is more subjected to ridicule, than the wounded Venus of Homer.

Kingdoms owe their power not to merit, but to fortune; Assyrians, Medes, Persians, Greeks, and Egyptians, succeed one another in order; and at last Rome, whose very origin is enough to excite a blush, succeeds: and whatever auguries may indicate, she shall hold her dominion for her appointed season, and no longer. Indeed, what so deceitful as the rites of divination? Regulus consulted the Augurs, and was taken prisoner; so did Mancinus, yet he passed under the yoke; and Paulus received a happy omen, and fell at Cannæ: but Caius Cæsar, who despised such indications of future events, seemed to be prosperous, and to conquer in proportion. The origin of all these things is in those wandering and lying spirits, which, being immersed in grovelling vices, and having lost their heavenly temper in the contact of earth, cease not to hurry others into their own depravity and perdition.

Your own poets and philosophers, continues Cyprian, know that there is one God, and that these all are but demons.[1] In this, Socrates, Plato, and Hermes Trismegistus, consent with us. These wandering spirits you attach to statues and images. They breathe their inspiration into your prophets, animate the entrails of sacrifices, direct the flight of birds, dispose lots, contrive oracles, jumble falsehood and truth together (for they are themselves deceived and deceivers), disturb your existence, infest your sleep, inject causeless and superstitious fears, convulse your limbs, injure your health, irritate diseases to bring you to their shrines, that they may feast on your sacrifices, and then by undoing their own work, seem to effect a cure. By such means do they seek to divert

---

[1] Perhaps the best account of the theology of the heathen, especially of their apparently inconsistent doctrine of many demons and one God, may be found in Bp. Warburton's account of the heathen mysteries, in his *Divine Legation of Moses demonstrated*.

you from the worship of the true God; and to involve you in their guilt, that they may have companions in their punishment. But even these demons, when adjured by us in the name of the true God, are obliged to leave the bodies which they have possessed, conquered and confessing their real nature. Under the influence and mighty operation of our exorcisms, you may hear them confess that they are beaten with stripes, bound in the fire, and more and more exceedingly tortured: and as they either depart by degrees, or flee away at once, according to the faith of the demoniac or of his exorcist, you may hear them declaring whence they came and whither they go. And hence the enmity of the common people against us; for these demons instigate them to hate us, without knowing what we are, lest if they should once know us, they should cease to be our persecutors.

There is, in short, but one God, and He is Lord of all. If in states and cities there can be no division of sovereignty without dissension, how much more is it necessary in the mighty universe that there should be one God. And what temple can contain God, whose temple is the whole world? If you ask His name, it is God: as He is but one, He requires no distinctive appellation. And indeed the common expressions of the people shew the innate sense of this truth in the mind: for do not all exclaim, O God! and say, God seeth, May God reward them, and the like?

What Christ is, and the dispensation of salvation through Him, may be thus briefly stated. To the Jews first the favour of God was vouchsafed, and His promises were made; and hence their ancient sanctity and prosperity. But they became at length, as they themselves confess, disobedient and idolatrous; or if they confess it not, their present condition is a token of the wrath of God. Now God had long ago declared that He would choose for Himself another people who should serve Him faithfully, and be blessed with the highest privileges. Of this dispensation, Christ is the Messenger, and the Mediator: and as such He was foretold long before He came, by prophets of the Jews. Hence the

Jews themselves expected Him : but as He was to come twice ; once in humility, and again in power and great glory ; they in their pride and folly overlooked His first coming, being blinded judicially for their past offences: and now they suffer their due reward.

Then, after a slight sketch of the life, and death, and ascension of Jesus, Cyprian proceeds to declare the appointment of disciples to preach the religion of which He is the head; and points out the fact that they are manifestly doing this, in the midst of sufferings and persecutions, which are but the filling up of the measure of the sufferings of Christ Himself in His followers. Suffering, which is the test of truth, we endure, that Christ the Son of God may be proclaimed not only by the preacher's life, but by the martyr's passion. Him we accompany, Him we follow; He is our Leader, our Light, our Salvation : He will open to us the gates of Heaven, and make us partakers of the Father. We Christians *shall be* hereafter what Christ *is*, if we imitate Christ in this world.

Such is Cyprian's tract on the vanity of idols, which affords a very fair specimen of that kind of work in the early days of the Christian Church. We return now to his personal history, and to the first steps of his singularly rapid ecclesiastical career.

Cyprian soon lost his friend and spiritual father; for Pontius has scarcely named Cæcilius, before he mentions his death; adding, that on his death-bed, Cæcilius left his wife and children to the care of Cyprian ; thus making him, who was heir to his piety and religious attainments, the guardian of his dearest relations.

Even in the short interval, however, between his own baptism and the death of Cæcilius, Cyprian had been admitted into the order of Deacons ; for Pontius, who was himself of that order, says, "while he was *one of us*,[1] he dwelt with Cæcilius, a man of honourable report, whose memory is yet held in reverence; who had already been the means of his

---

[1] Erat ille etiam de nobis, &c. Pontius.

conversion to the faith of Christ." The interpretation of this passage of Pontius is not without importance, since it is the only *direct* testimony which we have to the admission of Cyprian into the Diaconate, before he filled the higher orders of the Church. Eusebius thus speaks of him: Cyprian, first a Rhetorician, afterwards a Presbyter, and at length Bishop of Carthage, eventually received the crown of martyrdom; and St Jerome says, that being early elected into the Presbytery, he was afterwards made Bishop of Carthage:[1] while Pontius, whose duty it was to be more explicit, only says in general terms, that he passed through *each honourable step*, to the highest order of the priesthood. Hence, contrary to all probability, which should surely be the interpreter of the silence of historians, some have chosen to deny that Cyprian was ever a Deacon. The silence of Pontius may, I think, be accounted for, from the exaggerated stream of panegyric, in which the life by that author is composed; for he seems determined to mention nothing which he cannot convert into a *singular* mark of honour in his idolised master. Hence, while his own modesty prevented his speaking of the order to which he himself belonged as an honourable distinction, he could scarce find fit words to express the fact, that Cyprian had passed through it. In such general terms as these, then, Pontius speaks of Cyprian's advancement: "He rose rapidly from the order of Priests to that of Bishops; for who would hesitate to advance such an one through the highest degrees of honour?" And again; "this surely is a sufficient commendation of his excellence, that he was elected to the honour of the Priesthood, and of the Episcopate, by the judgment of God, and the favour of the people, even while he was yet accounted but a Neophyte." We cannot wonder, however, that some should make use of such expressions to prove, in spite of probability, that Cyprian was never a Deacon;

[1] Christianus factus, omnem substantiam suam pauperibus erogavit, ac post non multum temporis electus in Presbyterum, etiam Episcopus Carthaginiensis constitutus est. Hieronymi, Cat. Script. Eccl. vol. i. p. 187. Editio Francofurti, 1684.

when we find Blondel asserting, in spite of a yet greater probability, and in opposition even to these plain assertions, that he became a Bishop, without ever having been a Priest.

But though St Cyprian was doubtless a Deacon at the time of Cæcilius's death, it is certain that he was not yet advanced to the Priesthood; for in that case, neither could Cæcilius have committed to him, nor could he have accepted, the guardianship of his wife and children, without breach of ecclesiastical discipline; which debarred Priests and Bishops from taking upon themselves any secular duties, especially those of a guardian or executor. The Deacon, not as yet permitted to consecrate the Eucharist, or to administer Baptism, except under peculiar circumstances, was not rigidly tied down by the sanctity of his office to purely spiritual avocations; indeed his duties, even in respect of the Church, required some degree of intercourse with the daily offices of common life; to him, therefore, such a charge was permitted. And there was nothing inconsistent in these regulations; as there might seem to be if they were still enforced, when the Diaconate has become a step soon passed over, and taken almost invariably rather as an approach to the Priesthood, than for its own sake: for in the early Church many remained for life in the order of Deacons; while others passed through it, with a rapidity as little known among us as the opposite continuance in it. Cyprian, who passed hastily through the Diaconate, and his panegyrist Pontius,[1] who probably never advanced beyond it, afford examples in point.

It was during the reign of the Emperor Philip, while the Church was free from persecution, that Cyprian was thus adorning the progressive states of a catechumen, of a lay communicant, and of the Diaconate, by his personal and active piety and charity, and by his works in defence of Christianity, and in illustration of Christian doctrine. Meanwhile one of his great contemporaries was advancing, in a distant part of

---

[1] Jerome, speaking of Pontius, calls him only "Pontius Diaconus Cypriani." Cat. Script. Ecc. vol. i. p. 187. Nicholas Ferrar is an example of the like kind in our Church.

Africa, to the summit of his dignity and reputation; for it was at this time that Dionysius was appointed to fill the Episcopal throne of Alexandria, vacant on the death of Heraclas, who had been its occupant for sixteen years.[1] The Epistles of Cyprian and of Dionysius form a large part of the authentic materials for the ecclesiastical history of this age: and we shall often have occasion to cite the authority of the Prelate of Alexandria.

It was probably in December of this year (247) that Cyprian was made a Presbyter. Without distinctively referring any of his acts or writings to this part of his life, Pontius tells us, in general terms, that as he had been active as a layman, so he was also as a Priest. To this season we may probably refer his three books of Testimonies against the Jews: this at least is the conclusion of the Benedictine editors of Cyprian's works, who have well remarked, that the contents, or rather the omissions, of this work, indicate the time at which it was composed; since it contains no allusions to those events in which the interest and energies of Cyprian were so deeply engaged, during all the remainder of his life; while even some of his principles are less vividly displayed than they would have been at any subsequent period. In the third book, for instance, he collects several Scriptural testimonies against heretics and schismatics; but he would have been fuller and more vehement on this point, had he written amidst the very flames and commotions which were excited by heretics in his own diocese.

The three books into which this work is distributed are addressed to Quirinus, who was probably a young Christian, for Cyprian calls him his dear son. It seems that Quirinus had requested his more accomplished friend to furnish him, from the Scriptures, with the evidences of Christianity; in consequence of which request these books were written. The two first books were given to Quirinus, accompanied with an introductory Epistle, in which Cyprian thus unfolds his plan. "I have comprised the subject of this work in two books of

[1] Pearson's Annals. Eusebius, vi. 35.

nearly equal size; in the first book I have endeavoured to shew, that the Jews, as it had been foretold, had departed from God, and forfeited the favour of the Lord, which had been at first granted to them, and promised to their posterity; but that Christians, whose faith is the ground of their acceptance with God, have succeeded in their place, out of all nations, and from every quarter of the globe. The second book contains a statement of the mystery of Christ; shewing that He is come, as the prophets had foretold, that He has done and suffered all that had been presignified concerning Him." In the third book, in conformity with another request of Quirinus, Cyprian presents in the words of Scripture, a summary of the duties of Christians; following the same plan which he had pursued in the two former books, and adding nothing of his own to the citations from holy writ, but the connecting heads of the several sections.[1] For a better understanding of these

---

[1] Some notion of the contents of these books may be derived from the following heads.

### BOOK I.

1. That the Jews grievously offended God, by leaving the Lord, and following idols.
2. And also because they believed not the prophets, but slew them.
3. That it was foretold that they should neither recognise, understand, nor receive the Lord.
12. That the old baptism should cease, and another be instituted.
16. That the old sacrifice should cease to be offered, and that a new one should be offered in its stead.
17. That the old Priesthood should be extinct, that a new Priest should come, whose Priesthood should be eternal.

### BOOK II.

1. That Christ is the first-begotten of God, and Himself the wisdom of God, by whom all things were made.
6. That Christ is God.
11. That He was to be of the seed of David according to the flesh.
19. That Christ is the bridegroom, and the Church His bride, from whom a spiritual progeny should spring.

### BOOK III.

16. The benefit of martyrdom.
24. That we can approach the Father only through Christ.

matters, he remits Quirinus to the Scriptures themselves, assuring him that strength will be given to him as he reads; and that his insight into sacred things and all spiritual truth will be increased, as he goes through the contents of the Old and New Testaments.

Thus was Cyprian preparing himself, by a diligent and useful career in the inferior stations of the Church, for the highest order of the Christian hierarchy, to which he was soon most unexpectedly raised.

25. That no man can enter into the kingdom of God unless he be baptised and regenerated.
26. That it avails little to receive Baptism and the Eucharist, unless we advance in good works.
53. That the secrets of God are inscrutable, and that our faith therefore should be implicit.
54. That none is free from sin and corruption.
65. That all sins are cast off in baptism.
111. That the sacrifices of the wicked are evil.
116. That he loveth God more, to whom the more sins are remitted at Baptism.
120. That we should continue instant in prayer.

## CHAPTER III.

Cyprian chosen Bishop.—His attempt to escape.—The part of the People in his Election.—The Constitution of the Church in the Cyprianic Age.—The state of Morals and of Discipline in Cyprian's Diocese, and the Acts and Writings which arose out of the Condition of the Church.—The Epistles of Cyprian.—The Case of Geminius Victor:—Commemoration of the Dead:—The Primitive Practice a Witness against Romish Errors.—The Case of the Player:—The state of the Stage in Cyprian's Time.—The Case of the Rebellious Deacon.—The Case of the Συνεισακτοι.—"Ancient Christianity."

THE elevation of St Cyprian to the Episcopal throne of Carthage, followed very soon upon his admission to the Priesthood: for at the death of Donatus,[1] in the year 248, the whole body of the people, with the concurrence of by far the greater part of the clergy, demanded Cyprian for their Bishop; overlooking the youth of the Christian, in the singular merit of the man. The modesty of the young Presbyter, however, would have given place to his seniors; and he actually withdrew, concealing himself for a while from the eager search of the people. But the providence of God had marked Cyprian as their Bishop; and when the people had for some time surrounded his house, besieging the door, and searching every passage and retirement in their officious zeal, he appeared at last, baffled in his concealment, before the assembled crowd. The people received him with transports

---

[1] It is only from a casual expression of Cyprian in one of his Epistles to Cornelius, that we learn the name of his predecessor: *Antecessorum nostrorum Fabiani et Donati.* Agrippinus, of whom we shall afterwards have occasion to speak, is, I believe, the only Carthaginian Prelate before Cyprian and Donatus, whose name has descended to these times.

of joy, proportioned to the earnestness of their hopes and expectations. Yet his consecration was not wholly free from opposition; for certain Presbyters, who seem to have had some previous pique against him, opposed his election, and contrived to embitter a considerable portion of his Episcopate with their factious and schismatical opposition. So far from rigid truth is the boast of Pontius on behalf of his patron, "Quidam illi restiterunt, etiam ut vinceret:"—some opposed him, that his dignity might be graced by his overcoming their opposition; unless indeed it was Pontius's meaning, that he overcame evil with good; for he presently adds, that it was a wonder to many how patiently he endured this opposition, and how readily he pardoned it, so as to receive his opponents into the number of his most intimate and friendly acquaintance.

St Cyprian is not the only example that antiquity presents, of one avoiding the Episcopate so pertinaciously, as to resort even to concealment or flight. Indeed there was so much of personal risk, so little of temporal advantage, and so great a weight of spiritual responsibility, attached to the highest pastoral office in a persecuted Church, that it is no wonder that many were anxious to escape from the invidious dignity. We shall presently find the see of Rome vacant for some months, because of the danger which must inevitably beset one who should fill it; and when the election was at last made under a favourable aspect of affairs, we shall find Cyprian magnifying the virtuous and disinterested courage of the man who did not shrink from the mingled duties, dangers, and honours, of that station. In the mind of Cyprian, however, the fear of danger could have had no place; and it was doubtless his unaffected modesty which prompted his intended rejection of the dignity which the acclamations of the people of Carthage would have conferred on him. St Athanasius, like Cyprian, a man too bold to flee from danger, and indeed in no immediate apprehension that it would await his elevation to the Episcopate, affords a parallel example. Apollinaris the Syrian, as quoted by Sozomen,[1] tells us, that

[1] Sozomen, ii. 17.

Alexander, Bishop of Alexandria, being near his end, was divinely moved to appoint Athanasius his successor. As he lay, therefore, expecting his death, he called aloud for Athanasius, who had fled to avoid the choice which was to fall upon him. An attendant of the same name answered the dying Prelate, who only said, that it was not he whom he called, and continued still to call " Athanasius ! Athanasius !" At length the good Alexander exclaimed with a prophetic impulse, "Thou thinkest to escape, Athanasius; but thou shalt not escape." And he was accordingly found by the direction of Providence.

Nor was the part which the people had in the choice of a Bishop in Cyprian's case at all unusual. SS Ambrose and Augustine present remarkable instances of a like choice. Indeed this seems to have been one of the methods in which God designated certain persons for this high office; as He did also in other ways, quite beyond our present experience; and, since He has established the Church in a settled form and order, beside the necessity of the case. It would be almost as unreasonable to wait for the expressed consent of the people in the choice of a Bishop now, or even to give to their acclamations a very material influence, as it would be to expect that his successor should be appointed by Divine admonition in a dream to a dying Bishop, or that a dove should alight upon the head of the person to whom God would direct the choice of His Church. Cyprian, Athanasius, and Fabian,[1] were designated by such means; but we therein find, not a rule of discipline, but a manifestation of God's special purpose; not a principle of general application, but a particular interposition of Providence.

Having now accompanied Cyprian in his elevation through the several orders of the Apostolic Ministry, to the Episcopate, the *Sacerdotii sublime fastigium*, we may pause for a moment to take a rapid view of the polity of the Church, as it appears in ecclesiastical records of that period.[2]

[1] Eusebii, *Ecc. Hist.* vi. 29.
[2] Those who would acquaint themselves with the minutiæ of this ques-

The whole body of the Church was divided first of all into two grand divisions, Clergy and Laity: a distinction which was first made by Jesus Christ Himself, and which was guarded most reverently by His Apostles, and by the whole of Christendom for many ages: yet Dodwell has to meet the objections of Rigaltius against the primitive authority of this division of the Church, which he does with his usual learning in his first Cyprianic dissertation, *de voce cleri sacri ordinis propria*. Dodwell's arguments are still important, for they bear on the position of all those sects who trace their origin, or that of their Ministry, to lay interference; in short, to any thing but Apostolical derivation. If there is a Clergy in the Church of Christ, and if the office of the Clergy is not only to minister *for* men, but to minister *from* God, then it is clear that something more than the choice of the people or the assumption of the individual is required to give a man a place in the Clergy: and it is equally clear, that the intervening of a few or many successions to an usurped office does not better the position of the last intruder. If A, having no power to ordain, that is to transmit the office of a minister *from* God, pretends to ordain B, and B to ordain C, and so on to M or N, since none of the intervening persons can transmit more than he received, and B in fact received absolutely nothing from A, who had absolutely nothing to give, then are M and N mere laymen, with this only addition, whether it be of honour or of shame, that they are assuming a sacred office which belongs not to them.

How many sects are now without Clergy, I will not pretend to say.

In St Cyprian's time, the distinction between the Clergy and the Laity was so strictly guarded, not only by ecclesiastical laws, but also by popular opinion and feeling, that it would have been morally impossible for a single person to usurp a single pastoral function without ordination: an in-

tion, will consult Bishop Sage's principles of the Cyprianic age, with his vindication of that work. Stillingfleet, in his Unreasonableness of the Present Separation, is also pretty full upon the subject.

truder even into the Deacon's office would have been rejected everywhere with scorn and indignation, and his temerity would have found its proper reward in excommunication. But nothing can be more unjust than to suppose that the Laity were therefore depressed, or deprived of their proper place and influence in the Church: so far from it, that the very plainness of the line of demarcation by which they were separated from the Clergy, giving them a definite position, ensured them also definite privileges. Were the Laity confused with the Clergy, all ecclesiastical affairs must inevitably fall, sooner or later, into the hands of the Clergy; for they would be the best fitted for them by the habits and opportunities of their office; and having this direction pointed out to their ambition, they would certainly follow it, unless they were more than men in virtue, and as certainly succeed, unless they were less than men in conduct:[1] but with a defined province for each, Clergy and Laity have their proper place, from which neither the one nor the other will advance or retire, if they know the real strength of their own position, or consult the real welfare of the whole body.

We have seen indeed already, in the election of St Cyprian to the Episcopate, how great a voice the people had in those days, when the distinction between Clergy and Laity was most marked; and many other proofs might be added, shewing that they had a more effectual influence in the ecclesiastical polity of those times. St Cyprian himself always appears most anxious to save their privileges, and to give them their proper place in the body of the Church.[2]

The Clergy, who were set apart for the pastoral office by a solemn Ordination, of which the Bishop was the sole dispenser, were distinguished into three ranks, Deacons, Pres-

---

[1] The immense influence of the Clergy in secular affairs during the middle ages, when the case just supposed was reversed, and the Clergy were more secularised, instead of the Laity being more confused with the Clergy, fortifies this reasoning with an *ex abundanti* example.

[2] I may refer on this head to a little Pamphlet published anonymously by myself some two years past, *On the admission of Lay Members to the Ecclesiastical Synods of the Protestant Episcopal Church in Scotland.*

byters, and Bishops. These had each its defined province distinct from the rest, just as clearly as the Laity distinct from the Clergy. The Bishop was the chief ruler in the Church under God, and the fountain of authority to all the rest; especially he was the channel through which whatever partook of a sacramental efficacy or character was transmitted from God to the Church. Hence the rule, that nothing should be done χωρὶς Ἐπισκόπου, or ἄνευ γνώμης τοῦ Ἐπισκόπου: which means something more than that it ought not to be done without the Bishop's sanction; but that if it were so done, it would be as if not done at all, illegal, and even invalid. So St Ignatius says, that without the Bishop there is no communion; and such passages from other primitive authors might be cited almost without end.

The distinctive theological office of the Bishop, that which could under no circumstances be committed to any other, that which not only must not be done χωρὶς Ἐπισκόπου, but which must be done *by* the Bishop, was Ordination. In this were the Bishops always reckoned more especially the successors of the Apostles, and the express ordinance of God. The Presbyterate, which was the next order, had its own functions also, which were derived from the Bishop, but could not be committed to the Deacon, especially the consecration of the blessed Eucharist; and this order also was referred to the immediate ordinance of Jesus Christ. The last order of the Pastoral Clergy was that of the Deacons, which was instituted by the Apostles themselves, and to which were committed other functions and offices, into which the Laity were not permitted to intrude, though they were below those of the Presbyterate. The highest office for which the Deacon was held competent was the administration of Baptism, to which he was ordinarily appointed by permission of the Bishop on the greater festivals, at which the number of candidates was so great, that the Presbyters and Bishops were not sufficient for the task: in some places it seems to have been the common practice for Deacons to baptise.[1]

[1] Bingham, Orig. Ecc. II. xx. 9.

Thus then, in St Cyprian's time, and for all the generations in the Church before it, a proper Episcopacy, in its strictest theological sense, was established. That this Episcopacy was also diocesan, or such that the authority of the Bishop extended over many separate congregations, is equally clear from the whole history of the Church in those days. In Rome there were at this very time forty-six Presbyters, seven Deacons, seven Sub-Deacons, forty-two Acolyths, fifty-two Exorcists, Readers and Ostiarii, with above fifteen hundred widows and poor, dependent on the bounty of the Church. All these were under the Episcopal jurisdiction, that is, in the diocese of Cornelius:[1] and when the number of Christians at Rome is estimated from the number of Clergy, officers and poor among them, it will be too absurd to suppose that they were not many Churches, or separate congregations.

The Churches of Rome [2] and Carthage, together with many others, were also at this time Metropolitan, or Archiepiscopal, as will appear abundantly during the course of this work. This is indeed rather a question of polity than of theology; the Archbishop or Metropolitan being elevated above the Suffragan Bishop not in theological order, but in ecclesiastical rank and power: it is however very satisfactory to see our own ecclesiastical form so exactly paralleled in the primitive Church, and before the alliance with the State can have secularised the Church, or in any way modified her constitution.

Thus far, then, we are wholly in accordance with the primitive Church; for even the place of the Laity, and their influence in the councils of the Church, which escapes a careless search under another form, is yet found not too minute, but, on the contrary, rather exaggerated, in the alliance of Church

---

[1] See the letter of Cornelius in Eusebius, Ecc. Hist. vi. 43. In Cyrus, the diocese of Theodoret, there were 600 parishes, or Churches under the government of separate Presbyters.

[2] The highest rank to which the Church of Rome ever attained by right, was to that of a Patriarchal See, which is to Metropolitan Churches what they are to the Suffragan Sees. But it is to be observed, that Britain is not in the Patriarchate of Rome.

and State, and in the King's supremacy:[1] and nothing can be clearer than the identity of our constitution both theological and ecclesiastical; of our Churches Episcopal and Metropolitan, our Episcopate, Presbyterate, and Diaconate, with those of the Church of Carthage in St Cyprian's time.

The only question which occurs is suggested by the enumeration of ecclesiastical officers before mentioned, who were subject to Cornelius in his Church of Rome; and we shall meet with the same frequently in Carthage, and other Churches. Even here, however, the difference is not so great as at first sight appears. For first of all, the inferior orders, Subdeacons, Acolyths, and the rest, were never suspected to be of divine appointment, or of necessary use in the Church; nor were they entrusted with any charge approaching to a pastoral or sacramental character. In the next place, though under different names, we have very nearly the same servants of the Church; Churchwardens, Parish Clerks, Vergers, Sextons, &c., succeeding to all the offices of Subdeacons, Readers, Ostiarii and the rest. One difference we confess, and would gladly see removed, but it is rather in the character of the times, than in the spirit or constitution of the Church:—that whereas in Cyprian's time whatever was at all connected with the service of God was regarded with greater reverence; and so it was required that all persons engaged within the precincts of the Church, even the very servants, should be separated to their occupation by a religious ceremony: now we have reduced religion within the confines of the smallest province in which she can maintain her state; and the Apostolic principles, and the sentiment which led to consecrations having languished, the very thing itself seems out of date.

But we must return to St Cyprian in the discharge of his Episcopal office. His attention seems to have been turned, immediately on his elevation, to the restoration of discipline,

[1] See Hooker, Ecc. Pol. viii. 8. It is well to find a saving of important principle in what seems our weakest point.

which had been much relaxed during the long peace which the Church had enjoyed;[1] and in some instances to the correcting of most serious abuses, which had crept into the manners even of ecclesiastics. To this end he called in the advice and assistance of his clergy and people, and wrote his Tract *de habitu virginum*, together with several Epistles, adverting to particular cases which called for his interference.

And now our attention is arrested by the first of those Epistles of St Cyprian, which throw so much light on the history, laws, and principles of the Church in his days. Geminius Victor, an ecclesiastic of the Church at Furni, and not improbably its Bishop, at his death appointed Geminius Faustinus, then a Presbyter, the guardian or executor of his will. The necessity of keeping the Clergy free from the cares of this world, and especially from those duties which would bring them within the precincts of the court of the heathen magistrate, had suggested laws to prevent any of the Clergy from undertaking such an office, under pain of degradation. The civil law, on the other hand, on account of the difficulty with which persons were found to take on themselves places of such trouble and responsibility (the discharge of which, however, was necessary to the proper transaction of affairs), had made it penal to refuse them. The Church, therefore, was obliged to inflict the penalty, in some instances, not on the Clergyman who executed, but on the testator who imposed, such an office; and now Cyprian was called upon to enforce the laws of the Church against Victor, who had nominated Faustinus his executor. Accordingly in a letter to the Clergy and people at Furni, he expresses his regret at such a breach of discipline; cites the decision of a former Synod condemning the practice, of which Victor had been guilty; and reasons, in general terms, on the necessity on which the Ecclesiastical Canons on that head were founded.

---

[1] Sulpicius says, that after the persecution under Severus, the Church enjoyed a peace of thirty-eight years, except when Maximinus persecuted some particular Churches. Africa did not, in all probability, suffer in this partial affliction. *See Pearson's Annals.*

*No man that warreth entangleth himself with the affairs of this life, that he may please him who hath chosen him to be a soldier:* and if this rule should regulate the life of every Christian, much more of every ecclesiastic, that he may give himself the more entirely to the service of the Altar: on the same principle proceeded the exemption of the Levites, under the Mosaical law, from the cares of this life: and all this was maturely considered by those who made the ecclesiastical rule which Victor has disregarded. "Wherefore," continues Cyprian, "since Victor has dared, contrary to the law lately enacted in Council, to nominate Faustinus his executor, no oblation ought to be made for his death, nor any prayer be offered in his name in the Church: that so we may maintain the decree of the Bishops which was religiously made, and of necessity; and that a warning may be given at the same time to the rest of the brethren, not to call off the Priests and Ministers of the Altar and Church of God, by the distracting cares of this world."

This method of enforcing an Ecclesiastical Canon, by forbidding the mention of the offender, even after his death, in the service of the Church, leads us to consider another primitive rule and custom. The oblations of the faithful in the Holy Eucharist were made not only for themselves individually, but for the whole Church; and, of consequence, for the dead in Christ; who were ever held to be a portion of the Church, as certainly as those who were still living in the flesh: and though the ancient Fathers, with their characteristic caution in handling sacred and mysterious subjects, did not venture to describe what was the specific advantage which the faithful dead might receive from this act; yet they held it highly congruous to suppose (as who will not?) that when the memorials of Christ's death and sacrifice were solemnly celebrated on earth, it was not without some benefit to all who were truly interested in that stupendous act of His love. The Angelic Host they believed to be present at the Holy Eucharist: and as the celebrants communicated with seraphic spirits by their presence; why should they not also with those with whom they might certainly be present in spirit, being mystically joined with them in one body, even Christ's; and so all His whole Church on earth and in paradise be united by a mutual benefit.

Nor was there any superstition in the belief, that the prayers of the righteous, especially when assembled as a Church, and sanctified by the celebration of the most sublime mysteries of our faith, might benefit the souls of those who awaited, in their separate state, the full fruition of the bliss. But here, as in the case of oblations, the primitive Church pretended to unravel no mystery; and sought not to explain or to particularise what was most excellent in its sacred obscurity and generality. As they *offered* for the blessed dead as well as for themselves, so also they *prayed* for them, but in both cases without fanaticism, and without superstition.

In order to the greater interest in this part of the service of the Church, the names of those, for whom offerings and prayers were made, were recited aloud, out of the diptychs or sacred rolls of the Church. Patriarchs, Prophets, Apostles, the Blessed Virgin, and the Martyrs of the Church, were first mentioned; and then those pious men who had departed in immediate communion with that particular Church were enumerated in order; especially the Bishops, and other ecclesiastics. Besides the mysterious benefits which might thence accrue to the departed, it was not doubted that this was a fit honour to their name and memory: and to the living, it had this assured benefit; that it was a great inducement to them to cultivate that unity of the faith, and those virtues which were thus rewarded :—that it kept up in their hearts the memory and affections of the dead, with a pious hope of a reunion with them at the resurrection :—that it was a marked confession of the great truth which Christ Himself taught, when He said, that God was not the God of the dead but of the living; viz., that all saints live in and to Him :—that even if the dead received not a blessing, yet at least this service performed by the living, in piety and charity and hope, was acceptable to God, and so would not miss its reward :—that it was an instrument of discipline in the hands of the Church, by which the living might be encouraged to a godly life; for they could not choose but be excited to virtue by the pious memorial of the blessed, and affected sadly, yet profitably, by the solemn verdict of the Church, which refused the wicked a participation in these honours and benefits.

The judgment, then, of St Cyprian against Geminius Victor amounted to this; that his name should not be inserted in the diptychs of the Church, nor any memorial be made of him at the Altar, at which he had once communicated. If this should seem a severe sentence, the necessity of the case should be considered, and the importance of supporting, by every possible means, a canon which seems at first sight wanting in the more rigid moral sanctions. Moreover it should be considered, that this excommunication of Victor after his death, was the infliction only of an ecclesiastical form of discipline, and by no means amounted to a judgment of his state before God; to whom mercy was still left, though disapproval was the duty of the Church. The conduct of Cyprian is justified, moreover, by the constant practice of the Church, and even by an act of General Council; for the sixth Council having anathematised Pope Honorius, as a Monothelite, after his death, together with several other Bishops, ordered that their names should be erased from the diptychs. And the judgment of a particular Bishop or Church might afterwards be reversed, as in the case of a person excommunicated in his lifetime without sufficient cause: thus when Chrysostom had been unjustly condemned and excommunicated, the Western Bishops would not communicate with the Bishops of Egypt, the Bosphorus, Thrace, and the East, until they had restored the name of Chrysostom to the diptychs of his Church. Arsacius, the successor of Chrysostom, was actually deprived of their countenance; which Atticus, the next Bishop, only obtained, by submitting to their just demands.[1]

To those who give only a cursory attention to such matters,

[1] Theodoreti, *Ecc. Hist.* v. 34, vol. iii. p. 1076. Ed. Halæ, 1769.

what we have just said may seem to array the Church in the days of St Cyprian on the side of Rome, in her custom of oblations and prayers for the dead, and in her doctrine of purgatory, which grew out of that custom. I must, therefore, point out the difference between the Roman and the primitive practice; and shew that the latter does not presuppose, but actually refute the doctrine of purgatory.

The oblations and prayers which were offered for the dead in the Primitive Church were offered not for the unholy, but for the blessed dead; not for those concerning whose state the Church was in doubt; but for those concerning whom there was never any question, but that they were received into Abraham's bosom, or Paradise; not, therefore, that they might be delivered from any, I know not what torments, but that their joy might be more full even in their state of expectancy; and that the time of the consummation of their glory might be hastened: a petition which we make expressly in the words of our Funeral Service, and virtually, whenever we pray, *Our Father, Thy kingdom come.*

And therefore it was that the primitive Christians prayed for the *greatest* saints, and for those *only* whom they believed to be in their rest in Paradise: and even though they had believed in a purgatory, it was not to such as might be supposed to be in that place that these prayers referred; else Geminius Victor, before mentioned, should rather have been the more than the less remembered in the prayers of his Church, for the offence which he had committed. But, in fact, there is not a single vestige of any thing like the doctrine of purgatory till long after the days of Cyprian: and though Augustine certainly gave occasion to the less modest assertions of subsequent doctors, by his very guarded expression of a *question*, whether a place of intermediate purgation *might not by possibility exist;* yet even Augustine's modest opinions were not in accordance with the Romish dogmatical assertions, guarded by eternal sanctions.[1]

[1] "Constanter teneo purgatorium esse, animasque ibi detentas fidelium suffragiis juvari." "Hanc veram Catholicam fidem, extra quam nemo salvus esse potest." Creed of Pope Pius IV.

But if prayer for the dead, according to the primitive notion, is incongruous with the doctrine of purgatory, it is perfectly irreconcilable with the practice of praying *to* the saints, or of using their mediation with God. It were almost impossible to pray first *for*, and then *to* or *through*, any being: but the primitive Christians actually did pray *for* the Blessed Virgin, the Holy Apostles, and such other saints as Rome now prays *to*, and makes her mediators.[1]

The Bishop of Exeter, in his letters to Charles Butler, has proved at length that Augustine's notion of purgatory was not the same as that of Rome at the present day. Even Augustine would *scarce* escape the penalty of damnation for the rejection of this Article; and *certainly* all the preceding Fathers of the Church cannot but be condemned.

[1] It is very instructive to see the change made by the gradual perversion of doctrine, in those public Prayers which are the very best records of the tenets of a Church: I therefore transcribe the following passage from Bingham's Orig. Ecc. book xv. iii. 15, which bears directly on this point.

"It appears from all the ancient Liturgies under the name of St Basil, Chrysostom, Gregory Nazianzen, and Cyril, that they prayed for all saints, the Virgin Mary herself not excepted. And it is remarkable, that in the old Roman Missal they were used to pray for the soul of St Leo, as Hincman, a writer of the ninth age, informs us, who says the prayer ran in this form, 'Grant, O Lord, that this oblation may be of advantage to the soul of thy servant Leo, which Thou hast appointed to be for the relaxation of the sins of the whole world.' But this was thought so incongruous in the following ages, that in the later Sacramentaries or Missals it was changed into this form: 'Grant, O Lord, we beseech Thee, that this oblation may be of advantage to us by the intercession of St Leo,' as Pope Innocent the Third assures us it was in his time. And such another alteration was made in Pope Gregory's Sacramentarium. For in the old Greek and Latin edition there is this prayer: 'Remember, O Lord, all Thy servants, men and women, who have gone before us in the seal of the faith, and sleep in the sleep of peace; we beseech Thee, O Lord, to grant them, and all that rest in Christ, a place of refreshment, light, and peace, through the same Jesus Christ our Lord.' But in the new reformed Missals it is altered thus, 'Remember, Lord, Thy servants and handmaids N. and N. that have gone before us, &c.' That they might not seem to pray for saints as well as others that were in purgatory. Which makes it very probable, that St Cyril's Catechism has also been tampered with, and a clause put in, which speaks of their praying to God by the intercession of Patriarchs, Prophets, Apostles, and Martyrs:

It seems then, on a careful review of this matter of prayers and oblations for the dead, that we of the English Church are far nearer to the doctrine, principles, and practice of the Primitive Church, than the Church of Rome is: for Rome, apparently continuing the same custom, has connected it with principles and doctrines, together with which the precise custom of the ancients could not stand; while we, not so obtrusively retaining the custom, yet *have* retained it in part; and for the doctrine and principles, maintain them still entire. For we expressly commemorate the dead in the Eucharist; and with regard to oblations for the blessed dead, for those, that is, for whom they were presented in St Cyprian's time, I defy any one to point out a single principle or doctrine of the English Church which is opposed to it. On the contrary, the commemoration being made in the very prayers in which the oblation also is made, leads obviously to the conclusion, that the offering is for them, as well as for the living mentioned with them: and so far as prayer for the dead is concerned, it is only not condemned, but actually used by the Church over the grave of every departed brother, when she saith, "That it may please Thee of Thy gracious goodness shortly to accomplish the number of Thine elect, and to hasten Thy kingdom; that we, with all those that are departed in the true faith of Thy holy Name, may have our perfect consummation and bliss,

since the ancient Liturgies prayed for them as well as for all others. St. Chrysostom says expressly, 'they offered for the Martyrs.' And so it is in his Greek Liturgy, 'We offer unto Thee this reasonable service for the faithful deceased, our forefathers, fathers, Patriarchs, Prophets, and Apostles, Evangelists, Martyrs, Confessors, religious persons, and every spirit perfected in the faith; but especially for our most holy, immaculate, most blessed Lady, the Mother of God, and ever Virgin Mary.' Though, as Bp. Ussher has observed, some of the Latin translators have also given a perverse turn to these words, rendering them thus, 'We offer unto Thee this reasonable service for the faithful deceased, our forefathers and fathers, by the intercession of the Patriarchs, Prophets, Apostles, Martyrs, and all the Saints.' For it sounded ill to the Latin ears to hear St Chrysostom say, the ancient Church prayed for Saints and Martyrs. And yet he says it, not only in the forementioned places, but over and over again in others."

both in body and soul, in Thy eternal and everlasting glory; through Jesus Christ our Lord." Thus we have commemoration of the dead, and, if I be not greatly mistaken, an oblation for the dead, and prayer for the dead; the only difference being, that we pray for none by name.

Now when it is considered that we have *so much* of the primitive custom, and *all* the primitive doctrine upon this question; and that whatever of this custom we have not, we have been obliged to forego on account of the false doctrines which Rome had so connected with the custom, that there was, humanly speaking, no possibility of avoiding her error without modifying her usage: the blame of our partial deficiency, if such it be, will surely be laid on those who have robbed us of our right, by their perverse adherence to wrong.[1]

A player, who had left off the exercise of his profession when he embraced Christianity, but still continued to teach it to others, gave occasion to the second of Cyprian's Epistles; in which he gives the following answer to Eucratius, an ecclesiastic, who had asked, whether such a person ought to be admitted to communion. "I hold it to be inconsistent with sacred and evangelical discipline, that the modesty and honour of the Church should be tainted with the contact of such a person: for if it be contrary to the divine law for men to wear women's garments, how much more so must it be for them to imitate also the manners and gestures of the most abandoned of that sex: nor is the excuse to be heard, that he does not himself appear thus before the public, while he continues to teach others to do so; for he can scarce be said to have retired from a profession, who is training up to it many successors. If, however, he makes poverty a pretence, let him receive sufficient for his wants, so they be moderate, from your Church; or if you are poor, he can be amply provided for here: and instead of leading others into the paths of perdition, he may himself learn that which shall be for his everlasting peace."

[1] See on this subject PALMER's *Origines Liturgicæ*, vol. ii. chap. iv. §. 10. p. 94 *et seq.* 2d Edition.

The licentiousness of the theatre St Cyprian had already touched in his Epistle to Donatus. He observes, with evident truth, that while the stage was occupied with the representation of the most monstrous actions that had ever been perpetrated, and while the repetition of the scenic story was accompanied with loud applauses, men were habituated to the forms of vice; and began to fancy, that what was applauded as done in the days from whence the fable was borrowed, might always be done, and that with honour. Thus crimes, which ought not so much as to enter into people's imagination, were not only not permitted to sink into oblivion, but were converted into examples. Other parts of the dramatic scene were direct stimulants to vice; so that the woman who went thither virtuous, might return, in inclination at least, thoroughly depraved; while all was rendered worse, by the gods themselves being represented as criminals, in many cases, so that the people who are ready enough to follow bad example, and to find an excuse for sin, would be led to consecrate every perpetration of wickedness into religion.

Without at all advocating the modern theatre, I must yet remark, that much of this reasoning of Cyprian is not applicable to our times; though it was loudly called for by the state of things in his own. Women not being permitted to appear on the stage, all the female parts were sustained by men; there was a degree of licentiousness and obscenity in the representations of many pieces, which would not now be tolerated on the stage of the most abandoned cities: and above all, the drama was so intimately linked with idolatry, that a Christian could not have taken his part in it, consistently with his duty to God, even though there were no other and more direct immorality, inseparable from the profession of a player.[1] Still, however, it will be obvious that the

---

[1] The profession of an actor was always by the Primitive Church held to be inconsistent with true religion. In the African code of Canons (45) players are grouped with apostates. And the Apostolical Canons (14 *al* 18) deny Holy Orders to one who has married an actress.

moral question and its solution is not now wholly different from that which Eucratius put to Cyprian, and Cyprian's answer. If the general tendency of the stage, as it is now conducted, be deleterious to the public principles and morals, we need not doubt on which side such an one as Cyprian should and would place the weight of his authority.

Cyprian's third Epistle is to an aged Bishop, named Rogatian, who asked his advice as to the course which he ought to pursue with a Deacon, who had so forgotten his station and his duty, as to insult the person and despise the authority of Rogatian. In strict accordance with the principles of Church government and discipline in his age, Cyprian, declared most explicitly, that it was wholly in Rogatian's power to proceed against the rebellious Deacon, either to degradation, or to excommunication, as the case required: yet he recommended, first of all, the milder methods of persuasion and reproof; since it is better to overcome reproaches and injuries with patience and clemency, than to overwhelm the offender with the weight of the Episcopal authority.

But the most painful delinquency against which Cyprian had now to exert his Episcopal authority forms the subject of his fourth Epistle. The experience of the Church during two centuries of persecution had fully justified St Paul's assertion, that for the present distress, celibacy was the better state. It was also recognised by the word of inspiration as an acceptable discipline and instance of self-denial. From these concurring circumstances and Scriptural declarations, a single life was by this time looked on as a state of greater privilege and sanctity, and many of each sex had voluntarily embraced that condition, not binding themselves by any vow, but simply purposing to themselves a religious celibate.[1]

[1] Such persons in Cyprian's days, and till long after, did not subject themselves to any particular regimen: this is clear from the directions and exhortations in Cyprian's book, *de habitu virginum*; and also from the circumstances to which we are now directing our attention, which must have arisen out of the most unbounded licence in the voluntary celibates of both sexes, to follow their own inclination as to the place of

From this condition, those who were already married were of course excluded: but for those there was a greater refinement of asceticism open, by a voluntary continence; and to this some of them resorted. This discipline, like that of the voluntary celibates, was neither scandalous, nor in itself otherwise than innocent: though it had too much the appearance of going beyond what was required by God, to seem wholly wise and safe. But out of it arose a most criminal practice; for it seems to have suggested to those who had already professed celibacy, the dangerous expedient of choosing one of the other sex, bound by the like vows, with whom they might form a kind of spiritual nuptials, still maintaining their chastity, though, in all things else, living as freely together as married persons.[1]

That there were unworthy motives at the bottom of such a course it would be difficult not to believe: it is however fair to suppose that the delinquents were self-deceived. They had prevailed on themselves to believe that they might thus,

their residence, and their general deportment. The difficulties also which Chrysostom notes (*de sac.* III. xvii.) in the sacerdotal government of virgins in the Church, arise out of the same liberty. The following words of Bingham (*Orig. Ecc.* VII. iv. 3.) will sufficiently indicate the progressive restraints which were laid upon professed virgins. Having observed that in Cyprian's days they were not even positively forbidden to marry, he proceeds: "But in the following ages, the censures of the Church were inflicted on them. The Council of Ancyra, [Anno 314.] determined universally against all such as having professed virginity, afterward went against their profession, that they should be subject to the same term of penance as digamists were used to be; that is, a year or two, as we learn from one of the Canons of St Basil. The Council of Chalcedon [451] orders them to be excommunicated, if they married, but leaves the term of their penance to the Bishop's discretion. The Council of Valence [374] in France is still more severe, forbidding them to be admitted immediately to penance; and when they were admitted, unless they made full and reasonable satisfaction to God, their restoration to communion was still to be deferred . . . . ."

[1] Non deesse qui Dei templa et post confessionem sanctificata et illustrata membra turpi et infami concubitu suo plus maculent, cubilia sua cum fœminis promiscua jungentes. Ep. vi. p. 12. see also Ep. lxii. pp. 102-104.

even more effectually than in any other way, strengthen their religious character, by preserving their celibate, in the midst of such temptations: and there was something in the spiritual union which they did not conceal, not unapt to excite admiration, and to fill them with self-complacency. The world, however, refused to view the matter in this light; and much scandal, as might be expected, ensued.[1] Pomponius, then, a brother Bishop, wrote for St Cyprian's advice, as to the course which he should pursue, and the manner in which he should treat those who had been guilty of this scandalous custom in his diocese; one of whom it seems was a Deacon. Cyprian, after his usual manner, takes a decided view of the case, and does not for an instant temporise with the deceitful reasonings by which such a practice was excused. He declares at once, that the professed celibates with their *agapetæ* had placed themselves within the snares of the devil; and laments that many had already, as might be expected, fallen a sacrifice to his wiles: he recommends, that those who had offended in this matter, without reference to the truth or falsehood of their assertions of purity, should undergo penance; that they should then resume their state of professed celibacy, if they still thought it conducive to their Christian character; but otherwise, that they should marry, since, as St. Paul says, *it is better to marry than to burn*. But if any refused to forego their scandalous custom, they were to be excommunicated, without hope of reconciliation.

As for the Deacon who was among the number of the delinquents, he had been already excommunicated by Pomponius, whose judgment Cyprian approves.

This whole matter affords us a most useful general lesson, and an awful example of the deceitfulness of sin. It was under the pretence of a singular sanctity that the συνείσακτοι, voluntarily placed themselves in a position so full of scandal to the Church in general, and of danger to themselves; and

---

[1] Quando etsi stuprum conscientiæ eorum desit, hoc ipsum grande crimen est, quod illorum scandalo in aliorum ruinas exempla nascuntur. *Ibid.*

many of them doubtless, when they were on the verge of losing the very purity which they estimated so highly, were priding themselves on the constancy with which they resisted temptation, and maintained their Christian life.

We are also forcibly reminded here, that God is the wisest dispenser of our duties; not only when He is apparently rigid and severe, but also when He is so merciful to our infirmities, that men fancy they can advance in their obedience even beyond what He requires of them. Every step towards the extreme criminality of some at least of the συνείσακτοι, was beyond the law of God, though taken with an avowed intention of pleasing Him; and had this course of conduct stopped but one or two steps sooner, we might have been almost disposed to believe, that the voluntary yoke was good to be borne: in other words, that man was in this case wiser than God. But the principle of the mischief was in the voluntary exercise of the married, opposing as it did a plain precept of holy writ; and it advanced still farther in the asceticism of the celibate, also contrary to the spirit of many of the sacred declarations. I need proceed no farther; I will only observe, that we have still, in the Roman Church, a memorial before us of the truth of the remarks which I have now made: for though Rome has so far profited by the fall of the συνείσακτοι, as to take her celibates under the peculiar protection of the Church, and to enforce a separate habitation for the two sexes, the whole system is scandalous and dangerous; and she had certainly better revert to obedience to the word of God, than proceed to the organizing of human devices. *We* will not deny to Romanists the merit of a good intention, at least in a vast majority of instances; neither surely can *they* deny, that some of the blackest stains that ever came upon any Church, or upon any body of men whatever, have proceeded from their system of celibacy.

Thus far I had written, before an extraordinary attack upon the Church appeared, under the title of *Ancient Christianity*. The character and the writings of St Cyprian are strangely distorted in this work; and the case of the συνείσακτοι, with

St Cyprian's Tract on the attire of virgins, are made, by perversion, abundantly useful in supporting the slanderous representations which are wanted for the suppport of the argument. Mr Taylor's system required, that the celibacy of persons of either sex should be the effect if not of actual, yet at least of moral, force: and so, without the shadow of proof, he speaks of the "rash and unwarrantable vow of perpetual celibacy, or virginity, taken or forced upon multitudes of young women, in some moment of artificial religious excitement."[1] To this representation we have simply to say, that it is false; and without it the whole scheme totters.

The work of all others in which one would expect to find St Cyprian labouring to produce an artificial religious excitement, which should force virgins to devote themselves to a perpetual celibate, is the tract above named, *On the Attire of Virgins.—Nuns,* Mr Taylor explains it; though he ought to know, that *nuns,* in the sense in which his reader will understand the word, had then no existence; and though he is manifestly aware, that unless it be thus understood, his reasoning will lose half its force. This is dishonest, and should have been avoided by one who speaks in this very same page of a similar sophism with becoming reprobation: "How much," he exclaims, "turns often upon an insensible substitution of a *technical,* for the general and genuine sense of an ethical, term!"[2] How much, we may retort, here turns on the artful substitution of a name, which has been appropriated to an institute unknown in Cyprian's time, and associated in our minds with a large catalogue of evil, which had no place in the world until ages after, for a simple term, sufficiently expressing its object, and not adapted to suggest suspicions, and opprobrious thoughts!

Then, again, there is the accomplished management by which a few isolated passages are made to stand as the representatives of the whole Tract, and of the character of all St Cyprian's writings. To a mind at all versed with the subject,

[1] *Ancient Christianity*, p. 72.  [2] P. 75.

and imbued with the necessity of giving at least some meaning to the words of our Lord and of St Paul on the subject of a life of religious celibacy, even the passages adduced, as they stand in their isolated form, will cause no unfavourable impressions. But when it is remembered, that the treating of any particular virtue almost necessarily leads to the giving to that virtue an undue preference at the time;—the balance being justly struck not on a view of a particular Tract or Homily, but of the whole series of moral discourses of an author or an age; when it is remembered, that St Cyprian is there expressly speaking of a religious celibacy, and there only in all his works, instead of almost every where, as a careless reader of "Ancient Christianity" would suppose; and when it is remembered, that even that work alone does really stand free from the blame which Mr. Taylor attaches to it, if it be read as a whole; when all this is remembered, the argument of "Ancient Christianity" will gain but little from the Tract *De Habitu Virginum*.

And if we were to judge of the whole Church, or of any portion of it, by the invectives which are pronounced against certain vices in certain members of it, what would the indignant remonstrances of Bishop Latimer lead us to suppose was the state of England in his day:—of the Protestant Court of Edward VI., and of the reformed Church of our fathers?

And, if the characters of the very preachers against iniquity were always to be involved in the stain of which they speak (and unless it be on that principle, I know not whence the stigma falls upon those names which Mr Taylor delights to mention); where again would be the character of every bold reprover of vice in every age?

And what can be a more satisfactory proof of the purity of the Christian Church, as a society, from any particular vice, than the indignant reprobation of that vice by all who hint at it, and its denunciation by several Councils?[1] Perhaps it

---

[1] The learned reader may turn to Dodwell's third Cyprianic Dissertation, for much learning on the whole of this matter; and for the voice of Fathers and Councils, to sect. 3 of that Dissertation.

may signify little to Mr Taylor, that there is in the Apostles' Creed such an Article as "THE HOLY CATHOLIC CHURCH;" but we confess that we should scarce prove its *holiness* very satisfactorily, if we found in all its safeguards of virtue, and all its repudiation of vice, nothing but the symptoms of leprosy, or the indications of a moral plague.

If Mr Taylor himself had not zealously laboured to disabuse us of such an opinion, we should have been in danger of taking his book for the work of a man half learned at most, who had heaped together by the use of indexes all the passages which seemed to serve his impure purpose by some *mention* at the very least of impurity, though to condemn it: and that without reading a single entire page, still less a single entire treatise, he had concluded, that all was alike impure, or capable of easy misrepresentation.

But this at least is certain. That Mr Taylor has commenced the study of the Fathers with a sinister purpose, with a mind early infected with the spirit of dissent, at an age when it was too late for him to acquire that tact, without which the theological, and even the profane literature of an age, can never be understood and appreciated. Such being his object, and such his qualifications for the task, the irreverent and the impure will revel in his pages, if they be unlearned; but all the really learned will see through his artifice or imperfect information, whichever it may be: and the Church of God, which has withstood the attacks of moral persecution from many a stronger hand, will weep as she receives the blow, not at her own discomfiture, but at the impiety of her son.

## CHAPTER IV.

Revolutions in the Roman State.—Their influence on the condition of the Church. — Edicts of Decius.—The Persecution commences. — Some retire from Carthage—among whom St Cyprian himself.—Cyprian's reasons for retiring.—His care of the Church while absent.—His letter to the Confessors.—The insinuations of the Roman Clergy against Cyprian: and Cyprian's answer to their Epistle.—The Progress of the Persecution.—The sufferings of Mappalicus, and other Confessors and Martyrs.

WHILE St Cyprian was engaged in restoring that discipline which a long peace had relaxed, the Roman state was convulsed by a rapid succession of rebellions. Within the space of six months the two Philips were slain; a traitor, who had assumed the imperial name, expiated his treason with his blood; and the imperial dignity descended on one no better entitled to it than the rebel whom he had chastised. Early in the summer of the year 249 a rebellion broke out among the legions of Mœsia, who invested an inferior officer named Marinus with the purple. Decius marched against the upstart, who was soon after murdered: and Decius, who left Rome the general of Philip, returned in the imperial robes, to hurl his former master from the throne. The elder Philip met the traitor with an army of superior numbers, but the appeal to arms was unsuccessful: he was routed, and in a few days slain at Verona; and soon after, his son and associate in the empire, the younger Philip, was murdered at Rome by the prætorian guard. This was in August: in September, Decius proclaimed himself emperor, throwing off all pretences of allegiance, which he had hitherto affected to maintain; and in October he was received at Rome with the acclamations of the people and senate.

To the citizens of Rome it was comparatively unimportant whether Philip, or Marinus, or Decius, reigned; but to the Christians throughout the empire it was far otherwise. These revolutions were the signal of a bitter persecution. Philip had always been favourable to Christianity, and Eusebius tells us, that it was even reported by some that he was a Christian: but Decius was warmly attached to the superstitions of his forefathers; was alarmed *possibly* at the number of Christians who might be expected to resent the death of Philip, and *certainly* was not the more kindly disposed towards Christians, for Philip's encouragement of the Church. The reign of Decius commenced, therefore, with an edict against the Christians, directed to the magistrates throughout the empire; in which he commanded that the Christians should be driven to apostacy, and to the worship of the heathen deities, by every motive of fear and force; threatening the infliction of severe penalties, and even tortures, upon the magistrates themselves, if they should neglect to execute this decree in all its rigour. The officers in the several provinces, thus stimulated to a cruel persecution, immediately entered upon their odious charge; and seemed to make it an occasion of increasing their ingenuity, as well as cruelty, in the arts and infliction of torture. Many were thrown into prison, many were scourged, and new and strange instruments of torture were exhibited, to intimidate the appointed victims; and in many instances death was the only favour which the judge conferred on the trembling and agonised confessor and martyr.

The letters of Dionysius of Alexandria, preserved by Eusebius, give some account of the persecution which followed on this edict in Egypt; though he tells us at the same time, that a popular fury, which often ended in horrid violence and murder, had already been excited against the Christians of Alexandria by a poet, who had employed his art in upholding the ancient superstitions, and exciting his fellow-citizens against the Christians. This letter of Dionysius, together with the Epistle of St Cyprian, to which we shall presently refer, affords a sufficiently correct view of what was passing throughout Christendom: nor shall we find any lack of such descriptions of particular cases of suffering and constancy, as may give to the general history the necessary, though in this case painful, interest of individual and personal details.

The first step which was taken on the publication of the edict of Decius seems to have been, the appointing a day on which all who were accused or suspected of being Christians should be required to renounce their faith, and sacrifice to the heathen gods. Meanwhile they were suffered to remain unmolested in possession of their own property, and without any farther sacrifice of their rights, as subjects and citizens. There was sufficient leniency here towards *the persons* of the brethren, but a cruel policy *against the faith of the Church;* for there was no more likely method than this to make apostates. The measure of suffering which he might have to expect on the appointed day, was yet unknown to the Christian; and he had no ground to look for anything short of the most cruel torments and a lingering death. Space was given to brood upon this danger; and the Church had not been composed of men, if there had not been found many to shrink from torture and death by a denial of their holy faith; especially since this, too, was made easy to them by many devices, which ensured to the apostates the safety, without the public exposure, of their recusancy.

Many, in express obedience to the precept of our blessed Lord Himself, who taught His disciples, when persecuted in one city to flee to another, retired from Carthage, leaving their possessions as the price of their life; and perhaps (since some of them doubtless fled from their distrust of their own fortitude), as a price of their Christianity also. These certainly did well, and reasoned justly, and received a reward in proportion to their integrity and faith; although, as we shall find hereafter, they avoided not the sneers and reproof of their more courageous brethren. "Let no one, my beloved brethren," says Cyprian, in his Treatise on the Lapsed, "let no one derogate from the honours of those who thus maintained their integrity, nor cast any reproach upon their confession. When the appointed day had passed, whoever had not yet denied himself to be a Christian, had in fact confessed the faith of Christianity. The first title to the crown belongs indeed to those who confess their Lord in the hands of the heathen; but to reserve one's self in the faith and service of the Lord, by a cautious retreat, is only second to that highest point of glory. The first is a public confession, the latter is a private confession. The first is a conquest over the judge of this world; the latter is the maintaining a pure conscience, and integrity of heart, content with the testimony of God alone. On the one hand is the greater and more cheerful endurance; on the other a wiser and safer caution. One man is found ready, when the hour of suffering approaches; but another is perhaps only reserved for a future trial, having already sacrificed his fortune, that he might not abjure the faith."[1]

Those who fled of course suffered proscription, and confiscation of goods; while those who remained, but neither sacrificed to heathen gods, nor otherwise denied their faith, were banished, or cast into prison, there to await the more vigorous proceedings of the proconsul, when he should arrive at his province. St Cyprian himself was among those who avoided persecution by an early retreat: not, however, before he had seen ample indications, that against him especially, as the Bishop of the Church, the fury of the heathens would be excited; not before the circus and the amphitheatre had again and again echoed the voices of the people, calling out that he should be cast to the lions; and not before (which is far the most important) he had become fully convinced by the best consideration, and, as he himself tells us, by a warning also from heaven, that he should thus be fulfilling his duty to God and His Church more perfectly. Under these circumstances it was, that he followed the precept of the Lord, as he himself assures the Roman Clergy;[2] and at the first outbreak

[1] *De Lapsis*, p. 182.   [2] *Ep.* xiv.

of popular fury, when the cries of the people were swelled with loud threatenings against him, consulting not so much his own safety, as the welfare of the flock committed to his charge, he made his retreat; lest by his inopportune and illjudged presence, the commotion already so violent, should be still more increased.[1] On this retreat Cæcilius Cyprian was proscribed by name, and his estate confiscated.[2]

We know not the place of St Cyprian's first retreat, nor the names of any of his companions, except Victor his Deacon: he tells us, however, incidentally, that he had not retired from Carthage, without leaving so much of his property, as he was enabled to appropriate, for the benefit of the poor of his diocese; committing it, for that purpose, to the Presbyter Rogatian: and we have presently sufficient indications, that if absent in body, he was yet in spirit present with his flock; sparing neither exertion, nor prayers, nor eucharistic commemorations, nor frequent directions, encouragements, and reproofs, to preserve them in the true faith of Christ, and within the bonds of Apostolical order.

He was careful, therefore, through the medium of Tertullus,[3] of whom he speaks with much affection, to receive constant intelligence from Carthage; and he made up for his absence, as much as possible, by his frequent letters to the Clergy, and to the people of his Church. He begins, in Epistle V. with the necessary provisions for maintaining discipline in his absence. Having acknowledged the good providence of God in his present security, he exhorts his Clergy to give the greater diligence to the affairs of the Church: since his part in them had now devolved on their management; and since the state of Carthage, and his own office, more obnoxious to popular vengeance, permitted not his return. With prudence,

---

[1] St Cyprian is not the only person who has avoided persecution by flight under the like circumstances. "His contemporaries, Dionysius of Alexandria, and Gregory of Neocæsarea, had fled also; as had Polycarp before them, and Athanasius after them." See chap. xii. of "The Church of the Fathers;" in which is an admirable view of the principles o the Church of Christ on this subject.

[2] *Ep.* lxix.       [3] *Ep.* xxxvii. p. 50.

and a total absence of all fanaticism, he exhorts them to a proper care to restore all things to peace and quiet, if it were possible; and he suggests a present rule of conduct to this end, that the Presbyters, whose office it was to visit the confessors in their prisons, should not crowd about them in too great numbers; but that they should go separately, each attended with his single Deacon; that the attention of the heathen might not be arrested, nor their suspicions needlessly excited; that the Priests might not be debarred the exercise of their duty in administering the Holy Eucharist to their imprisoned brethren, nor they be deprived of the privileges of communion: "for we ought," says he, "as servants of God, to adapt ourselves to the present times, meekly and humbly; to concert means of quiet, and to have respect even to the feelings of the people."

The same real wisdom is manifest in all his letters under these trying circumstances. In his seventh Epistle, for instance, he writes to his Clergy, "I salute you, dearest brethren, being through God's blessing in safety; and I would that I might soon obtain permission from heaven, and find fitting occasion to return to you, both to your joy and my own. For what would both my pleasure and spiritual interest point out as the best place for me, but that in which the providence of God made me a Christian. But however trying it may be to remain still separated from you, it is my first duty to promote the peace of the community, and to remain here; lest my return should excite the rage and malice of the Gentiles, and I, who ought to consult peace in all that I do, should become the chief occasion of violence." In this letter, St Cyprian makes mention of a supply out of his own patrimony, which he had left behind him for the use of the pensioners of the Church; and he mentions a farther supply which he thus sent by his Acolyth Naricus; and makes suitable arrangements for its distribution.

St Cyprian's sixth Epistle[1] is addressed to Sergius, Rogatianus, and the other confessors in prison; to those, that is

[1] *Ep*. lxxxi. in the Benedictine Edition.

who had refused obedience to the edict of Decius, before the magistrates of Carthage; and were remitted to confinement until the arrival of the Proconsul with higher powers. The terms of high praise and of respect in which he addresses these sufferers for the name of Christ, may prepare us to hear of their future elation, when we consider how very difficult it is for men to bear the praise of their fellow-creatures, without vanity and presumption: yet from Cyprian, whose adherence to the cause of Christ was of a different complexion, and though equally sincere, yet wanting in the splendour of a public confession, and continued sufferings before the eyes of the people, those expressions of deep reverence come with a peculiarly good grace. "Would," says he, "that the present state of affairs would permit me to visit you in person: for what could now fill me with greater joy, than to embrace you again, and to receive the pressure of those arms, which have retained their purity amid the temptations to idolatry, and still held fast the faith of our Lord? What so delightful, what so ennobling, as to touch those lips which have uttered a glorious confession: and to be seen by those eyes, which have looked down upon this world, and shewn themselves worthy of the beatific vision? But since so great a privilege is denied me, I send these letters to you in my place; at the same time congratulating you, and exhorting you to farther perseverance, that you may stand fast in your professions, and persist in your heavenly path, until you receive the crown of glory; having that God for your defender and keeper, who saith, *Lo! I am with you always, even unto the end of the world.* O blessed prison, which your presence has illuminated: O blessed dungeon, which is but as the next step to heaven! O darkness more splendid than the sun itself, so long as it contains living temples of our God, even your bodies sanctified by a divine confession! Now you need no other occupation than to meditate on those divine precepts and loving commands, with which the Holy Spirit has continued to animate you to the endurance of suffering. Think not then of death, but of immortality; think not of temporary torment, but of eternal glory; since it is written, *Precious in the sight of the Lord is the death of His saints:* and again; *A broken spirit is a sacrifice to God, a broken and a contrite heart God doth not despise:* and again; where holy writ speaks of those divine torments which consecrate the martyrs of God, and sanctify them by the very endurance of suffering: 'Though they be punished in the sight of men, yet is their hope full of immortality. And having been a little chastised, they shall be greatly rewarded: for God proved them, and found them worthy for Himself. As gold in the fire hath He tried them, and received them as a burnt-offering. And in the time of their visitation they shall shine, and run to and fro like sparks among the stubble. They shall judge the nations and have dominion over the people, and their Lord shall reign for ever.'"[1]

Cyprian proceeds to some appropriate exhortations; and we learn from his letter, that women and children were not free from this persecution, nor wanting in that divine grace, which enabled them to witness a good confession. He mentions with especial praise Rogatian and Felicissimus, two ecclesiastics, who had borne the first outrage of heathen violence, preparing as it were for their brethren, mansions in the prison house, and a way to heaven through violence and death: and he does not conclude without a prayer, that those whom God had made confessors, He would still continue to bless, until their first steps to glory should be consummated with the martyrs' crown.

While St Cyprian was thus earnestly engaged in fulfilling his duty towards his flock, though absent, reports had gone abroad to his disadvantage; and at Rome he had been represented rather as a renegade than as a faithful but prudent man, acting himself upon those high principles of duty, which he openly recommended to others in the like case.

It seems doubtful whether the Roman Clergy had heard of Cyprian's retreat from his enemies; or whether they had heard it only imperfectly, and without any of the peculiar circumstances which forced the Bishop to a temporary retreat

[1] Wisdom iii. 4-8.

for the benefit of his people. At any rate, they had not yet been told, for there had not been time for this, of that great diligence in his charge which, as they themselves afterwards confessed, made him as it were present with his flock, though in person he was absent from them. Looking upon Carthage, therefore, as a deserted Church, and being themselves deprived of their Bishop by the martyrdom of Fabian, they wrote to Carthage a letter, in which they offered many suggestions, in harmony with the directions which Cyprian had already given, for the better government of the Church; and in which they glanced somewhat severely at the conduct of the absent Bishop. There can be little advantage in transcribing strictures which evidently took their rise from a false report, or at least a misapprehension: one passage, however, I cannot refrain from copying (though it is not quite free from insinuations against St Cyprian), since it gives us a fair description of the Church of Rome at that time. "We do not," say the clergy of Rome to their brethren at Carthage, "send you bare exhortations, but they are enforced, as you may easily learn from those who have seen our state, by our example. By God's grace we have done, and yet do, according to our precepts, notwithstanding the extreme peril in which we stand; for we have the fear of God, and eternal torments, rather than man's anger, and a short suffering, before our eyes; and thus encouraged, we leave not the brethren forsaken, but continually warn them to constancy in the faith, and preparation to meet the Lord. Thus we have even recalled some to their duty, who were going up to the Capitol by restraint, to offer sacrifice, or openly to apostatise. Our Church stands firm; though some indeed have fallen, either from the extremity of terror, or because they were remarkable for their station, and the more exposed to the fear of man: whom, however, even in their separation from us, we do not utterly abandon; but we exhort them to repentance, that they may obtain pardon from Him who can alone bestow it; lest being utterly forsaken by us, they should become worse."[1]

[1] Ep. ii.

Crementius, the Subdeacon, who was the messenger of the Roman Clergy to Carthage, carried also a letter to St Cyprian, giving an account of the martyrdom of Fabian. This letter was so expressed, as to convey a tacit reproof to Cyprian for his retreat. I shall give Cyprian's answer entire.[1]

"Cyprian to his brethren the Presbyters and Deacons of Rome, Health! When there was an uncertain rumour, dearest brethren, among us, of the departure of that excellent man my colleague,[2] and we were doubtful what to think, I received your letters at the hands of Crementius the Subdeacon, by which I was fully informed of his glorious exit; and I was exceedingly rejoiced, that the honour of its close was worthy of the integrity of his administration. I congratulate you very highly, because you perpetuate his memory in so illustrious a testimony; so that through you I am acquainted with the splendid reputation of your Bishop, and an example of faith and virtue is thus afforded me. For the fall of a Bishop is not more pernicious as an example of defection, than his fidelity is useful and salutary for the imitation of his brethren. I have also read another letter, in which it is not clearly expressed either by whom or to whom it was written; and since both its character and contents, and the paper itself, raised a doubt in me, whether it had not been mutilated or corrupted, I have sent back to you the identical letter, that you may yourselves discover whether it is the same which you sent by Crementius the Subdeacon: for it is a matter of the utmost importance, if the integrity of the letters of the clergy is rendered questionable by deception or fraud. That I may know this, therefore, examine carefully, whether the writing and subscription be yours, and return to me the true account of the matter. I wish you, dearest brethren, continued health."

This mention of the death of Fabian, Bishop of Rome, opens to us an altered view of the present persecution. It was before observed, that the Christians were not, generally at least, immediately put to death; but that some days were

[1] Ep. iii.     [2] Fabian, Bishop of Rome.

allowed for them to determine whether they would sacrifice their rights as subjects, or their religion; and that those who confessed Christ at the expiration of that term, were then banished, or committed to prison, until the Proconsul of each province should arrive, to enforce a more rigorous sentence. But still death was the ultimate sanction of the imperial edicts: and in Rome, where they were first published, would the interval soonest expire between their mildest and their most severe execution. Accordingly, Fabian first fell a sacrifice to the inhuman edict of Decius: Alexander Bishop of Jerusalem, and Babylas of Antioch, succeeded in due time; and the persecution being directed more especially against the Bishops of the several Churches, as St Cyprian himself assures us, the Prelates of various Churches received the crown of martyrdom; while others, among whom were Gregory Thaumaturgus and Dionysius Alexandrinus, sought security, as Cyprian did, in a temporary retreat; the latter Prelate, as well as Cyprian, pleading an express revelation from heaven as his warrant.[1]

Fabian, who had filled the Roman see fourteen years, received his crown on the twentieth of January, in the year of grace 250. Soon after, Moyses and Maximus, of whom we shall hear more presently, and Nicostratus a Deacon, were cast into prison; and Celerinus, of a family of martyrs,[2] was summoned before Decius, and after many torments was imprisoned nineteen days. By the time that a report of these things had reached Carthage, the persecution had assumed there also the same violent form. The Proconsul arrived at Carthage probably about the beginning of April, nearly at the same time at which Crementius came from Rome, with letters to Cyprian, and to the Clergy at Carthage. Those who were already imprisoned were treated with greater rigour: they

[1] Eusebius, vi. 40.

[2] "Avia ejus Celerina jam pridem martyrio coronata est: item patruus ejus et avunculus Laurentius et Egnatius, in castris et ipsi quondam sæcularibus militantes, sed veri et spiritales Dei milites, dum diabolum Christi confessione prosternunt, palmas a Domino et coronas illustri passione meruerunt." Ep. xxxiv.

were macerated with hunger and thirst, and thus prepared to experience the most savage tortures, or death itself. A general view of this stage of the persecution may be collected from St Cyprian's Epistles, written at this time, which will also afford us some instances of individual suffering and constancy. I shall transcribe the first of his Epistles (No. X.) to the martyrs and confessors on this occasion, as affording not only a description of the sufferings of the Christians of these times; but also an example of the manner in which their Bishop fulfilled his part as a ruler of the flock, and as their friend and counsellor in all spiritual matters.

"Cyprian to the martyrs and confessors, continued health in Christ our Lord, and in God the Father.

"I am exceeding glad, and heartily congratulate you, brethren, most blessed in your great endurance, when I hear of your faith and courage, in which your Mother the Church triumphs. Indeed she triumphed before, when a judicial sentence drove the confessors of Christ into exile, without shaking their constancy. But your present confession is as much more glorious and honourable than that, as the sufferings have been greater, through which it has been maintained. The combat has been greater, and greater has been the glory of the combatants. You have not been deterred from the contest, but you have been rather the more excited to the battle, by the prospect of torture: and you have returned, firm and undaunted, with an unshaken devotion, to the struggles of the hottest engagement. Some of you, I hear, have already been crowned; some are pressing towards the crown of victory, and stand ready to grasp it; and all the glorious band, upon whom the dungeon has closed, are animated with an equal and mutual ardour to carry on the contest. This is as it ought to be with the soldiers of Christ in the army of the saints; that effeminacy may not enervate, that threats may not terrify, that racks and tortures may not move the integrity and stability of their faith: since He is greater who is in us than he who is in the world; and no earthly infliction has greater power to cast us down than the Divine help has to support us. Of this we

have the proof before our eyes in the glorious contest of those
of our brethren, who were the leaders in this conquest of tortures; and afforded an example of constancy and faith, while
they rushed again and again on the battle, until the battle was
overcome. In what words shall I proclaim your praises, O
brethren, most invincible! With what device of the herald
shall I blazon the strength of your fortitude, the endurance of
your faith! You have borne the most exquisite tortures, even
to the consummation of your glory; nor have you yielded to
torment, but rather torment has yielded to you. Your martyrdom has crowned those sufferings, to which your tortures
refused to put an end. The severity of infliction was thus
continued, not to the overthrow of a dauntless faith, but that
it might transport men more rapidly to their Lord. The spec-
tators wondering at the celestial contest, the contest of God,
the spiritual contest, the battle of Christ, saw His servants
standing, with a determined voice, with a mind untainted,
with heavenly virtue; without the arms of this world, indeed,
but strong in the panoply of faith. The tortured stood more
unmoved than their torturers; and the crushed and lacerated
limbs overcame the instruments of cruelty. The fierce and
often repeated lash could not overcome their invincible faith,
although their very vitals were laid open with repeated stripes,
and the frequent blow fell not on the body, but on the wounds
of the servants of God. The effusion of blood might have extinguished the flames of persecution, might have assuaged the
very fires of hell with its glorious stream. O how noble was
that spectacle! In the eyes of the Lord how sublime! How
great, how acceptable in the sight of God, that fulfilment of
the oath, that pledge of the devotion of His soldiers! since it
is written in the Psalms, the Holy Spirit speaking also to us,
*Precious in the sight of the Lord is the death of His saints.* This
is indeed a precious death, which has purchased immortality;
which has received the crown as the consummation of virtue.
How did Christ then rejoice! How willingly did He fight and
conquer in such servants of His; confirming their constancy,
and giving to all those who believed in Him according to their

faith! He was present, as if the contest were His own: He strengthened, encouraged, and animated those who fought for Him, and for the honour of His name: and He who once conquered death *for* us, continues to conquer death *in* us. *When they shall deliver you up,* says He, *think not what ye shall say; for in that hour it shall be given you what ye shall say; for it is not ye who speak, but the Spirit of your Father who speaketh in you.* The present combat afforded an evidence of this truth. A word full of the Holy Spirit broke from the mouth of the most blessed martyr Mappalicus, when he exclaimed, in the midst of his tortures, to the Proconsul, *To-morrow shall you see a struggle indeed!* And what he said with the witness of a courageous faith, the Lord Himself fulfilled. The heavenly struggle was seen; and the servant of God received his crown in the height of the anticipated contest. . . . This is the struggle which the Apostle Paul describes, in which we ought to run so as to obtain the crown of glory : *Know ye not,* says he, *that they which run in a race run all, but one receiveth the prize? So run, that ye may obtain. And every man that striveth for the mastery is temperate in all things. Now they do it to obtain a corruptible crown; but we an incorruptible.* Again, describing his own contest, and in immediate anticipation of being offered up, he says, *For I am now ready to be offered, and the time of my departure is at hand. I have fought a good fight, I have finished my course, I have kept the faith : henceforth there is laid up for me a crown of righteousness, which the Lord, the righteous Judge, shall give me at that day : and not to me only, but unto all them also that love His appearing.*

"This struggle, therefore, appointed by the Lord, undergone by Apostles, Mappalicus, in his own name and in the name of his companions, promised that the Proconsul should see. Nor did he disappoint the expectation that he had excited : he exhibited the contest he had promised; he bore off the palm which he deserved. Let me, then, exhort those of you who remain to follow that most glorious martyr, and the rest who shared in his engagement; who were patient in tribulation, who were victorious over the rack, and stood like soldiers and comrades unbroken in faith. That those whom the bond of one confession and the walls of the dungeon have already associated, may also be associated in the consummation of virtue and the heavenly crown. That you may dry, by your joy, those tears of your Mother the Church, which she sheds over the fall and ruin of many; and that you may confirm those, who are yet unshaken, by your example of endurance. When your turn shall arrive, and you too shall be called to the fight, quit yourselves valiantly, and endure with constancy; well assured that you fight under the eyes of the Lord, who is present with you, and that you march to glory through the confession of His name. He is not such a master as to look on His servants from afar; but He Himself struggles together with them; with them He advances to the conflict: He Himself, in the successful issue, both bestows and receives a crown.

"If, however, the Lord should grant peace to the Church, before your day of conflict arrive, still yours is the unshaken purpose, and yours a conscious deserving of glory. Nor let any of you be moved to envy by the apparent superiority of those who have endured torments before you, and arrived by a glorious journey to the Lord, having trampled a conquered world under their feet. The Lord is a discerner of the hearts and the reins; He sees through our secret thoughts, and looks into our inmost heart. The testimony of Him alone, who is to award it, will be sufficient to secure you the crown. Either condition, therefore, dearest brethren, is alike noble and illustrious; it is safer to hasten to the Lord fresh from the victory; it is more joyous, having served with honour, to receive for a while the praises of the Church. O how blessed is our Church become; bright with the approval of God, illustrious with the glorious blood of her martyrs. She was already white with the works of her sons; now she is red with the blood of martyrs: neither the lily nor the rose is wanting in her coronal. Now let each one of you contend for the full possession of either dignity: let him receive either a white crown for his works, or a purple crown for his passion. Peace and war have their garlands alike in the heavenly camp, with which the soldier of Christ may be gloriously crowned.

"Brethren, most courageous and most blessed, I wish you health in the Lord: continue to hold me in your remembrance. Fare ye well."

The history of a persecution is but an aggregate of the records of sufferings inflicted on separate individuals. I shall therefore best finish this part of the subject, by collecting from the works of Cyprian some other accounts similar to that of Mappalicus in the foregoing letter.

Celerinus,[1] descended from a family of martyrs, both on his father's and his mother's side, was the first who earned the glorious title of a confessor, animating his brethren by his example, and teaching them victory by his successful endurance. Yet, as Cyprian tells us, his struggle was not short nor light; but he triumphed by a miraculous constancy and courage: nineteen days and nights was he confined and tortured; but his body only was enchained, while his soul remained free and unshackled. His body was emaciated by hunger and thirst; but God kept his soul alive in faith and virtue, with spiritual food. While stretched upon the rack, he was stronger than his torturers; while in prison, greater than they who imprisoned him; prostrate so far as his body was concerned, he was more lofty than they who stood over him; in his bonds he was more unfettered than they who bound him; receiving his sentence more dignified than his judges. The marks of his wounds remained conspicuous in his glorious body; and his emaciated limbs long bore witness of his suffering. Such patient endurance received the honourable testimony even of the persecutor himself, and is worthy to stand foremost among the records of this season of affliction patiently endured to the glory of God, and the honour of the Church.

Aurelius also receives an honourable testimony from St

[1] *Ep.* xxxiv.

Cyprian, as one who had twice suffered for the faith; first of all, indeed, being banished only, but afterwards tortured, and victorious on both occasions. It should seem that the torture was often inflicted, and before several magistrates, since Cyprian tells us, that as often as the adversary would challenge the servant of God, so often was he found prompt and courageous, so often did he fight and conquer. To have suffered in banishment under the eyes of a few was little: he was reserved to display a greater endurance in the Forum itself, that he might be victorious over the proconsul, as he had before been over the inferior magistrates; and that after his exile, he might suffer tortures. The account which we have of Lucian tells us incidentally, that the torture inflicted on Aurelius had deprived him of the use of his hands; for he was one of those whose names Lucian used, (with that pretext,) in the letters of communion to the lapsed, with which Lucian is less honourably connected, than his place as a confessor would warrant us to expect.

For Lucian was a faithful and courageous witness for the truth; though not sufficiently imbued with those principles of order and discipline which might have handed down his name, with that of Celerinus and Mappalicus, his brethren in suffering, with unalloyed splendour. He himself thus speaks of his sufferings, with those of several others, his companions.[1] Bassus died in the quarries: Mappalicus on the rack: Fortunio in prison. Paulus from the effects of torture; and Fortunata, Victorinus, Victor, Herennius, Credula, Herena, Donatus, Firmus, Venustus, Fructus, Julia, Martialis, and Aristo, were all starved to death in prison. With these I shall myself probably be numbered, adds Lucian, before this day is over: for now we have been for eight days past confined with still greater rigour than heretofore; though for five preceding days, our only allowance was a morsel of bread each day, and a small measure of water.

With this enumeration, by one of the sufferers, of the various tortures and hardships inflicted on the brethren, I shall conclude the account of this persecution. Those who

[1] *Ep.* xxi.

estimate duly the immense moral influence of courage in suffering, combined with unshaken virtue, and mildness of demeanour, will not be at a loss to understand the assertion, that the blood of the martyrs has ever been the seed of the Church : and those who know and feel that even in Christians the remains of corruption, of fear and self-indulgence continue, will not wonder that many were found unable to stand against so violent an assault. The constancy of those who patiently endured to the end, striving even unto blood, we must ascribe to the grace of God, operating in them marvellously, almost miraculously; and sometimes, indeed, with an evident manifestation of an Almighty hand, that neither persecutors nor persecuted might fail to see, that it was not the might of man, but of God, which was thus put forth. For those who fell we may mourn; but proudly or harshly we may not condemn them. It is God that maketh us to differ; and He who glorified His power in the strong, may hereafter glorify His mercy in the feeble.

## CHAPTER V.

The Number of Apostates in the Decian Persecution.—The *Sacrificati*, *Thurificati* and *Libellatici*.—The Discipline of the Lapsed.—Its Rigour, —and its Occasional Relaxation.—The Privilege of the Martyrs :— Abused in this Instance.—The Clergy chiefly in Fault.—Cyprian's own Determination of the Case of the Lapsed.

IN this persecution, which was the fiercest to which Christianity had yet been exposed; and which found the Church less prepared than it had been at any previous time to resist its spiritual enemies; a proportionate number of the brethren, in all parts of the Roman empire, apostatised from the faith. We have several indications of the multitude of the lapsed, not in Carthage only, but in Egypt, and Spain, and in Rome itself: and now it was that by the united effort of the sound part of the Church in all Christendom, the ecclesiastical regulations concerning the treatment of the lapsed, on their return to a better mind, were reduced to the most perfect form that they ever assumed. This was not effected, however, without very serious divisions in several places; and the exigency of the times, in this as in other cases, called out and exercised the master mind of St Cyprian.

Those who lapsed in times of persecution, had been called formerly, from the kinds of abjuration which had been demanded of them, SACRIFICATI, and THURIFICATI; according as they had approached the heathen altars with a sacrifice, or only with incense: but in the present persecution, another kind of apostates arose out of the circumstances of the times, called LIBELLATICI. The two former classes of persons had plainly and unequivocally denied their Saviour and the one true God; the *Libellatici* found a way of avoiding the penalties of persecution by a more indirect, yet still a real, denial of their faith, and by a virtual dereliction of their religious principle. It is probable that Decius had decreed that every one who was accused or suspected of being a Christian, should be called on to produce a certificate, or *libellus*, from the magistrate, attesting that he had abjured his faith in Christ, or declared that he had never been a Christian. The cupidity of the magistrate, and the pusillanimity of some of the accused (fearful alike to deny their heavenly Master, and to confront a heathen judge), conspired to erect on this foundation a system equally disgraceful to both; yet one which should enrich the one, while it ensured safety to the other, at the expense of such a measure of temporising, as might probably evade all censure and inquiry. The timid Christian was eager to purchase, and the venal magistrate was not unwilling to sell, such a testimonial, or *libellus*, as was required to ensure a freedom from farther molestation: and the *Libellaticus*, or person who had purchased the *libellus*, returned to his occupation and his patrimony, no longer obnoxious to the laws.

The sale of these *libelli* was more profitable to the magistrate than the shedding of Christian blood: and it was more subversive, whether or no it was suspected to be so at the time, of the true interests of the Church; which flourished while it was watered with the blood of martyrs, and encouraged by the voice of confessors; and only languished in the sad but silent defection of cowardly pretenders. Every facility seems to have been given to those who would thus purchase immunity from suffering; and it is more than probable that many were permitted to purchase the *libellus*, without being subjected to a public examination, or to any inquiries. The number of those who were detected by the circumstances of their defection, was sufficient to overwhelm the Church with sorrow and shame; and we need not now speculate on the multitude, who may have secretly enjoyed their purchased freedom from suffering, together with the peace of the Church.

These *Libellatici* were numbered, equally with the *Thurificati* and *Sacrificati*, among the lapsed; although their crime was not held to be quite so great, and their ecclesiastical penalty was moderated in proportion. The discipline of the lapsed, which had been previously established by the usage of the Church, seems to have been as follows. Those who had denied the faith explicitly, or by offering sacrifice or incense, were at once excommunicated: no offerings were received from them, and no mention was made of them at the Eucharistic commemorations; nor were they received with the faithful into any ecclesiastical fellowship. They were not, however, utterly cast off, nor left to become hardened by escaping observation and rebuke; nor, if they came to a sense of their miserable condition, were they permitted to remain in despair of the favour of God, by being for ever shut out from the peace of the Church: but all those who would bear reproof and receive exhortation, seem to have been the object of vigilant and laborious attention from the Clergy of the Church; while all who came of themselves to a sense of their condition, and desired the peace of the Church, even though their fidelity did not return till all danger was past, were admitted, at the discretion of the Bishop, to a penance proportionate with their offence; and were afterwards formally received into communion with the faithful, by Episcopal imposition of hands.

Another and a more glorious way of retrieving their place in the Church, was by actual confession afterwards, and a martyr's death. In such cases as these, the long and formal penance which was usually necessary, which was profitable both to the returning lapsed, and to the Church in general, was fairly remitted; since no length or rigour of penance could be more effectual than such a confession or death, to attest their return to soundness of faith and Christian courage; nor could any exhibition of a humiliated condition, nor any solemnity of reconciliation, more effectually impress the whole body of the Church with the necessity of faithful endurance, and a good confession. In the case of those who actually attested their perfect restoration to the faith with their blood, none denied that they received a martyr's crown; especially since martyrdom was always accounted a kind of second baptism, in which all sins were purged away, at least on the Church's account, with blood; as they had been, in the ordinary laver of regeneration, with water.

There were also some cases, in which it would have been manifestly more rigorous than wise or charitable to withhold the communion of the Church from penitents among the lapsed; even though the whole term of their penance had not transpired, and though they had not received imposition of hands from the Bishop. Such was the case of those who were truly penitent, so far as man could judge, and who fell into any mortal sickness, before they were restored. And in cases in which extreme danger seemed to threaten a whole population, due provision was sometimes made for the frequent occurrence of such cases. Thus St Cyprian himself, in anticipation of a season of peculiar unhealthiness at Carthage, proposes in some degree to relax those rules which postponed the restoration of the lapsed, till the judgment of the Bishop in person had been heard: "Since," says he, in an Epistle to his Clergy (xii.), "summer has already commenced, which is a season abounding with serious sickness, I think that some indulgence ought to be granted to our brethren, and that those who have received letters of communion from the martyrs, and may hope through their privileges to be accepted by God, if they are seized with any grievous and dangerous illness, may make confession of their fault before any Presbyter who may be present, without waiting for my return; or if a Presbyter cannot be found, and death seems near at hand, before a Deacon, so that by imposition of hands, in order to their penance, they may approach the Lord in that peace of the Church, which the martyrs would have bestowed upon them by their letters. The rest of the people also who have fallen, I would have you support by your presence, cherishing them with appropriate encouragement, that they may not entirely fall away from the faith and from the mercy of the Lord: for they, who in meekness and humility and true penitence persevere in good works, will not be so forsaken by the gracious help of the Lord, as not to be partakers of the mercy of God."

Eusebius[1] relates an interesting case, which will illustrate this provision by the example of an individual. Serapion had led an irreproachable life; but having sacrificed to the heathen gods during the violence of persecution, he often implored remission, but in vain. Being taken ill, he remained three days speechless and insensible. On the fourth day coming to himself, he called a youth to him, and said, "How long shall I be detained in this world while absolution is withheld from me? Go, and bring me a Priest." After this he again became speechless. The child ran to fetch a Priest; but it was night, and the Priest was sick. His Bishop, however, (Dionysius of Alexandria, on whose authority Eusebius relates this story), had ordered, as we have before seen Cyprian doing, that Communion should not be withheld from those who implored it in their last moments (especially if they had asked for it while in health), so that they might die in hope of salvation. The Priest, therefore, gave the child a portion of the Eucharist, telling him to moisten it with water, and to put it into Serapion's mouth. The child returned; but before he had reached the house, the old man had come to himself. "My child," said he, "I perceive that you are returned, but that the Priest has not been able to come: do as he has ordered, so that I may be suffered to depart." The child moistened the portion of the Eucharist, and placed it in Serapion's mouth, who died almost immediately on receiving it. "Is it not plain," asks the historian, "that God had preserved his life until he should obtain pardon for his fault; and that, having been reconciled to the Church, he received the reward of his good works?"

Another medium of return to the peace of the Church, was

[1] *Liber* vi. 44.

the intercession of the martyrs; which was so prevailing (and founded indeed on such good grounds), as almost to amount to a command, when exercised with tolerable judgment, and consistently with good order. It was fair to suppose, that those blessed saints who were awaiting in the faith and hope of martyrs an immediate crown of glory, and admission to the beatific vision, and whose prison was sanctified to them by the presence of the Spirit of God, might especially prevail in their intercessions at the throne of grace; since an Apostle had said that *the fervent effectual*[1] *intercession of the righteous man availeth much:* and the privilege of those whose souls should soon cry from beneath the heavenly altar, against the persecutors, was thought to extend in some degree to a prevailing intercession for the persecuted. St Cyprian himself, reminding the martyrs of their duty in this respect, does not forget that they were such as should sit as judges with Christ: a consideration as proper to exalt their privilege in this case, as to prompt them to a careful and holy use of it. In these considerations there seemed sufficient grounds to attribute no slight efficacy, even with God Himself, to the intercession of martyrs; and as concerns the Church, none certainly ought to prevail so greatly with her, as those her most holy and most faithful children; whose confession was her glory, whose endurance was her strength, and in whose blood she was more than conqueror.[2]

To prevent those evils which might be expected in the exercise of such a privilege by the martyrs (and every privilege

---

[1] *Inwrought*, ἐνεργουμένη, James v. 16.

[2] These considerations prevailed with the Church in very early times. Tertullian twice alludes to the privilege of the martyrs to restore those to the peace of the Church by their intercession, who had been cut off from it by sin or apostasy, but whose repentance and desire to be restored was manifest: and there is this evidence, at least, that the custom was not new, even in Tertullian's time; that it had begun to be in part abused, as we may collect from the twenty-second chapter of his book *De Pudicitia*. Origen also has several passages bearing on the same point. But for the learning on this head, I must refer to the eighth of Dodwell's Dissertationes Cyprianicæ.

entrusted to men, however pious, is liable to abuse), it was the custom of the Priests and Deacons, who were engaged in visiting the martyrs in prison, to instruct them in the proper exercise of their privilege; to shew them the necessity of doing everything in subordination to the Church in general, and in accordance with her laws; and, in this instance, so to express their recommendations to the mercy of the Church, as to leave them to be ratified by the Bishop, the proper minister of ecclesiastical reconciliation. It was the duty of the Clergy, too, to suggest, and to approve, the individuals who should receive this great favour through the recommendations of the martyrs; an office for which they were prepared by the exercise of their pastoral care, in which they became acquainted with the character, the penitence, the reformation, of those who had yielded, indeed, to the violence of persecution, but whose tears and submission marked them out as proper recipients of the favour of the Church. Under these limitations the privilege of the martyrs, of which we have been speaking, was a great benefit not only to individual penitents, but also to the Church in general; affording a fair and constitutional method of remitting the severity of Ecclesiastical Canons, in those peculiar cases in which they were too rigorous for the particular occasion, though neccessary for the general health of the Church. It was the exercise of the royal prerogative of pardon, whereby the law is not weakened, and yet the offender is received into favour, and the community gains a subject. None could question that the peace of the Church was well bestowed upon Numeria and Candida, for instance, who had fallen, but sincerely repented; and manifested their recovery not by tears only, but by good works: whose brother Celerinus, too, a most noble confessor, himself in his prison bewailed their fall with unspeakable grief, and besought on their behalf the restoration of the Church's favour, through the mediation of Lucian, whose spirit was then vibrating, as it were, between heaven and earth.

Nor should it be forgotten that in this, as in every other case in which a rule of discipline is applied by the Church, it was never supposed that God's pardon was necessarily withheld from those who were not restored to Church communion, provided that they were really penitent. This principle, which Cyprian expressly lays down in the eleventh Epistle, sufficiently defended the practice of the Church from any taint of tyrannical severity; while it left to her laws those sanctions, by which her purity and fidelity must be guarded.

Thus, whatever there was of leniency in the treatment of the penitent lapsed, was not without reason and without profit; and whatever there was of austerity and extreme rigour, was sufficiently counteracted by the assurance, which we need not doubt was industriously afforded to all whom it properly concerned, that though the Church might not relax her rules of communion; since what was formal and external was a part of her charge; yet God, who seeth the hearts of His penitent servants, might receive those to His favour whom the Church dare not, without some indication of His will, re-admit into her fellowship. In a word, the treatment of the lapsed was a part of Church discipline, and not a judgment upon the eternal state of individual Christians. But it will be better to express this in the words of St Cyprian himself. "I know," says he, to the laity of his Church, "from my own grief, that you, dearest brethren, lament and bewail the fall of our brethren. For my part, in the words of the Apostle, *Who is weak, and I am not weak? who is offended, and I burn not?* and again, *If one member suffer, all the members suffer with it; and if one member rejoice, all the members rejoice with it.* I sympathise, therefore, and lament with you, over those of our brethren who have fallen away under the terrors of persecution: tearing away with them, as it were, a part of mine own bowels, and inflicting on me equally the pain of their wounds. *To these indeed the Divine mercy may apply a remedy;* yet I think that we ought not to judge incautiously, or to act hastily in their case; lest while the peace of the Church is rashly invaded, the Divine wrath be the more incensed against them."[1]

But during the present persecution of the Church in Africa,

[1] *Ep.* xi. p. 21.

the salutary laws, which should have restrained the exercise of the martyrs' privilege, were in many instances disregarded by all persons concerned; by the lapsed, by the Presbyters and Deacons, and even by the martyrs themselves: and hence arose miserable divisions in the Church, with all the heart-burnings and lasting evils of party spirit; some proceeding even to actual violence, and others taking occasion from this excitement and division, to add fury to a previous faction, and strength to a subsequent schism. In a word, the question of the lapsed is more or less connected, henceforth, with almost every incident of importance in which we shall find St Cyprian involved. We must therefore trace the history of these sad disputes with considerable care.

So soon as the end of April, before, that is, the extremity of persecution had lasted a month, we find Cyprian lamenting the pride and presumption of some confessors; and again, soon after (Ep. vi.), he rebukes some of the clergy for a spirit of insubordination, and contention. And in an Epistle written in June to his clergy, he feelingly laments, that the beauty and excellence of confession was so often tarnished by these vices; and having recommended humility and obedience, and regretted his own necessary absence at so trying a season, he enters at once upon the great question which then awaited his decision, touching the reconciliation of those who had received a recommendation from the martyrs, without sufficient proof of penitence on the part of the lapsed; without sufficient caution on the part of the martyrs; and wholly without a sufficient care, to say the least, on the part of the clergy, to maintain due order and discipline. "I regret," says he, "to hear that some of you, actuated by pride, and impudence, employ yourselves in exciting discord . . . . and that they cannot be governed by the Deacons or the Priests; but so demean themselves, that the illustrious splendour of many and excellent confessors is tarnished by the disreputable manners of a few. Such persons ought to dread, lest they should be expelled from the society of the good, being condemned by their testimony and judgment. For he is the truly illustrious confessor, for whom the Church has not to blush afterwards, but in whom she still glories. As for that which my brother Presbyters Donatus and Fortunatus, Novatus and Gordius, have written to me, I have been able to answer nothing alone; since I have determined, from the beginning of my Episcopate, to do nothing by my private judgment without consulting you, and without the consent of the people. But when God shall permit my return, we will determine what ought to be done together, as our mutual dignity demands."[1]

Although, however, Cyprian would absolutely determine nothing in this case for the present; yet he found it necessary to exert the authority both of his office and of his character, to regulate matters as far as possible in the meanwhile. For this purpose he wrote presently after his last Epistle three others, to the martyrs and confessors; to the clergy; and to the laity of his Church; recommending to each the course that they should pursue, in the present exigence. It is from these Epistles, chiefly, that we collect the proper and ordinary rules of the Church; and from them we also collect that these rules were in every possible respect disregarded in the present case.

The first fault seems to have been in the negligence of the clergy, in not affording to the martyrs sufficient advice and assistance in the exercise of their privilege, and the choice of the objects on behalf of whom it should be exerted. It will be well if the reader does not come to the conclusion, that in this instance the martyrs were made the tools of an ambitious and factious party among the Presbyters, who actually instigated them to an unworthy use of their licence of recommendation, in favour of men to whom they knew that Cyprian could never conscientiously concede the privilege of communion: thus associating with themselves, in their opposition against their Bishop, a body of overweening martyrs and confessors, and a clamorous party of the lapsed; while they flattered the pride of the one, and excited the hopes and passions of the other.

[1] *Ep.* v. pp. 10, 11.

For in his (tenth) Epistle to the martyrs and confessors, Cyprian expressly declares, that the fault is not so much with the martyrs themselves, as with the clergy, who ought to have so directed them, as to cut off all occasion of such disorder: whereas, in fact, the clergy were so far from setting before the martyrs the rules of the Gospel, and of ecclesiastical discipline, that they actually, and intentionally, misrepresented them; so that when the martyrs themselves would have exercised a proper caution with due respect to the authority of their Bishop, certain Presbyters rather excited them to insubordination, and made their care ineffectual. Thus many were actually admitted to communion, whom the martyrs had only recommended to the lenient judgment of the Bishop; and that before any penance had been exacted of them, or any sufficient ecclesiastical reconciliation had taken place. Thus Cyprian, while he does not wholly excuse the martyrs, yet lays the greatest blame on some of the clergy: and it is remarkable that, presumptuous and unwarrantable as some of the demands of the martyrs were, yet still, had they been precisely obeyed by the Presbyters, they would not have led to so great a breach of discipline, as the restoration to communion of the lapsed, without the Bishop's consent or knowledge. This will appear even from the following most haughty letter of the confessors to Cyprian.

"All the confessors to Pope Cyprian, Health! Be it known to you, that we have granted peace to all those, concerning whose good conduct since their fall you may be well persuaded; and it is our will that this measure of ours be made known by you to other Bishops. We would that you should maintain peace with the holy martyrs. Written by Lucian in the presence of an exorcist and reader."[1]

But if Cyprian did not condemn the martyrs so much as certain of the clergy in this matter, still less did he compare the guilt of the lapsed themselves, with that of the factious Presbyters. "As for the lapsed," says he, "they may be pardoned. Who would not seek for life, feeling himself to be

[1] *Ep.* xvi.

dead? who would not, knowing his danger, seek earnestly for safety? But those who are placed over them should restrain their impetuous desire, and keep them within the bounds of proper discipline: or else they who should be the shepherds, become rather the butchers of the flock." In another Epistle (xxvii.) Cyprian expressly tells us, that some of the lapsed, who had received the recommendations of the martyrs, yet maintained the humble and Christian bearing which was due to him as their Bishop: and these he very highly commends.

But of those of the clergy who were involved in these errors, Cyprian speaks very differently; as will appear from his ninth Epistle, of which the following is an extract.

"I have long forborne, dearest brethren, to interpose in this affair; hoping that my silence would rather tend to the peace of the Church: but now, since the rash and hasty presumption of some, threatens to disturb the honour of the martyrs, the modesty of the confessors, and the peace of the whole body of the people, I can remain silent no longer, without danger to the Church in general, as well as to my own authority. For what danger may we not anticipate, when some of the Presbyters, forgetful both of the Gospel and of their place, and slighting both the judgment of God which is to come, and His Bishop now placed over them, arrogate to themselves the sole authority with an unprecedented impudence. And I would that the injured Church were not a sufferer by their arrogance. The insulted dignity of the Episcopate I could overlook and bear, as I have often done: but now there is no place for forbearance, while the brethren are being led astray by some of your body, who endeavour to win upon the lapsed by their groundless pretences of restoring them to the peace of the Church, and in fact cajole them to their ruin. The very apostates themselves know, that they have committed the most heinous offence: and he who withholds from them the judgment of God, deceives those who are already most miserable: for then, those to whom a true repentance is open, and who may appease God, their merciful Father, by prayers and by their future obedience, are deluded to their greater damnation; and they who might otherwise retrieve themselves, are more miserably fallen. For whereas, even for smaller offences, a stated time of penance is imposed; and confession is required according to a certain rule of the Church; and the penitent is restored to his place by imposition of hands of the Bishop and clergy; now, at a brief interval, before the persecution has ceased, the Church herself not enjoying peace, they are admitted to communion, and their name is offered with those of the faithful at the altar: and without penance, without confession, without imposition of hands, the Eucharist is given to them, though it is written, *He who eateth the bread or drinketh the cup of the Lord unworthily, is guilty of the body and blood of the Lord.*

"But now the chief guilt falls upon those who are placed over them, yet neglect to inform them how they should act in this case with due reverence to God, and to the authority of the Church. Hence the blessed martyrs are exposed to envy, and the confessors are set at variance with their Bishop: so that whereas mindful of my dignity, they had originally expressed their wish that their petition might be considered when the Church was restored to peace, and I had returned to my place; the Presbyters, forgetting that honour which the martyrs had accorded to me, and despising those divine laws which they had regarded, communicate with the lapsed, before any one necessary preliminary has been observed.

"For these things the anger of God is expressed against us night and day. For not only in visions of the night are we reproved, but young children, moved by the Holy Spirit, recount to us day after day those rebukes, which the Lord will have to be uttered against us. Of these things I will give you a more particular account when the mercy of God shall restore me to my Church: meanwhile, if those among you who act so rashly and proudly, with such forgetfulness of their duty to man, and of their fear of God, still continue such a perverse conduct, I am determined to put forth that power with which the Lord hath endued me, and to suspend them from their office, until they may be heard and judged before me, and before the confessors themselves, and the whole body of the Church."

From such statements as these, we have no difficulty in determining, that the chief fault in the matter of the premature restoration of the lapsed lay with certain Presbyters. The names of some of them we collect from Cyprian's fifth Epistle; in which he mentions a letter, which evidently displeased him, from Donatus, Fortunatus, Novatus, and Gordius. Two of these names we shall find often hereafter, among the schismatical opponents of Cyprian: and we can hardly doubt that they were all among those original opposers of his election to the Episcopate, of whom Pontius tells us. It may be well to bear this in mind, for the character of these men gives a colouring to the whole history of Cyprian's Episcopate; and the perpetual recurrence of their persons and of their party affords a remarkable instance of the same moral depravity, exposing itself in various ecclesiastical offences, and falling into divers theological errors, of opposite tendencies; alike only in being evil.

It is impossible, indeed, to state the conclusion of this whole affair of the lapsed, without entering into the history of an actual schism which arose out of it; or which at least took it as its avowed origin. It will be sufficient here to state, that St Cyprian continued firm in his determination to maintain the discipline of the Church, such as I have before stated it; moderating the strictness of general rules only where particular cases required; and giving repeated injunctions to his clergy, to seek the real good of the lapsed, by setting before them the danger of their state, or encouraging them to hope in the mercy of the Lord, according as each individual might require to be treated; and all along proposing to settle the whole matter by his Episcopal authority (not, however, without the counsel and consent of his clergy and people); when peace should be restored to the Church, and when he should be enabled to return to the personal superintendence of his diocese; an event which was long protracted by the cabals of his enemies.

## CHAPTER VI.

*Cyprian's return prevented by a Schism in his Church.—The Origin of the Schism.—Novatus :—His Character :—His Crimes.—He is cited to appear before Cyprian.—He escapes under cover of the Decian Persecution.—He makes a Party, and forsakes the Church.—He obtains the Ordination of Felicissimus :—It is questioned by whom.—The five Presbyters Companions of Novatus in Schism.—Cyprian appoints Deputies to put his Regulations in force.—The place which voluntary Seceders hold, in respect of the Church.—Novatus goes to Rome.— Novatian :—His Character.—His secret Cabals :—Fostered by Novatus. —Election of Cornelius to the See of Rome.—His Character.—Novatian's Schismatical Ordination.—His practices at home and abroad.— The spread of his Party.—Novatus returns to Carthage.*

CYPRIAN had now remained more than a year[1] in his retreat. He lamented his forced absence with deep and unceasing regret; day and night with tears and groans regretting, that he who had been chosen their Bishop with so great and zealous affection, was still deprived of the presence of his flock. He found consolation, however, in the hope that he should celebrate the approaching Easter among them : for at this high festival, and at the solemn season preceding it, it was the custom of all Bishops to be present with their spiritual children; and all ecclesiastical affairs were so ordered, as not to interfere with this arrangement. But the promised pleasure and privilege was denied to Cyprian and his flock, by the miserable secession and rebellion of certain of his own people, who so disturbed the peace of the Church, and excited

---

[1] Non suffecerat exilium jam biennii, &c., *Ep.* xl. the last Epistle to his people before his return, p. 53.

so much passion and violence, that Cyprian compares the effects of their machinations to another persecution : and as he had before remained absent from his city, lest his presence should too much excite the avowed enemies of Christ and His Church, and lest he who ought to be the bond and conservator of peace, should become, however unwillingly, the occasion of tumult ; so now he declares it was inexpedient for him to return, lest the authors of schism, though professed Christians, should be excited to some sudden ebullition of violence, by the return of their own Bishop.

The seeds of these disturbances had fallen on a soil fruitful in evil, before the commencement of the Decian persecution ; but we omitted to notice them at that time, that we might give a tolerably connected account of the growth of this fatal schism. But after the usual manner of such noxious words, it branched into so many separate factions ; each united in itself, but separated from the Church by various errors ; that we shall be called off more than once from the main tenour of the history of Cyprian and the Church, to expose the crimes and follies, or to trace the adventures, of some wanderer from the doctrine and fellowship of the Apostles.

In the Church of Carthage, at the time when our history commences, was a Presbyter named Novatus. He was doubtless among those who opposed the election of Cyprian, and disturbed the beginning of his Episcopate ; for a rancorous and persevering hostility to whatever was right, seems to have been habitual in him. We find him avowedly connected with Donatus, Fortunatus, and Gordius, in proposing a factious question to Cyprian, touching the lapsed :[1] and these, with whom Novatus was then associated, were among the Presbyters of whom Cyprian says, that they still retained the recollection of their former conspiracy, and their opposition to his Episcopate, though sanctioned by the whole Church, and by the judgment of God Himself. This Novatus was a lover of novelty, of insatiable avarice, proud and overbearing, of ill report among the Bishops of his

[1] *Ep.* v. p. 11

province, and accused by common report of peculation in the temporal, and error in the spiritual deposit of the Church; he was fawning and treacherous, a firebrand of contention, in the Church a destroying tempest, and a disturber of all peace.[1] This man, about the end of the year 249, seems to have become obnoxious to ecclesiastical censure, by specific acts of violence and injustice. We have the following catalogue of his crimes; but it is not clear for which of them he was called to give an account. He had appropriated to himself a part of the funds appointed for the relief of widows and orphans: he had occasioned his wife's miscarriage, by kicking her when she was pregnant; and he had suffered his father to die of hunger in the street, and had not even taken the charge of his funeral.

For these crimes, or some of them, Novatus was cited to answer before Cyprian; and there is little doubt that he would have been convicted, and deprived of his ecclesiastical dignity, and even of lay communion. But when the day for his trial was near at hand, the Decian persecution broke out with such fury as to disturb all the arrangements of the Church, for its internal purity and peace.

Nothing could have fallen out more opportunely for Novatus: he thus avoided the present censures of the Church, and found time also to make a party to maintain his cause against his accusers and his judge, and abet him in his future plans. He was not content with impunity; he must also have notoriety, influence, and revenge: and he turned the difficulties of the Church under persecution into an opportunity not only of covering his own retreat, but of collecting round him a factious multitude, chiefly composed of those who were disgusted with

---

[1] *Ep.* xlix. p. 63. Mosheim warns us against taking Cyprian's account of Novatus without question. It is out of all doubt the testimony of an adversary; and we know that the best men are not free from liability to mistake the character of their opponents: but if we do but judge Novatus by the specific charges which Cyprian adduces against him, without taking his comments upon them (and surely we shall not accuse Cyprian of deliberate falsehood, though Mosheim does not hesitate to do so), we shall find Novatus branded with indelible infamy.

the rigour with which the discipline of penance had been exacted from the lapsed. So soon as he had gathered about him a sufficient number of clergy and laity to make his party formidable, he separated, by his own act, from the Church; and not only braved her censures, but even opposed to her body a conventicle of his own, and retorted her condemnations and warnings with insolent and rebellious threats.

His appropriate charge as a Presbyter was over a congregation separate from that of the mother Church, but in the diocese, and under the episcopal jurisdiction, of Cyprian. This congregation met on some eminence in the suburbs of Carthage, whence the place of their assembly was called "*on the hill.*" At this Church, Novatus collected around him five other Presbyters, together with a large body of the people; taking advantage to this end of the commotions which followed on the decision of Cyprian concerning the lapsed, which he himself fomented, and had perhaps originated, that they might subserve his personal ambition. Among his acts of insubordination, that in which schism and rebellion were most formally involved, was the procuring the ordination of Felicissimus as his Deacon, without the consent of Cyprian his Bishop, and even without his knowledge. This Felicissimus became afterwards his tool and most active partisan: indeed he was a worthy associate of Novatus; for he too had been a peculator, and was charged with repeated adulteries, and the most heartless debaucheries.[1]

The order of these events is obscure; and the facts, though in themselves undeniable, are so denuded of circumstances in the accounts which we have of them, as to suggest many difficult questions. How, for instance, being only a Presbyter, could Novatus ordain Felicissimus? or, if he did not himself usurp the episcopal function in that instance, how could he obtain so irregular an ordination for one of his own choice, at

[1] *Ep.* xxxviii. p. 51, and *Ep.* lv. p. 79. Mosheim here endeavours, as before in the case of Novatus, to take off the edge of Cyprian's censures: indeed he is the self-constituted apologist of every one whom Cyprian condemns.

the hands of any Bishop? or, if this office was really performed by a Bishop, how is it that that Bishop, becoming a party in the schism, is not associated with Novatus in the condemnation, nor so much as named by Cyprian? Mosheim supposes, that as a Presbyter of a separate charge Novatus had, or thought that he had, power to ordain a Deacon for his own Church: and that he did so in this case. Blondel had before expressed the same opinion. Baronius supposes, though in direct contradiction of all history, that Novatus was himself a Bishop; and so, not by an usurpation of office, though schismatically, conferred orders on Felicissimus. Of these two opinions, which are founded on the false assumption that Novatus ordained Felicissimus with his own hands, that of Baronius is the least improbable: for it is just possible, though only just possible, that an error may have been committed in stating the place of Novatus in the Hierarchy; but it is not possible that Novatus should have supposed himself endowed with the authority to ordain, being but a Presbyter, or that he should have acted on such a presumption, being the first Presbyter who had ever ventured on such an anomalous act, without its being specially noted in the history of the Church. Aërius was the first person who adventured upon such a theory or practice, and he did not live till the next century.[1]

But Novatus most assuredly did not ordain Felicissimus. He probably took advantage of the presence of a strange

---

[1] Aërius, as Augustine tells us (*de Hæres.*, vol. x. p. 21), was mortified at not himself attaining the Episcopate; and having fallen into the heresy of Arius, and having been led into many strange notions by impatience of the control of the Church, he taught among other things that no difference ought to be recognised between a Bishop and a Presbyter. Thus Aërius revenged himself upon the dignity to which he had unsuccessfully aspired: and he has left his history and his character to future ages, as an argument almost as forcible as direct reasoning and evidence, of the Apostolical ordinance of the Episcopate. Aërius, like some others who have succeeded him, was a self-erected reformer, actuated by personal pique, and regulated by Anti-Catholic principles. See Hooker's *Ecc. Pol.*, VII. viii. 9.

Bishop at Carthage, whom he found some means of influencing, to obtain the ordination of his satellite: and perhaps in his own Bishop's protracted absence, it was not very difficult to make out a probable case, and one which would satisfy a person unsuspicious of evil, for the ordination of a Deacon, in a congregation separate from the mother Church. Or, reasoning from what *was* in another case, to what *might be* in this, perhaps Novatus procured the co-operation of some Bishops, by such disgraceful arts as Novatian soon after employed, to procure his consecration at the hands of three obscure Italian Prelates. But it seems to me most probable, that some lapsed Bishop, attached to the cause of Novatus by community in error, might have given the necessary orders to Felicissimus: for such Bishops were employed, as we learn from Cyprian himself, in the schismatical consecration of Fortunatus.[1] This supposition, which is in itself probable, will solve all difficulties; and will sufficiently account for no mention being made of the ordainer of Felicissimus, or of his being involved by this schismatical act in the condemnation of Novatus; for such a Bishop as I have supposed would have been already implicated in the whole guilt and sin of separation; and Cyprian would scarce have condescended to mention the name of a person thus situated, except for some very special purpose. The Church knows nothing of heretics and schismatics.

The extent to which this schism was already carried is sufficiently apparent from the fact, that it rendered Cyprian's return to his own diocese a matter of danger,[2] or at least of imprudence: a consequence however monstrous in itself, yet naturally enough flowing from a schism which separated a large portion even of the clergy of Carthage from the communion of the Church Catholic. Of the eight Presbyters, besides Novatus,[3] of whom alone we have any mention as

[1] Tanta apud eos etiam malorum penuria est, ut ad illos nec de sacrificatis nec de hæreticis viginti quinque colligi possunt. *Ep.* lv. pp. 84, 85.

[2] Fustes et lapides et gladios, quos verbis paracidalibus jactitant, non perhorrescimus, &c. *Ep.* lv. p. 80.

[3] Bishop Pearson, the Benedictine Editors, and Mosheim, all enumerate five schismatical Presbyters *exclusive* of Novatus.

attached to the Church of Carthage, and who perhaps formed the whole of the Bishop's consistory, five, that is, the majority of the whole number, adhered to the party of Novatus, and to his Deacon, surreptitiously ordained. These five were Fortunatus, Jovinus, Maximus, Donatus, and Gordianus, Presbyters of long standing, and the same who had been the old oppugners of Cyprian's Episcopate; while of the three who remained faithful, Britius, Rogatianus, and Numidicus, the last had been lately, and indeed during the very progress of the schism, added to the list of the Presbytery of Carthage.[1] Encouraged by so large and important an array of Ecclesiastics, this party presumed so far, as to declare that they would refuse the communion to all who maintained the fellowship, or obeyed the mandates of Cyprian; and this assumption, though without the shadow of lawful authority, though in fact a sentence of excommunication against themselves, yet was not to be despised; for it wanted not that kind of power which the people can most readily appreciate, that of numerical strength.

Cyprian, though absent in person, had not left his flock without pastoral charge. He had placed the care of the poor and of strangers in the hands of a Presbyter, Rogatianus; having himself provided for their need in the first instance, and added to his former supply by the hands of Naricus, an Acolyte: and afterwards he sent Caldonius and Herculanus, two of his colleagues in the Episcopate, and Numidicus the Presbyter before mentioned, associating them with Rogatianus n such parts of the charge of his diocese as could be executed by deputies.[2] The charge of these persons extended to the enforcing of those laws concerning the lapsed, which it was the policy of Novatus and his faction to oppose; and Felicissimus ventured openly to deny the authority under which they

---

[1] See *Ep.* xxxv. written by Cyprian to his clergy and people to inform them, that he had added Numidicus to the Carthaginian Presbytery. Numidicus had already adorned the same station in some other Church by remarkable courage and fidelity.

[2] See *Epistles* xxxvi. and xxxviii.

acted, and to threaten excommunication to all who obeyed them. Such extreme audacity and insolence defeated its own purpose, and wholly overreached the mark; for it so far opened the eyes of the people, that many thenceforth retraced their steps. Cyprian himself at once recognised the happy consequences of their avowed separation of themselves from the communion of the Church; which was far better than their continuing its members in name, while they were in fact enemies to the body of Christ; and was even preferable, on the whole, to the sentence of excommunication proceeding in the first instance from the Church. "Let him," says Cyprian to his before-mentioned deputies, "abide by his own sentence, and hold himself as separated from our communion, his voluntary act being ratified by us."[1] And, writing to his people, he says, "It seems nothing short of an interposition of Divine Providence, that these men have brought upon themselves, by their own act, without my will or even knowledge, the punishment which was due to their crimes; and that they who must otherwise have suffered the sentence of excommunication at our hands, and with your suffrage, have themselves left the pale of the Church."[2]

It is scarce possible to record this judgment of Cyprian, without a mental reference to parallel cases in our own times. Our Church is subject, as that of Carthage was in Cyprian's days, to the insolence of voluntary seceders from her body: we are attacked and maligned and opposed with every available weapon; and the terms of the communion of each sect involve our condemnation and exclusion. Now, that all this is very sad, let no one deny who bears in mind the frequent exhortations of the Apostles and of Christ Himself, to unity and charity and humility:—let no one deny, who recognises in the Church a divinely appointed medium of spiritual gifts; and who must believe, therefore, that those who are without her pale are deprived of great and inestimable privileges: but I think that we invest it with a kind and character of evil which it does not possess, and render it still more painful,

[1] *Ep.* xxxviii.     [2] *Ep.* xl. p. 52.

when we view it as an attack upon us by part of our own body; as if there were a continuing schism *within* us and *among* us, and *brother divided against brother*. If any just concession on our part, in the first instance; if any fair and honourable terms of union even now, were able to reunite these dissevered limbs to the Church, it would be the part of Christian charity to concede, or to reflect upon the terms which might be offered: and if the schismatics had been thrust out by us with unnecessary contumely, and irritated by improper severity, a burden would indeed rest upon us. But when we can appeal to history, that *we* have not been the separatists either actually or in temper; when we can call each sect to witness for us, except in the particular question in which it is itself involved; when we can, with pious confidence, approach God, as loving our brethren, as protesting against error and divisions, as in no way and in no degree affording sufficient grounds for leaving our communion; when in a word we may look on all who have left us as self-erected enemies, and self-constituted aliens from our body; we may pity them indeed, and we may lament the evil of disunion in general; but we stand so far above their insolence, and so far beside their malice, that we need not feel nor express irritation, and that peculiar tone of sorrow, which is excited by the treachery of brethren and of friends.

In the censures before mentioned, Cyprian includes Augendus (a layman I suppose, who had been led away by the faction of Novatus; who was perhaps singularly violent, and so obtained an unenviable conspicuousness notwithstanding his private station), and all others who were alike criminal were equally obnoxious to the same sentence, unless they should repent. All this we collect from Epistle xxxviii., which is a precept or commission to Caldonius and Herculanus, and Numidicus with Rogatianus, to pronounce this sentence of excommunication: and this we find by the next Epistle that they immediately proceeded to do. Thus Felicissimus and Augendus, with two or three others who were of the number of the confessors, but whose presumption had linked them in affections and pretensions with the schismatical party, were formally separated from the Church.

Novatus, who had before escaped the censure of his Bishop, under cover of the persecution, on this occasion avoided a formal excommunication by absence. He was in Rome, whither he carried his iniquitous character unchanged; and where he found, or soon made, equal occasions of exercising it to the peril of the Church.

For it was now the beginning of the year 251, and the chair of Rome had been vacant for a whole year, Fabian having suffered martyrdom in the preceding January, and Decius being so furiously set upon the extirpation of the Christian priesthood, that the brethren at Rome had not dared to proceed to the election of another Bishop. Decius, however, was now in Macedonia, and Julius Valens had assumed the purple, and was gone into Illyricum,[1] and the Church at Rome being left in comparative quiet by civil commotions, proceeded to the election of a successor of their late Bishop.

One of the most remarkable of the members of the Church of Rome at this time was Novatian. He commenced his public career as a professor of the philosophy of the Stoics; and his mind was naturally attuned to the austere system of that sect. A lover of solitude, and given to severe moral speculations, and morbidly excitable by the suggestions of those evil spirits which attack us through the medium of a vain imagination, he came first under the notice and discipline of the Church as an energumen; for it was not till he had been long vexed by an evil spirit that he sought the faith and help of Christ.[2] In this condition he remained until his death seemed to be approaching, and then he received clinical Baptism. The singular and striking character of the man

[1] Bishop Pearson's Ann. Cyp., p. 29.

[2] Beside the Cyprianic Epistles, the materials for the history of Novatian are found in Eusebius, especially in an Epistle of Cornelius to Fabius, Bishop of Antioch, which Eusebius has transcribed in the forty-third chapter of his sixth book.

had invested him with so great interest and factitious importance, that he was too incautiously raised by his Bishop to the order of Presbyters, when it seemed that this favour was necessary to retain him in that Church, which he had entered under such strange circumstances, and with the spirit of which his rigid temper and harsh morals were so incompatible. The whole body of the Clergy, however, and many of the people, protested against his ordination, properly objecting against him his clinical Baptism.[1] But what was morose in his disposition, and what was irregular in his conduct, was not in the least altered by his elevation: for now, involving the true God and the true religion in the rigorous principles of his philosophy (instead of reducing his philosophy into subordination to the truth, and his mind into submission to God), he imagined a system of divinity which had all the faults of his miserable ethics,[2] and gloomy speculations. According to this system, all offences were equal, and all inexpiable; and such attributes were ascribed to God, as could not be imagined without equal harshness and temerity.[3] He exacted of Christians as a condition of communion, a more rigid perfection than the best men were able to maintain; and declared them utterly cut off from the privilege even of penance by their

---

[1] Whether this objection was founded on any Canon yet actually made in any Church, or whether it was only from the reason of the thing, I know not: but afterwards (in the beginning of the fourth century), the Bishops assembled at the Council of Neo-Cesarea ordained in their twelfth Canon, that those who had received clinical Baptism should not be admitted Priests, since their faith was not of choice, but of necessity.

[2] Magis durus secularis philosophiæ pravitate quam sophiæ dominicæ lenitate pacificus, &c. *Ep.* lvii. p. 95.

[3] Quis ante crudelissimum Novatianum, crudelem Deum dixit, eo quod mallet mortem morientis, quam ut revertatur et vivat? Vincentii Lirinensis Com. cap. xxxiv.

I ought not to withhold the confession that there is some difficulty in determining how ar Novatian personally carried these monstrous principles. In the sect which originated from him they were certainly carried to the extremest length. Mosheim, as usual, is learned and industrious in his enquiries into thi matter. See his *Commentarii de rebus Christ. Sec.* iii. 16 pp. 520 et seq.

first fall; especially by an apostasy, though in the bitterest persecution.

Yet Novatian himself followed not so rigid a rule of conduct; nor maintained his courage and fidelity without suspicion: and no marvel; for after his baptism he rejected the ordinary discipline of the Church, refusing to receive the holy unction[1] from the Bishop, which was the appointed vehicle of the highest grace, and the confirmation of his baptismal privileges:[2] and how then was he a partaker of the Holy Ghost? And during persecution he was betrayed by terror into the denial of his office; for when the Deacons besought him to leave the solitude in which he had immured himself, to engage in the active duties of his station, and to exhort the brethren to perseverance and courage; he answered their entreaties in a rage, and declared that he would no longer be numbered with the Presbyters, but that he would return to his former profession of philosophy.[3]

The inconsistency of his conduct with his professions did not rest here; for while he was covertly seeking the Episcopate, he denied with tremendous adjurations (ὅρκων φοβερῶν) that he desired that dignity: an incident which Mosheim endeavours to turn to his advantage, as if it was a proof that he really sought not that elevation, nor had manifested any ambitious pretentions: whereas it was plainly an attempted expurgation of himself of intentions and practices already imputed to him; for who solemnly desires that of which he has never been

[1] Cornelius apud Eusebium, ut ante.
[2] Ἀνάμνησον σαυτὸν τῆς ἱερᾶς μυσταγωγίας, ἐν ᾗ οἱ τελούμενοι, μετὰ τὴν ἄρνησιν τοῦ τυράννου, καὶ τὴν τοῦ βασιλέως ὁμολογίαν, οἱονεὶ σφραγῖδά τινα βασιλικὴν δέχονται τοῦ πνευματικοῦ μύρου τὸ χρῖσμα· ὡς ἐν τύπῳ τῷ μύρῳ τὴν ἀόρατον τοῦ παναγίου Πνεύματος χάριν ὑποδεχόμενοι. Theodoret, in Cant. i. 2. vol. ii. p. 30.
[3] This conduct of Novatian brought him within the meaning of the sixty-second Apostolical Canon; if the code, of which it is a part, was so soon framed. "If any Clergyman from fear of man, Jew, heathen, or heretic, deny the name of Christ, let him be excommunicated: if he deny his clerical character, let him be deposed; and on repentance be received only as a layman."

accused? His eloquence was abundantly sufficient for all his purposes :[1] but that which chiefly won upon the people was his rigorous adherence to the theory of Church discipline, and his severity to the lapsed. The confessors especially, flattered with the exclusive dignity and prerogatives which he awarded to them, but from whom his ambition and inconsistency were at present concealed, were especially moved by his eloquence and pretentions to a singular piety. Thus Moyses, a most glorious professor, and one who eventually died in prison after torture, was at first one of his nearest associates; but on a farther knowledge of the man and his designs, this holy martyr repudiated him entirely. Others, however, continued their false estimate of the man and his principles, and Novatian gathered around him a large number of persons, who imagined that in him—in him who had not been brought up in the Church, nor scarce regularly admitted into it—in him who had endured no conflict for the faith; nay, who had avoided all question by a cowardly and ignominious solitude, and now at length showed himself when all danger was passed —that in him they had found a proper successor of the holy Bishop and martyr Fabian, and a worthy competitor with Saint Cornelius.

Affairs were in this posture when Novatus arrived at Rome; and his love of faction overcame all principle in him, as ambition had already done in Novatian. Novatus, who had before excited and organised a schism against Cyprian at Carthage, on the pretence that the lapsed ought to be received with a short penance or none; now at Rome joined the party of Novatian, who denied communion to the lapsed, even after the most rigid discipline, and on their death-bed, not even allowing them the privilege of penance. Novatian

---

[1] Cyprian more than once speaks of the eloquence of Novatian; not indeed in terms of admiration, but so as to prove the fact that this quality was usually attributed to him. Some notions may be obtained of Novatian's parts, from the Epistle of the Roman Clergy to Cyprian (inter Epis. Cyp. xxxi.), which was written by him, as Cyprian himself tells Antonian. We have also a work of his remaining on the Trinity.

also had changed his opinion on that subject, though not quite in the same degree, having joined the Roman clergy in their sentence that the lapsed should be restored, though indeed with just caution, and after the most severe discipline;[1] a judgment which he now altogether repudiated, and even made his opposition to it an occasion of disturbing the repose of the Church, and himself breaking off from her body.

Novatus entered at once into all the designs of Novatian, and even outran the ambitious demagogue, spurring him to a more hasty breach from the Church, and a more determined opposition to its laws. So long as the vacant see was yet open to a fair competition, there is no reason to suppose that Novatian, though actuated by Novatus, proceeded beyond the usual arts of those who court popularity by crooked ways indeed, yet without the breach of any express laws but those of honour and conscience. But the eloquence and ambition of Novatian, seconded by the unprincipled violence of Novatus, were insufficient to compete with the established character and sterling virtues of Cornelius; and accordingly the latter was elected to fill the chair of Rome, with the consent of the whole body of the clergy, and the greater part of the laity; and Cornelius was canonically ordained by sixteen Bishops.

If contrast can add blackness to the character of Novatian, and criminality to his schism, we have that contrast in the sterling worth of Cornelius, and in the unimpeachable justice of his cause. St Cyprian, in a letter to Antonianus, gives an account of Cornelius, against the truth of which I know not that ecclesiastical history has anything to oppose. Of the qualifications and election of that Prelate he thus writes: "You will more safely collect the character of this man from the judgment of God, by whose providence he fills his present station, and from the unanimous testimony of his brethren in the Episcopate throughout the world, than from the inventions of malignant slanderers. It is not a little in his favour, that he rose not suddenly to his present position, but that he has

[1] See *Epistle* xxxi.

passed through all the inferior ecclesiastical orders: and having approved himself faithful in the functions of each, has now attained through them all to the Episcopate, the pinnacle of priestly dignity. He sought not, he did not even desire, this elevation; still less, like some who are inflated with arrogance and self-conceit, did he usurp it. With the quiet and modesty which are among the usual characteristics of those who are divinely appointed to this office, and which accorded well with his native humility, purity, and worth, he rather yielded to force in ascending the throne, than used force, like Novatian (*ut quidam*), to obtain it. With such qualifications, then, with the judgment of God and of his Christ, with the consent of almost all the clergy, and with the applause of the crowd of bystanders, and with the full concurrence of assembled Prelates, Cornelius was made Bishop, when the chair of Fabian, that is the chair of Peter, and the sacerdotal office was yet unfilled. . . . And how great was his courage and constancy, that he took his seat undaunted, at that very time when the tyrant (Decius) was uttering the most malignant threats against the whole of the Episcopate; and when he could have endured with more patience to hear of a competitor for the purple, than of a new Bishop of the Church in Rome. Is not Cornelius, then, to be applauded as a pattern of faith and virtue? Is he not to be numbered with the greatest martyrs and confessors? He, who awaited so long and so resolutely the approach of executioners and tormentors, braving their vengeance, though it should be enforced with fire or the sword, with the rack or with the cross? And though the power of God has hitherto protected His servant in his appointed elevation, yet so far as peril and devotedness is concerned, he has suffered whatever can be inflicted: and thus in his unstained priesthood he first conquered that tyrant, who was so soon to fall beneath secular arms in other hands." [1]

The election of Cornelius excited Novatian to a degree of criminality, of which it is probable he had scarce conceived himself capable: for the Episcopate which his ambition had

[1] *Ep.* lii. pp. 68, 69.

failed to reach, he would now compass by actual usurpation. He sent, therefore, two of his wicked party to some obscure Italian cities, and thence fetched three Bishops, pretending that he required their intercession with Cornelius.[1] Having got these persons into his power, Novatian engaged them in so free indulgence at a feast, that the close of the day found them intoxicated; and then, by the imposition of the hands of the three Bishops, he obtained Episcopal Orders. But he was not a whit the nearer his end, until he could obtain the influence as well as the name of a Bishop; until he could find a diocese to govern, which the three Italian Bishops had not to bestow. We must now follow him through his arts to get himself recognised Bishop of Rome, in spite of the canonical election and consecration of Cornelius.

Novatian had now to support his cause both at home and abroad. At home, besides the usual arts of demagogues, he employed one method of revolting impiety, at which we almost shudder while we relate it. In administering the Eucharist, he exacted of each communicant an oath of adhesion to his cause; and while he held their hands, together with the body of Christ, between his own, he said, "Swear to me, by the Body and Blood of our Saviour Jesus Christ, that thou wilt never abandon my party, nor return to that of Cornelius." And thus those unhappy men could not communicate, without uttering maledictions against themselves; and instead of the accustomed "AMEN," at the receiving of the sacred bread, their response was, "I will not return to the communion of Cornelius."[2]

In supporting his cause abroad, the first business of Novatian was to despatch letters of communion to all Christian Bishops, according to the manner of those times: and since

---

[1] Οὗτος ὁ Ναυᾶτος, ὀλίγους τινὰς καὶ λίαν εὐαριθμήτους κοινωνῆσαι τῆς αἱρέσεως πείσας, εἰς τὴν Ἰταλίαν ἐξῆλθε, καὶ τρεῖς πολιχνίων ἐπισκόπους ἐξαπατήσας ἦγεν, ὡς δῆθεν πρεσβευσομένους ὑπὲρ αὐτοῦ πρὸς τὸν τῆς Ῥώμης ἐπίσκοπον. Theodoret. de Hæret. Fab. III. v. vol. iv. p. 345. See also the Epistle of Cornelius to Fabian, in Eusebius.

[2] Eusebius vi. 43.

herein he had been of course anticipated by Cornelius, he took occasion not only to recount the fact of his own election and consecration, (which we may well suppose he did with less regard to the truth of the matter, than to the object which he had in view,) but also to throw all the odium he could on the character of Cornelius; and to affix on him if possible such specific offences, as would nullify his election.

The contents of these letters of Novatian may be collected from the notice of one of them to Antonianus, an African Bishop, which occurs in an Epistle of Cyprian to that Prelate; who it seems had been shaken by the representations of Novatian in his adherence to the Catholic communion of Cornelius. From Cyprian's answers to the scruples of Antonianus, we collect, that besides the general accusation against Cornelius, of an undue lenity towards the lapsed, the particular charge was added, that he had communicated with an ill-judged and indecent haste, and with some circumstances of peculiar impropriety, with one Trophimus;[1] and besides, that he was himself stained with the crime of the *libellatici*. This last and most scandalous article of accusation seems to have been an unqualified falsehood; the rest were founded on certain apparent grounds, but were magnified and distorted, so as to seem criminal, whereas they were in fact commendable.

"You ought not," says Cyprian to Antonianus, "to wonder, that you receive scandalous and malignant reports of Cornelius; for you know that it is the constant work of the devil, to wound the reputation of the servants of God with false accusations, and to asperse the noblest names: so that they, whose conscience is the most unstained, may be defiled with the slander of others. But be assured that our colleagues

---

[1] Bingham, by a singularly strange supposition, makes Trophimus one of the Bishops who ordained Novatian; and that to be the crime for which he was deposed, though the lenity of his Bishop still maintained him in the communion of the Church. But it is scarce possible that Novatian should have accused Cornelius of too great mildness towards one, whose only crime had been the ordaining of Novatian himself. See Bingham's Scholastical History of Lay-Baptism, chap. ii. sec. 3. and chap. v. sec. 3.

have most clearly proved, after patient investigation, that Cornelius is untainted with the ignominy of the *libellatici*, notwithstanding what you have heard; neither hath he received into communion those who sacrificed at the heathen altars, but those only whose innocence has been established after sufficient inquiry. As for Trophimus, of whom you wish me to write, the affair has been maliciously and falsely reported to you: for our dearest brother has done in this instance no more than his predecessors have often done, in yielding to a necessary expedient for collecting his scattered flock: and because with Trophimus a large portion of the Church had seceded, now, at his return to the Church with satisfaction and penance, and a confession of his past error, and on his bringing back with all humility and submission that portion of the brethren which he had separated, his prayers are granted; and not so much Trophimus, as the great body of the brethren who adhered to him, have been readmitted; none of whom would have returned at all, had they not had Trophimus as the companion of their reconciliation. After advising therefore with many of his colleagues, Cornelius received Trophimus to communion; and the return of his brethren with him, and the restoration of many to salvation, was his sufficient justification in this proceeding. And yet after all, Trophimus was received only into the place of laymen, and not, as the libel of Novatian would insinuate, to the exercise of his priestly functions."[1]

We may judge from hence how far Novatian's account of the proceedings at Rome was from the truth, even when he pretended to detail facts. Perhaps, however, if we proceeded even with Cyprian's vindication of Cornelius, we might be disposed to believe, that that Prelate had been somewhat more lenient in his treatment of the lapsed, I say not than was right, and perfectly within his power as a Catholic Prelate, but than seemed exactly fitting to most of the Bishops of his age, and to Cyprian himself, as his opinion had been expressed again and again. But whether this was so, could never have

[1] *Ep.* lii. p. 69.

a legitimate place in the discussion of the validity of the election and Episcopate of Cornelius; nor could any degree of lenity in a Bishop, which transgressed no rules already laid down by the Church, or no principles by which the Church universal would not be bound in the declaration of her judgment, be a sufficient excuse for disturbing his government, still less for breaking communion with him, and with the Church, and for usurping his Episcopate.

These lying letters were not the only vehicle of the poison of Novatian. Messengers were sent from Rome to the different Churches, expressly commissioned to carry a report favourable to Novatian, and subversive of the authority of Cornelius. The bearers of Novatian's letters to Carthage, and of his accusations against Cornelius, played their part most pertinaciously, even after they had been rejected by Cyprian and a synod of Bishops: and we have no reason to doubt that their impudence was equally great in other places. By all these means a great effect was produced in the Churches of many parts. We have already had occasion to notice the hesitation of Antonianus; which is little important in itself, compared with that of some other Prelates, but which called forth a vindication of Cornelius from Cyprian's pen, from which we have derived much valuable information. We learn from Eusebius,[1] that at Antioch some Bishops leaned so much towards the Novatian cause, that a council was necessary to suppress his party; and the schism which originated with him was not entirely healed until the sixth century.

But we are anticipating the times at which the party of Novatian prevailed in distant parts of Christendom: at present we find it struggling for a bare existence in Rome; where Novatian, his error, and his schism, were formally condemned, and the three Bishops who had ordained him were punished: two of them being deposed, and their sees filled by new Bishops, and the third being restored to his ecclesiastical functions only after he had humbly confessed

[1] Ecc. Hist., vi. 46.

his fault with many tears, and at the unanimous petition of the people.

Novatian's party had been already treated with equal rigour in Africa: for Maximus, Longinus, and Machæus, his emissaries to that province, and the first of them the Bishop whom he had endeavoured to obtrude upon the Church of Carthage, were expelled from that country. But he was only incited to greater exertions by these severities; for he still maintained himself as the centre of the schism at Rome, and laboured more and more tō disturb the peace of the whole Church, sending Bishops of his party, with other emissaries, into several cities. Of these, Evaristus a Bishop, together with Nicostratus[1] a Deacon and Confessor, and Priscus and Dionysius, accompanied Novatus, his ever-active and ever-dangerous ally, to Africa, whence his party had been before driven with ignominy.

[1] In Evaristus and Nicostratus we have characters of like depravity with that of Novatus. Nicostratus had defrauded his secular patrons, and had robbed the Church to a great amount. As for Evaristus, he had been already deposed from his Episcopate for schism. See *Ep.* xlviii. p. 62. Bingham, with less improbability than he asserts the same of Trophimus makes Evaristus, one of the Bishops who ordained Novatian; but I find nothing approaching to evidence on this point. Bingham's Scholastic History of Lay-Baptism, chap. v. sec. 3.

## CHAPTER VII.

Proceedings touching the Election of Cornelius, and the Schismatical Ordination of Novatian, at Carthage ;—At Hadrumettium.—The Episcopate of Cornelius finally Recognised.—Felicissimus and the five Presbyters Excommunicated.—St Cyprian's Letters to the Schismatical Confessors.—His Treatise *de Unitate Ecclesiæ*.—Letter of Dionysius of Alexandria to Novatian.—A Synod at Carthage, and in Rome.—The Return of the Schismatical Confessors.—Letters of Cornelius, the Confessors, and Cyprian.—Reflexions on the Novatian Schism.

HAVING now brought Novatus back to Carthage, we shall take occasion to describe the conduct of Cyprian in that see, and the means which he took for the suppression of the party, in the organising of which Novatus had been so deeply implicated, and still continued so actively engaged.

We have said that Cornelius, as was usual, immediately on his election sent letters of communion to the several Bishops of the Church, notifying what had been done, and seeking from them a recognition of his Episcopate. The letters of Cornelius to Carthage found a Synod of Bishops there met, and to this ecclesiastical assembly Cyprian communicated their contents, which intimated not only the election of Cornelius, but also the disturbances which had since arisen, though they had not yet proceeded so far as to the election of a schismatical Bishop. Upon this important occasion, Cyprian sought the counsel of his colleagues; and it was agreed that Caldonius and Fortunatus, two of their number, should be sent to Rome to collect information on the spot of what had passed, upon which the African Bishops might frame their definitive sentence. Caldonius and Fortunatus had also in charge to do what they could towards restoring peace to the Church in Rome.

It was in the absence of these Carthaginian deputies, that Maximus, Augendus, Machæus, and Longinus, the messengers by whom Novatian sent his letters, arrived at Carthage, claiming on behalf of their pseudo-Bishop, that he should be received as Bishop of Rome. There was sufficient evil manifested in this appearance of legates from another person pretending to the Episcopate of Rome, after Cornelius had been elected and ordained, to warrant the rejection of those legates from the communion of the Church; and to make it necessary to oppose their mission, and to refute their pretences, even before the fuller information which might be desired should arrive. This accordingly Cyprian and his colleagues did. They soon discovered that they were amply justified by the real merits of the case: for while Caldonius and Fortunatus were still absent, Pompeius and Stephanus, two African Prelates who had been present at the election and consecration of Cornelius, came to Carthage, and furnished Cyprian and his associates in the Church with a true account of the disturbances at Rome.

The arrival of Pompeius and Stephanus was most opportune; for the emissaries of Novatian, not satisfied with their repulse, had still laboured with pertinacious boldness, and by the use of slanderous reports against Cornelius, to obtain their end. They proceeded so far as to present themselves riotously at the religious assemblies of the Carthaginian brethren; by whom it was their object that their accusations against Cornelius should be heard, and their libels read. The conduct of Cyprian was most prompt and judicious. He doubtless employed the information which he possessed to support the cause of Cornelius in the proper way and place; but to the importunate and unquiet Novatus, and in the presence of the crowd, he only deigned to reply, that it was not according to his principles of government to suffer the character of one who was already chosen and ordained Bishop, to be publicly aspersed or his conduct to be so much as called in question before the people. The letters, however, of Cornelius, which seem to have been free from invective and a bitter spirit, were freely read to the people.

Thus repulsed in all their public attempts, these unhappy men went about from house to house, and from city to city, seeking to divide the Church, and to gain adherents to their schism. That they were not wholly unsuccessful is certain; but they found no countenance any where with the well-affected of the Church, or with those who understood those principles of government and order, by which she was then and ever had been, and we trust ever will be, regulated.[1]

The Synod of Bishops, who sent Caldonius and Fortunatus to Rome, had adjourned for a season, after determining that the final sentence should be deferred until the return of their emissaries; that it might be pronounced at last upon more ample assurance and information: hence, though there was a moral certainty of the result, yet the members of that Synod were not at liberty, as yet, to pronounce individually on the Episcopate of Cornelius. This will account for a little incident, to which we now proceed.

The letters of communion of Cornelius to Hadrumettium had been received and answered by Polycarp, Bishop of that colony, in an Epistle to Cornelius himself, in which he was recognised as the Bishop of Rome. But Cyprian and another Bishop, Liberalis, had gone together into that part of the country, during the recess of the Carthaginian Synod; and they communicated to Polycarp the present state of the question, with the determination of the Synod to defer their final sentence till Caldonius and Fortunatus had reported the result of their inquiries. In consequence of this, Polycarp directed the letters which he had occasion to send to Rome, not to Cornelius individually, but to the Clergy of that Church; thus avoiding a specific acknowledgment of the Episcopate of Cornelius. Cornelius was wounded by this change in the conduct of Polycarp, consequent on Cyprian's visit to him,

---

[1] We learn all this from a Letter of Cyprian to Cornelius, sent by Primitivus a Presbyter.

and expostulated with Cyprian accordingly: the answer of Cyprian, though not written till a somewhat later stage of the history, we shall take this occasion to notice, because it affords an intimation of the point at which things were left in Carthage, at the recess of the Synod.

Cyprian denies not the circumstances to which Cornelius adverts with displeasure: but declares that they proceeded from no inconstancy or indecision on his part; but that the Synod assembled at Carthage had determined to proceed to no definitive arrangement, until Caldonius and Fortunatus should return with an account of restored peace at Rome, or at least with an authentic report of what had been done there. Of this arrangement the Clergy of Hadrumettium were ignorant at the time; but they immediately acceded to it, when it had been explained to them by Cyprian and Liberalis.

And as Cyprian had before acquainted Cornelius with the steps which he had taken on his behalf: so now he is careful to show, that this, which seemed less directly in his favour, was not done except upon good grounds, and such as were consistent with, and even prudently arranged for, the confirmation of Cornelius's Episcopate. "I suffer none," says he, "to leave me, without an especial charge to avoid the dissemination of scandalous reports, and without an exhortation to maintain the unity of the Church: but because of the great extent of my province, which stretches into Numidia and Mauritania, lest a division in my city should be of ill consequence with those at a distance, we determined, when by means of the Bishops whom we sent we had been placed in full possession of the truth, and had the more irrefragable arguments of your canonical ordination, and after every shadow of doubt should have been removed from every mind, that letters should be sent from all the Bishops who reside in that province, as has now been done; so that all our colleagues might acknowledge you, and your communion, and maintain at the same time the unity and love of the Church universal. And I rejoice that this has so happened, according to my intentions, as to seem an instance of providentia interference: for now by these means, both the validity and the dignity of your Episcopate are placed in the clearest light, and rest on the strongest possible confirmation; since, by the answers of my colleagues who have written an account of these things from the spot, and from the relation and witness of Pompeius and Stephen, of Caldonius and Fortunatus, our brethren in the Episcopate, the propriety and entire justice of your title from first to last is more fully manifested."[1]

This letter of Cyprian shows us how great stress was laid in those days on the acknowledgment of a new Bishop by the whole body into which he was elected: which was, indeed, the most assured safeguard of a Bishop's authority; and to the Church, the most assured warrant of his orthodoxy. Nor is it unworthy of remark, that whereas in these days Rome has usurped the whole authority of this confirmation in all Churches subject to her sway; and has even, if not verbally yet by implication, declared that without her confirmation there cannot be a theologically valid, still less an ecclesiastically legitimate and canonical Episcopate; in a word, that there cannot be a valid Episcopate in any Church not subject to her; as, for instance, in the whole Greek Church[2] in Cyprian's days the Bishop of Rome was fully as dependent on the recognition of others, as others were on that of the Bishop of Rome; nor could afford to despise the countenance or overlook the least shadow of defection of a poor Prelate of a remote colony.

We have already collected from Cyprian's account of the matter to Cornelius, that on the return of Caldonius and Fortunatus, the whole subject of the Roman Episcopate was set at rest in the minds of the Bishops who met again at Carthage to receive the report of their messengers; that they directed their letters of communion to Cornelius, and declared that the same should be done by the whole province.

[1] *Ep.* xlv. p. 59.
[2] Yet in *fact* Rome acknowledges the Orders of the Greek Church; as do many of her best divines of our own Church. I only speak above of what she would do, if she were in all cases consistent in her own principles.

The same Synod which took these important steps for the confirmation of the authority of Cornelius, and the peace of the Church in Rome, took steps equally important to the peace of Cyprian, and to the repose of their own province, in the excommunication of Felicissimus the deacon, and the five Presbyters his adherents in his schism. Of this they sent an account to Cornelius.

And the same messengers who carried these accounts from the Synod, and the letters of Cyprian to Cornelius, also took with them a letter from Cyprian to those confessors in Rome who had been enticed into the sect of Novatian; in which he deplores most feelingly that schism, to which their accession gave its chief strength and influence. In this letter he exposes the full heinousness of their crime; and impresses on their minds a theological verity (to all most practically important in principle, but to them, in their present situation as confessors yet schismatics, most unpalatable in its application): that though the constancy of confessors is an additional honour even to the Church herself, glorious as she is, if they continue faithful to her; it ceases to be an honour even to the individual sufferers, from the instant of their defection. "Repress, I beseech you," says he, "this schism, respect your own confession, respect the divine tradition, and return to your mother, from whom you have seceded. Remember that it was from her body, and to her exceeding joy, that you advanced to the trial of your faith, and attained the glory of confessors. But now:—think not that you are maintaining the Gospel of Christ, while you are living in voluntary segregation from the fold of Christ, and from its peace and unity; since it would better become you, as good and illustrious soldiers, to sit down together in the camp at home, and to act and consult for the common good. *Our* unity and agreement cannot be disturbed: we cannot leave the fold of the Church, and go out and join you; therefore it is that we beseech you the more earnestly to return to your mother, the Church, and to the fellowship of her sons."[1]

[1] *Ep.* xliv. p. 58.

Mettius, a Subdeacon, the bearer of this letter, was especially charged to read it to Cornelius, before he delivered it to the confessors to whom it was addressed.[1] This was a proper attention on the part of Cyprian, to the courtesies of the Episcopal order.

It seems probable, too, that Mettius, though without any commission, conveyed a copy, or at least a report, of Cyprian's Tract on the Unity of the Church; which was occasioned by the present disturbances, and was certainly known at Rome, before the Author himself sent a copy thither. This Tract, which is one of the most elaborate of St Cyprian's works, and indeed one of the most valuable remnants of Ecclesiastical Antiquity, is so important, that a review of it must have a chapter to itself. We only observe now, that it seems to have materially subserved the cause for which it was written.

The impression produced by the Epistles and writings of Cyprian, was deepened by a letter of Dionysius of Alexandria to Novatian. This letter affords another, and an evidently independent testimony, to the paramount importance of Church Unity, which we have seen so effectually urged by Cyprian, and which it is now so much the fashion to despise as a mere fantasy of dreaming theologians; or as something worse, an engine of intriguing priestcraft. Perhaps Novatian might judge equally hardly of it. "If, as you declare," says Dionysius, "you were compelled to separate, in spite of yourself, you will manifest your sincerity by a voluntary return. It had been a sufficient motive for suffering anything that the Church might not be divided: nor had it been less glorious to suffer martyrdom for the Unity of the Church, than to avoid offering to idols. Nay, I even hold that it would have been the more illustrious of the two: for while the martyr in general suffers for his own salvation, he who suffers in the cause of unity, suffers for the salvation of the whole Church. Even now, if you can persuade your companions in separation to return to the bosom of the Church, your merit will more than equal your offence: you will avoid the imputation of the

---

[1] *Ep.* xliii. p. 58.

one, and of the other you will receive the praise: but if they should continue obstinate, and you cannot save them, at least save your own soul. I wish you health in the Lord, and that you may learn to love peace."[1]

This letter of the Alexandrian Prelate shall introduce us to better prospects, and to the view of that peace which he so ardently desired: for now the question of the lapsed was fully determined at Carthage, according to the rule of St Cyprian and Cornelius, which we have already sufficiently explicated. This was in August [257]: and Cornelius, having received from Cyprian an account of what was done at Carthage, both in the matter of the lapsed, and in that of Novatian, summoned a provincial Synod, to consult on the same subjects. Sixty Bishops, with many Presbyters and Deacons, obeyed his summons, and the same course was pursued by the Church at Rome, as had been already pursued at Carthage by the ecclesiastics of that province; those Prelates who were absent from the Synod signifying their consent to its decrees, so soon as they were acquainted with them. And now, the case of Novatian being so plainly condemned by all authority; and the exhortations of all good men seconding the principles of sound ecclesiastical discipline, and the express decrees of the Church; the confessors who had joined the party of Novatian would no longer persist in their separation, and they sought and obtained admission into the fold from which they had wandered.

Of this joyful event Cyprian received intelligence, first from Cornelius, and afterwards from the restored confessors themselves. The following extracts from the letters which conveyed this intelligence to Cyprian, with his congratulatory replies, will be interesting.

"I received in the first instance," says Cornelius,[2] "vague accounts of symptoms of compunction, and of a return to a better mind, in some of the adherents to Novatian's schism, from persons of approved integrity, and well-wishers to the Church: and by and by this report was admirably con-

---

[1] Euseb. vi. 45.   [2] *Ep.* xlvi. p. 60.

firmed; for two confessors, Urbanus and Sidonius, came to our brethren of the Presbytery and declared that Maximus, also a confessor, and a Presbyter, was desirous of returning with them into the Church; but since many things had occurred which made it imprudent to trust too entirely to their good faith, I determined to hear from their own mouths the proposal which they had sent by others. Accordingly they appeared before us; and when they had been charged with their criminal conduct by the Presbyters, and especially that they had very lately despatched letters full of scandalous and false reports, to the disturbance of peace and unity through all the Churches; they affirmed that they had been deceived, and that they knew not the contents of those letters: yet they confessed that they had been implicated too deeply in schism and heresy, when they were induced to suffer the imposition of hands upon Novatian. And when the heinousness of these and the like actions had been exposed to them, they earnestly petitioned that they might be remitted and forgotten. When this had been reported to me, I summoned an assembly of my Presbyters; with whom also five Bishops were associated, so that it might be determined with the consent of all, what course should be pursued with the returning confessors. At the close of these proceedings, Maximus, Urbanus, Sidonius, Macharius, and several others of the brethren who had joined them, were admitted into the presence of the Synod. With earnest prayers they besought us to bury their delinquencies in silence and oblivion, and promised for their part to present to God thenceforth the sacrifice of a heart undefiled, in accordance with the Evangelical benediction; *Blessed are the pure in heart, for they shall see God.* It still remained to inform the people of all these events, that they might see those, who had been formerly wandering in error, established in the Church. There was accordingly a large assembly of the people: and with one voice they rendered thanks to God, weeping for very joy, and embracing the restored confessors, as if they had but that instant been liberated from prison. As for the confessions of the restored brethren, I send you their very words. 'We know that Cornelius is a Bishop of the most holy Catholic Church, elected by God Almighty and Christ our Lord. We confess our error: we have been deceived, we have been carried away by captious and fraudulent misrepresentations. For even while we seemed to be holding some kind of communion with a heretic and a schismatic, our mind was still faithful to the Church. Nor are we ignorant that there is one God, and one Christ the Lord, whom we have confessed, and one Holy Spirit: and that there should be one Bishop in a Catholic Church.'

"Who," continues Cornelius, "would not, by such an acknowledgment, be moved to admit those who had confessed before the powers of this world, to the full proof of their confessions in the Church? Maximus, therefore, we restored to his former dignity; the rest we received to communion, with the applause of the whole multitude: all judgment we committed to God, to whom all judgment belongs. . . . We believe, moreover, nay are confident, that others who are at present involved in the same error, will soon return to the Church, when they see that their former leaders are again associated with us."

The following is the letter of the confessors themselves to Cyprian:—

"Maximus, Urbanus, Sidonius, and Macharius, to their brother Cyprian, Health! We are sure, dearest brother, that your joy will equal our own, at the step which we have taken; that consulting the good of the Church, and passing by former events, and committing them to the judgment of God, we have made peace at once with Cornelius our Bishop, and with the whole body of the Clergy. And we write this letter that you may be well assured, that we have done this to the great joy of the whole Church, and so as to carry with us the affections of all. We wish you health, dearest brother, for many years to come."[1]

[1] *Ep.* l. p. 64.

Cyprian's answer to the confessors shall close this series of letters.

"Cyprian to his brethren Maximus the Presbyter, Urbanus, Sidonius, and Macharius, Health! I confess, dearest brethren, that the perusal of your letter, in which you give an account of your return to the obedience and peace of the Church, gave me as much joy, as the report of your glorious confession had formerly done. For to confess the unity of the Church, is another witness of your faith, another token of your virtue; to maintain that the Church is free from possible participation in the error or wickedness of any, is to seek again the same encampment, from which you before advanced to the battle, and rushed eagerly to meet the foe, and to lay him prostrate. The trophies of your success ought to be suspended in that Church, from the armoury of which you were arrayed for the victory; lest the Church of Christ should lose the glory of those, whom Christ had prepared for glory. And now at last, you have returned to a path worthy of your faith, and of the love and reverence for the divine law which burns in the hearts of each of you; and you have given an example also of love and peace to others, that the truth of the Church, the sacrament of unity in the Gospel, which was before maintained by us, might be knit together also with the additional bond of your consent: and that the confessors of Christ who had stood out as the foremost in virtue and in honour, should not become leaders in error. Others are doubtless conscious of a great joy at your return; but I confess that I feel singularly interested in it, and my congratulations fall short of none, in sincerity and joy. Let me open to you my feelings with all simplicity. I was greatly and oppressively afflicted by the thought, that I could no longer hold communion with those whom I had begun to love with my whole heart. When a schismatical and heretical error received you, as it were, out of prison, whither you had been carried with the praise and gratulation of the Church, it was as if your glory had remained in the dungeon. For though there are evidently tares in the Church, this ought not so to subvert our faith or love, as to induce us to forsake the Church. It . . . labour, that we may be wheat; that when the w... red into the barn of the Lord, we may receive the r... r labour. The Apostle says, *In a great house there a...  'y vessels of gold and of silver, but also of wood and of ...  nd some to honour and some to dishonour.* Be it our dearest brethren, so to labour, that we may be vessels o... ld or of silver: but to break the vessels of earth can be c... mmitted to the Lord alone, to whom is given the rod of iron. The servant cannot be greater than his master: nor may any one arrogate to himself what the father has given to the son alone; nor think himself at liberty, by human judgment, to fan the floor, or drive away the chaff, or separate between the wheat and the tares. This were nothing short of madness, of obstinate pride and presumption: and while some will be always assuming to themselves a greater authority than justice and mildness will allow, they themselves fall away from the Church; and while they are boasting themselves of their greater light, their very pride shuts them up in impenetrable darkness. Bearing these things in mind, and endeavouring to follow the indications of God's will, in His justice and in His compassion, after long and deep consideration, I have myself arrived at a moderate judgment in these matters: as you will see on the perusal of the accompanying treatise, which I have lately read to my own people, and now commit affectionately to your perusal; and in which there is neither wanting just censure upon the lapsed, nor such milder remedies as may effect their cure. I have also, to the best of my power, written upon the principle of unity in the Church Catholic: and I have the more confidence that you will approve of that treatise, now that your own actions and affections may be in accordance with it: for you have now, by your return to the peace and unity of the Church, exemplified in your conduct, that which I have committed to writing. Dearest and most beloved brethren, I wish you eternal health."[1]

[1] *Ep.* li. p. 65.

Here            ect history of Novatian and his party;
though i        hat these events must give a colouring to
the futur

If any          ospect of the whole matter, be disposed to
ask, Wh         sy did Novatian teach, that he fell under such
heavy c         es and punishments, and eventually under such
universa        xecration of all good men? I shall return the
answer c Cyprian to this very question, when it was proposed
to him by Antonianus. "It is not fitting to inquire too narrowly what he teaches, since, whatever it is, he teaches it out of the Church. Whoever and whatever he may be, he cannot be a Christian who is not in the Church of Christ.[1] Let him pride himself as he will on his philosophy or eloquence; and let his boasting equal his vanity; he who hath held fast neither brotherly love nor Church unity has lost even that which he before possessed."[2]

That Cyprian's principle is *startling*, I admit; but the more we think upon it, the more likely we are, I suspect, to believe that it is *true*. It is moreover of very general application. It is so far from being a sufficient vindication of a separatist, that he carries the *doctrine* of the Church with him, that it is in fact the very extreme form of sinful schism, or causeless separation, to do this. So far as their separation is concerned (abstracting from it all its antecedents and consequents), the Manichæan or the Arian was excusable; the Quaker or the Socinian is now excusable; in comparison of any who may think to plead in their justification, that they teach no doctrines which ever were or ever can be condemned by the Church as heretical.

Nor will it be sufficient to take away this opprobrium from separation, that though there is no sufficient cause for it in a conscientious difference of doctrine; yet conscience is *pretended*, in respect of discipline. For the regulation of discipline is the proper province of the visible body of Christ's Church: and all individuals are bound to obey, and not to cavil, still

---

[1] Quisquis ille est et qualiscunque est, Christianus non est, qui in Christi Ecclesia non est.
[2] *Ep.* lii. p. 73.

less to rebel: and those who *pretend* conscience in this matter, too often mean obstinate opinion, or at best weak scruples. Cyprian gives a case in point, when he says to Antonian, "Among our predecessors, there were certain Bishops in this very province, who thought that the peace of the Church ought not to be given to adulterers, and cut them off from all the privileges of penance: yet they seceded not from the college of their brethren in the Episcopate, nor broke the unity of the Church by an obstinate severity and censure; so as that one who allowed not penance to adulterers, should secede from those who did. In such cases, the bond of unity being inviolate, and the peculiar mystery of indivisibility in the Catholic Church being preserved, each Bishop acts as he will, and on his own responsibility, as one who is hereafter to render his account to the Lord."[1]

Of course I do not deny, that by an hypothesis of unbridled and unchastened fancy, the Church may enjoin obedience to such rules of discipline, as may constitute a ground of separation truly conscientious: but in this case the Church itself would be schismatical, and in case of actual rupture, she would be the separatist;—which is in theology impossible, whatever it may be in imagination or logomachy;—and it is illogical to reason on any other than theological principles, in matters of theology.

But, in fact, there is so much of doctrine involved in discipline, though perhaps indirectly, that dissent on a pretended conscience against the Church's discipline, will usually end in downright heresy. In this light the schism of Novatian was very dangerous, and its consequences very instructive. Its pernicious effects were soon evolved. Pretending as its essential character a severer form of discipline, and avowing the intention of maintaining a more ascetical and uncontaminated piety, it might seem at first sight (especially if viewed as a matter of opinion or speculation), that the harshest judgment which could be pronounced of it was, that it was more rigid than was expedient: more honest than wise. But in fact' it

[1] *Ep.* lii. p. 72.

tended, and that presently, to obscure the character, and overthrow the reality, of the Church itself. Contrary to the universally received interpretation of the parables of the net, which gathered of all fishes good and bad; of the field, in which tares and wheat grew together until harvest; the definition of the Church which Novatian was obliged to assume as the ground of his separation, excluded from that body every assembly which contained a mixture of wicked men: and the obvious inference was, that the Church nowhere existed: nowhere, as he himself avowed, except with his own cabal; nowhere, as even his own party must soon discover, unless they should be judicially blinded to their own enormities. Moreover, the distinctive title which he assumed for his party, whom he called Cathari (Καθαροί) or *puritans*, while it sounded only as a profession and earnest of greater purity, in fact involved a reproach, and was intended so to do, of the Catholic Church. "Having obtained imposition of hands by robbery," says Theodoret[1] of Novatian, "he became the leader of a heresy; and gave to his followers not only the name of Novatians, but of Cathari: and he trembled not at the rebuke pronounced against some who say, *I am clean, touch me not;* to whom the Lord God saith, *These are smoke in My nose, a fire that burneth all the day;* for the Lord *resisteth the proud.*"[2] Perhaps some who to this day, would be distinguished by a name which casts opprobrium on all others, may not be free from the crime of the Novatians, nor undeserving of the divine rebuke thus applied to them by Theodoret.

It was a corollary of Novatian's doctrine concerning the Church, that the Baptism of the Catholics was invalid, or rather was no baptism at all. Hence his party was guilty of the sacrilege of rebaptising those whom they received into their number.[3] Again, they have their parallel in certain sec-

[1] Theodoreti Hæret. Far. compend. lib. iii. v. Περὶ Ναυάτου, vol. iv. p. 345.
[2] See Isaiah lxv. 5, and 1 Pet. v. 5.
[3] The Catholics received the Novatians without Baptism; but administered unction to them, on their conversion, as well as imposition of hands; for the Novatians rejected this part of the ceremony of Baptism.

taries of these days. The whole complexion, too, of their theology, represented God and Christ as cruel and implacable; and was therefore tinged at least with impiety. Have they no parallels again in these days? In a word, as Dionysius says, "We have cause enough to hate Novatian; for he hath divided the Church; he hath involved some of the faithful in his impiety and blasphemy; he hath brought in a dangerous doctrine; he hath taken away the mercy and beneficence of the Saviour; he hath rendered Holy Baptism useless, and hath thereby driven away the Holy Spirit, even though there might yet be hope of His return." [1]

[1] Eusebius vii. 8.

## CHAPTER VIII.

A Review of St Cyprian's tract "De Unitate Ecclesiæ.

It was on occasion of the disturbances in the Church, of which we have just given an account, and in the midst of those of which we are about to speak, that St Cyprian wrote his celebrated and most important tract "DE UNITATE ECCLESIÆ;"—"On the Unity of the Church."

The exordium is most appropriate to the times. Persecution was then the great and overwhelming temptation by which Christians were everywhere assailed: and as persecution was the temptation then most dreaded, so was open apostasy, and a return to heathen rites and superstitions, the sin most likely to abound; and the number of the lapsed was still reading to the Church a sad lesson of fear and humiliation on this head. On the other hand, since external assaults are usually found to cement a society in the bonds of a closer compact, schism would seem to be the sin least to be expected, and faction and cabals the temptations least to be feared. St Cyprian then begins his work against the evil of separation from the Church, by warning his readers and his hearers (for the tract in question was probably preached as well as published) against the deceitfulness and subtlety of Satan, who would now insinuate the temptations least expected, while the Church was watchful and prepared against the dangers more obviously impending.

To all the commandments of God, then, the Christian Bishop writing under these circumstances demands the obedience of his flock; and against all temptations, especially at that time against temptation to schism and heresy, he forewarns them; teaching them, that they who neglected God's law of unity imposed upon the Church, must perish equally with those who disobeyed any other divine precept.

The first point to be proved, according to this plan, is this. That unity is the appointment of God and of Christ. A visible unity of a visible body; not that factitious unity which was then pretended, and of which the liberalism of the present day dreams so vaguely, but *the sacrament of unity*,[1] or an outward and visible union of the Church, as a sign and conveyance, appointed by Almighty God, of certain spiritual gifts and privileges.

The first proof that St Cyprian offers of this is the typical character of St Peter, whereby he becomes (not as Bishop of Rome, but in his individual personal character) a type or figure (not an instrument) of the unity of the Church. The two limitations here expressed are most important, because it is by keeping them out of sight that the Romanists make it appear on a cursory view that St Cyprian favours their own Church in his present reasonings; whereas if either of those limitations be found or implied in St Cyprian's teaching, the whole scheme of Rome must fall to the ground, so far as Cyprian's testimony is concerned. But in truth *both* are most plainly indicated in this very treatise; much more therefore is the system of Rome, which cannot consist with *either*, unsupported by St Cyprian.

The passage in which the typical character of St Peter is thus adduced in proof of the will of God and of Christ that the Church should be one, is as follows: "Addressing Peter, the Lord saith, *I say unto thee, Thou art Peter and upon this rock I will build My Church, and the gates of hell shall not prevail against it: and to thee will I give the keys of the kingdom of heaven: and whatsoever things thou shalt bind on earth, shall be bound in heaven also; and whatsoever things thou shalt loose on earth, shall be loosed in heaven also.* And again to the same (Peter) He saith after His resurrection, *Feed My sheep.*

[1] Unitatis Sacramentum, p. 196. *bis.*

He builds His Church upon one, [and commits His sheep to him to be fed]. And although He committed an equal power to all the Apostles, saying, *As My Father sent Me, so send I you: receive ye the Holy Ghost. Whosoever sins ye remit, they shall be remitted unto him; whosoever sins ye retain, they shall be retained:* yet, for the exemplification of unity, He so disposed, by His authority, the original of that unity, that it might take its rise from one. The rest of the Apostles, indeed, were what Peter was; endowed with an equal fellowship both of dignity and of power; yet the beginning proceeds from unity, that the Church may be shown to be one."[1]

Now it will be observed, that while the last sentence is quite at variance with the Papacy, every word here uttered may be accepted by an Anglican divine; or at least, whether or no it agree with his private opinion, be permitted as harmless, in the controversy with Rome. But since the schism which gave occasion to the whole tract occurred at Rome, it is next to impossible that St Cyprian, if he had at all symbolized with the modern Romanists in the matter of St Peter's supremacy, should entirely forget to speak of St Peter the Bishop of Rome, as well as of St Peter the Apostle; and to make him *not a type only*, but also a *centre* and *instrument* of unity: for there lay the chief strength of this part of the argument, according to the Romish assumption.

The typical character of St Peter is prophetic of the Church's Unity, but we have also adduced by St Cyprian an older prophecy of the same thing; for in harmony with Catholic interpretation, he explains the words of the Bridegroom to the Bride in the Song of Songs; *My dove, my spotless one, is but one; she is the only one of her mother, elect of her that bare her*, as spoken by Christ to His Church. And afterwards he adduces many direct precepts of unity, all tending

[1] In this quotation I have followed the Oxford Edition of St Cyprian's Works. The reason why the Benedictine Edition and those which it follows are not to be relied on here, may be found in *James on the Corruptions of the Fathers and Councils*; in the note at the end of the tract on the Unity of the Church in the Oxford translation of St Cyprian's Works, and in the Appendix to my own "*Testimony of St Cyprian against Rome.*"

to set in the strongest light the intention and the command of God, that the unity of the Church should be visibly and inviolably maintained.

Besides these, there are many other indirect proofs of the divine origin of the principle of unity adduced by St Cyprian, such as the type of the seamless coat of Christ, which the very soldiers would not divide, and the unity of the ever-blessed and glorious Trinity. Many too are the warnings which he deduces from Scripture, as the case of Jannes and Jambres, and that of Korah, Dathan, and Abiram: and it is scarce necessary to add, that all those texts which are ordinarily cited for the same purpose, he does not forget to adduce as positive precepts to maintain the unity of the Spirit in the bond of peace; only this is observable, that it never seems to have suggested itself to his mind, that men could obey these precepts of love and charity and unity, while they were visibly separate, and actively employed in maligning and undermining the Church.

Hitherto we have St Cyprian indicating the duty of Church unity, but not mentioning any *instrument* or *bond of union*, without which the Church would be incomplete; and which Rome thinks that she finds in her own Bishop, while Ultra-protestants know not where to look for it. Now though Cyprian does not with modern Rome make St Peter personally or in his successor at Rome a centre or *instrument* of unity; neither does he, with the modern Dissenter, and with those members of the Church who are best designated perhaps as *invisible Churchmen*, forget, that an instrument of that unity is really provided, by means of which the command of God may be obeyed. This instrument of unity, or visible bond and centre of brotherhood, St Cyprian finds in the Episcopate: "which unity," saith he, "we should firmly hold and maintain; especially we, who as Bishops should preside in the Church, that we may approve the Episcopate itself to be one and undivided. Let none lead the brethren astray with a lie: let none corrupt the unity of the faith with treachery and prevarication. The Episcopate is one, and each Bishop so shares in it, as to have an interest in the whole."[1]  If any thing be wanting to make this doctrine of Cyprian plain, it may be gathered from his Epistle to the laity of his own Church, on occasion of the schism of Felicissimus. "God is one, and Christ one, and the Church one, and there is one Episcopal chair founded on a rock by the word of the Lord. It is impossible that any altar can be erected besides the one altar; or any new priesthood added to the one priesthood. Whoever gathers from other sources scatters. . . . Let no one, dearest brethren, induce you to wander from the ways of the Lord. Let none snatch you who are Christians from the Gospel of Christ. From the Church let none separate the sons of the Church. They who *will* perish, let them perish *alone*. They who have seceded from the Church, let *them alone* remain without the Church. They who have rebelled against the Bishops, let *them alone* be separated from the Bishops."[2]

To these passages might be added many others to show that St Cyprian makes the Episcopate not only what he had made St Peter, a type of unity, or an indication that God would have His Church one; but also more than He made St Peter, that is to say, an instrument of unity, by means of which the Church actually was what God had indicated in the typical character of St Peter that it should be.

The Church, he adds, after the express declaration of the oneness of the Episcopate, "The Church also is one, and by the increase of her fruitfulness, extends herself far and wide, still remaining one. So the rays of the sun are many, but its light is one; the boughs of a tree are many, but its strength is one, residing in the firm root; and when from one source several streams take their rise, though the copious fountain pour forth many rivers, yet unity is preserved in the source itself. Intercept a ray of the sun, and the principle of unity in its light no longer suffers it to shine. Tear a branch from

---

[1] Episcopatus unus est, cujus a singulis in solidum pars tenetur. Page 195.
[2] Extra ecclesiam soli remaneant, qui de ecclesia recesserunt, soli cum Episcopis non sint, qui contra Episcopos rebellarunt. *Ep.* xl. 53, 54.

the tree, and it cannot bud forth again. Cut off the stream from its source, and its channel is dried up. So the Church, pervaded with the light of the Lord, extends its rays through the whole world: yet the light is still one, in its universal diffusion, nor is the unity of the body disturbed: its exuberant fruitfulness extends its boughs over all the earth; it pours forth its streams far and wide: yet is there but one head, one source, one mother, present everywhere in her unnumbered progeny."

But there were some who thought to obtain the blessings promised to the one Church by a factitious unity among themselves; and those especially, who had gained over the Confessors at Rome, boasted of communion with these champions of the faith, and thought they might on the strength of it neglect the real Church Communion with the Bishop, and so, instrumentally, with Christ. In a word, they thought to receive *the grace* of the Sacrament of unity, while sacrilegiously rejecting the *outward sign*. With these St Cyprian thus reasons. "Let them not deceive themselves with a false interpretation of our Lord's words, *Where two or three are gathered together in My name, there am I in the midst of them.* This is to tamper with the Gospel, and to adapt it to a purpose which it does not support, by taking part, and omitting the remainder. And as they are themselves broken off from the Church, so would they mutilate the passage, and present it in fragments. For thus did the Lord say, when He would persuade His disciples to unanimity and concord. *If two of you shall agree on earth as touching any thing that they shall ask, it shall be done for them of My Father which is in heaven. For where two or three are gathered together in My name, there am I in the midst of them.* Indicating that the unanimity of the petitioners was of more avail than their numbers. . . . But how can he agree with another, who first agreeth not with the body of the Church itself, and with the whole brotherhood? How can two or three, manifestly separated from Christ and from His Gospel, be gathered together in Christ's name? [And such is their case.] For we departed not from them, but they from us: and heresies and schisms have a date posterior to ours, originating in the formation of separate assemblies, by those who have left the head and original of the truth. But, truly, it is of His Church that the Lord speaks; and to those who are in His Church that He says, that if they be of one mind, as He commanded, yet though they be but two or three, yet the majesty of God will hear their petitions."[1]

But not only do such men cut themselves off from the peculiar privileges attached to unity, but all other the peculiar blessings of the Church are to them of none avail. "What peace do they hope to receive who are at enmity with the brethren? What sacrifice do they offer who are opposed to the Priest? Do they who are assembled together, without the Church of Christ, dream that Christ is with them in their assemblies? Though such men should die in confession, not even their blood would wash away these stains. The sin of dissension is too weighty to be expiable by suffering. He who is not in the Church cannot be a martyr."[2]

And in respect both of criminality and of wretchedness of condition, he postpones the separatists even to the lapsed.[3] "Their crime is more than that with which the lapsed appear to be stained: for those do at least deprecate the wrath of God, with all the appointed offices of penance. The lapsed seek after the Church as suppliants: schismatics resist the Church. The lapsed yielded to force and compulsion: schismatics cleave with full purpose to their sin. The one injures

[1] Page 198. We may again find a parallel in one of St Cyprian's Epistles. Writing to Pupianus, he says, "The Bishop is in the Church, and the Church in the Bishop; they who are not with the Bishop, are not in the Church: and they miserably deceive themselves, who, not maintaining communion with the Bishops of God, think cunningly to insinuate themselves into the Church, by communicating with certain others; whereas the Church, which is one and Catholic, will not endure separation and schism, but is united and consolidated through all its parts by the cement of an united Episcopate."

[2] Page 198.

[3] This is in exact harmony with the Epistle of Dionysius to Novatian, upon his schism.

his own soul alone, the other perils the souls of many. The one sees that he has sinned, and weeps and laments; the other elated in his wilfulness, and rejoicing in his very crimes, separates children from their mother, allures sheep from their fold, and subverts the Sacrament of God; and whereas the lapsed has once sinned, the other offends daily. Finally, the lapsed may be received into the kingdom of heaven after martyrdom; but he who is slain out of the Church hath no part in the rewards of the Church."[1]

How terrible we may well say is the picture which St Cyprian presents, and to which all the saints of that age agree, of the state of heretics and schismatics! And since the very elect may be almost within the deceptive art of the tempter, how great reason that we should not be highminded but fear! Yet the temptation to schism, in St Cyprian's view of it, is only another way by which the great enemy destroys the souls of those who in truth are his, though other trials had failed to move them. "Let none," says he, "account it possible for the good to depart from the Church. The wind carries not away the wheat; nor does the storm tear up the firmly rooted tree. It is the chaff that flies before the wind; it is the rotten trunk that is shattered by the storm. Such are they whom St John transfixes with a curse: *They went out from us, because they were not of us: for if they had been of us, no doubt they would have continued with us.* . . . The Lord suffers these things to be, leaving still to each his free will; that while the choice of truth attests the sincerity of our hearts and minds, the unshaken faith of the approved may shine with redoubled lustre. The Holy Spirit forewarns us of this by the Apostle: *There must be heresies, that they which are approved may be made manifest among you.* Thus are the faithful proved; thus are the faithless detected. Thus, even before the day of judgment, are the works of the just and of the unjust divided, and the chaff separated from the wheat."[2]

After these copious extracts, it is scarce necessary to notice the grave and indignant warnings against separation, and the

[1] Page 201.  [2] Page 197.

affectionate and earnest entreaties to peace and unity, by which they are followed. But perhaps some one will ask, Is there nothing in the tract which we are examining about that charity, that bond of peace, which is as the soul, of which external visible unity is the body? I must remind those who should thus ask, that St Cyprian is expressly writing about the visible unity, about the *sacramentum unitatis;* so that he need not be accused of indifference to love and charity, though he had said but little about them: but in fact his ardent and affectionate spirit would not miss the opportunity of commending those Christian graces; and he again and again refers to them in very energetic terms. One passage (but it is one out of many) shall suffice. " In the house of God, in the Church of Christ, they dwell with united affections, in concord and singleness of heart. And therefore came the Holy Spirit in the form of a dove. A creature of cheerfulness and simplicity; bitter with no gall, fierce and violent with no savage beak and hooked talons, delighting in the dwellings of man, consorting together and rearing their young in an house: flying side by side in their wanderings from their nests, sweetening life with society and a mutual affection, betokening their peace with gentle kisses, and in all things living according to a law of love. Such simplicity, such love, should be seen within Church, and from the dove should the love of the brethren take its pattern."[1]

Such is an imperfect sketch of the tract of Cyprian on the unity of the Church. The abstract propositions which it maintains are and will ever be true. Their application to present circumstances may be difficult; and certainly is far more so than when St Cyprian wrote: for though the mystical holiness and truth of the Church remain perfect to the eye of faith; yet if She hath in any degree (and who shall dare to say that She hath not?) presented to the eye of sense a far different aspect; with *Her* assuredly is some part of the sin, and much of the shame, when Her weaker sons are scandalized. It is still their duty to live by faith; but if She

[1] Pages 196, 197.

hath made it harder to them, though they be not excused, surely Her own children will less readily cast the stone.

Against two extreme forms, however, of schismatical, proceeding, there can be neither hesitation nor danger in declaring all that Cyprian says to be just as true as ever, even in its direct application. If there be any who deny not the truth of the Church's doctrine, and the sufficiency of the means of grace, which she herself affords, or which may be had in perfect harmony with her laws; yet with unordained hands and with no Apostolic commission, present the mockery of an altar and of the Christian Sacraments; *they* are woefully deceiving the people, and feeding them with husks, whereas in their Father's house is enough and to spare for the meanest servants.

And again, the Romish Church, which first of all had so extremely overlaid the truth of Christ with error, and the purity of the Church with sin and crime, that its holiness and its catholicity was removed, except from the most piercing eye of faith; so that we might almost say, that even had we separated we should have been (dare I say justified; yet) at least forgiven: and at last, when we laboured earnestly to go back to a primitive faith and catholic practice, and would not, while we left the error, and escaped the sin, be driven, taunted, persecuted to separation; herself by her own act separated us from her communion: and then came hither by intrusion, and set up Bishop against Bishop, and altar against altar;—surely thus doing, the Romish Church does bring itself, and its adherents in this land, under the very meaning of St Cyprian's definitions of schism, and within the range of his reprobation.

## CHAPTER IX.

A Schism at Carthage.—Its Origin.—The Surreptitious Ordination of Fortunatus.—The Schismatics apply to Cornelius for his Support:—They are at first repelled, but afterwards too favourably heard.—St Cyprian expostulates with Cornelius.—The Extinction of Fortunatus's Party.—Maximus Ordained by the Novatians in Carthage.—His Faction contemptible.

WE have no sooner concluded the history of the attempt of Novatian on the peace of the Church in Rome, than we are called upon to record a similar series of events in Carthage. They were indeed of far less importance; nor did they originate any party which long existed as a separate communion: yet they gave some trouble to Cyprian; and called for the application of precisely the same principles of Church government and discipline, which were so fully elicited during the scandalous schism of the Novatians at Rome, and embodied with so great skill and judgment in the work we have just reviewed. And it is singular enough, that both these schisms should indirectly have occasioned for a while some mutual distrust of one another in St Cornelius and St Cyprian: for as Cyprian's having suspended his formal judgment touching the Episcopate of Cornelius, though for good purposes, had called forth a remonstrance from that Prelate, who knew not the motives by which Cyprian was actuated; so also did the hesitation which was occasioned in the mind of Cornelius by the false reports of the enemies of Cyprian, when there were no sufficient sources of authentic information at hand, give occasion to an expostulatory Epistle of Cyprian. From this Epistle we extract the following accounts.

Many years before, one Privatus, a notorious heretic, had been condemned at Lambesa, in Numidia, by a Synod of ninety Bishops; whose judgment had been approved by Fabianus and Donatus, the predecessors of Cornelius and of Cyprian in their respective sees. This man came to Carthage, accompanied by Felix (whom he had schismatically ordained Bishop), and by Maximus, Jovinus, and Repostus, who had lapsed in the late persecution. Privatus, thus accompanied, wished, it seems, or pretended a wish, to obtain a second hearing of his cause at Carthage; but this being denied him, he with his four companions, joining this party of Felicissimus, determined on constituting in the Church of Carthage an Episcopal head to their schismatical body. They fixed on Fortunatus, of whom we have already heard as one of the five presbyters who took part with Felicissimus in his schism; and they gave out that five and twenty Bishops were to join them from Numidia, to assist at his ordination. This, however, was a vain boast, for five only, and they excommunicated, assembled for this purpose.

Cornelius was already acquainted with the name of Fortunatus, and catalogues had been sent to him from Carthage both of those Bishops who were sound in the faith, and also of those Bishops and others who had been condemned and expelled the Church; Cyprian therefore deemed it hardly necessary to convey a particular account of these matters to Cornelius by a special messenger. He did, however, write to Rome soon after by Felicissimus; but in the meanwhile Felicissimus arrived at that city, together with other adherents of Fortunatus, there to appeal against the judgment of the African Prelates, and to produce the evidence on which they claimed that Fortunatus should be recognised as Bishop of Carthage.

At first Cornelius utterly rejected the claims of those impudent pretenders; but when they repeated the lies which they had forged at Carthage, and gave out that the number of Bishops assisting at the ordination of Fortunatus was that which they had at first promised to produce,—not five, but twenty-five;—and threatened to read the letters which they had brought with them in public, if they were not received by Cornelius, and to spread many scandalous reports: Cornelius was so far moved by their threats, that his determination was shaken, and he addressed a letter to Cyprian, seeking farther information upon the subject.

This application called forth the reply, from which this account is taken. All the circumstances of the ordination of Fortunatus, Cyprian relates as we have given them, and expostulates somewhat warmly with Cornelius, for his vacillation in so clear a cause. He tells Cornelius, in his own behalf, as he had before told Antonianus on behalf of Cornelius, that we are not to listen to the scandalous reports of factious and ungodly men, and such as the Church repudiates: he reminds him that such attacks upon his character by those who profess the same religion, are a part of the portion of a good Bishop in this world, as well as the open violence of Jews and heathens; even as Jacob and Joseph both suffered from the enmity of their brethren, and Christ Himself was betrayed by a disciple. The foul calumnies which the followers of Fortunatus vented, he turns to an evidence against them; for the evil man out of the evil treasure of his heart bringeth forth evil things: and especially when they are spoken against the priest of God; since it is written, "He that despiseth you despiseth Me;" and since our Lord Himself and St Paul illustrated by their conduct and precept the general rule, "thou shalt not speak evil of the ruler of thy people."

Thus having stated the source of such irreverence to the sacred office which he held, he goes on to point out its consequences also: that heresies have no other origin but this, that the priest of God is not obeyed, and that it is not sufficiently remembered, that there is but one Bishop at a time in a Church, and but one judge, in the place of Christ; that if the whole brotherhood would obey him, according to the divine institution, no one would be found to devise practices against the college of Bishops: no one, in opposition to the judgment of God, to the suffrage of the people, to the consent of the Episcopate, already declared in behalf of any, would erect himself into a judge not so much of his Bishop as of God Himself: no one would rend the Church of Christ by a breach of unity; no one would indulge his vanity and pride by the erection of a new heresy.[1]

Then he proceeds to set forth his own testimonies as the one Bishop in his see; his election, his constancy in persecution, and the like; and after giving an account of the proceedings of Fortunatus and his party, with a view of their characters; which we will gladly omit, or at least sum up in the single expression of Cyprian, that Fortunatus and they were worthy associates, he as a ruler, they as his people:—after having declared that the threats which they uttered against him personally made them murderers in the sight of God:[2]— after especially intimating their guilt, and largely proving its heinousness, in too readily receiving the lapsed; he enters upon another ground of complaint against them, and shows that the very fact of their carrying their cause to Rome, after it had been heard and determined in their own province, was in itself criminal, so that it ought not only not to be encouraged, but not so much as permitted by Cornelius.

St Cyprian's words are as follows : " After these schismatical proceedings, and when a false Bishop had been ordained for them by heretics, they dare to take ship, and to carry letters from schismatics and profane persons, to the see of Peter, and to a principal Church, from whence the unity of the Episcopate took its rise; forgetting that it was the Romans, whose faith is applauded in the preaching of the Apostle; to whom perfidy could have no access. But wherefore did they come, and tell you of their having ordained a pseudo-bishop, in opposition to the (true) Bishops? For either they are still pleased with their deed, and persevere in their crime; or if they regret it, and would retrace their steps, they know whither they should return. For since it has been determined by us all, as indeed is just and fit, that the cause of every man

---

[1] Neque enim aliunde hæreses obortæ sunt, &c. *Ep.* lv. p. 82.
[2] Fustis et lapidis et gladios—quod in illis est, homicidæ sunt apud Deum tales. *Ep.* lv. p. 80.

should be heard where his offence was committed; and that a portion of the flock should be attached to each pastor, to be by him ruled and governed, each having to render an account of his actions to the Lord; it is fit that those over whom we rule should not wander about, nor make a breach in the coherent concord of Bishops, by their own artifice and deceitful boldness; but that they should plead their cause where they may both find accusers, and witnesses of their crime. Unless, indeed, to a few desperate and abandoned wretches, the authority of the Bishops constituted in Africa, who have already judged their cause, and with the weight of their sentence confirmed the condemnation of their consciences, bound with many crimes, seem inferior. Their cause is already determined; their sentence is already pronounced: nor is it fit that the judgment of Bishops should be subject to the reprehension of inconsistency and change."

And afterwards: "They have not the face to appear before us, and to remain with us, so heinous and weighty are the crimes which are alleged against them. Yet, if they be willing to submit to my judgment, let them come. Let them show their penitence, for the Church is shut against none; and as for my personal accessibility and mildness, they cannot deny it."

These passages are not unworthy of note, as conveying expressly, what we shall find more than once implied in the following pages, the judgment of St Cyprian, and in him I will venture to say *of the Church Universal in his days and for ever*, concerning appeals to Rome, wherein consists one important branch of the supremacy usurped by that see.[1]

[1] The nearest approach that was ever made by any Ecclesiastical Synod, that could be deemed better than a party cabal, towards investing Rome with the privilege of hearing appeals, was made by the Sardican Council, about a hundred years after Cyprian's time. It was then determined, that if any particular Bishop felt aggrieved by the judgment of his comprovincial Bishops, he might apply to Julius, Bishop of Rome (observe not to the Bishop of Rome absolutely, but to Julius the then Bishop), in order to another trial (but observe), not before Julius personally, or in his courts, but before such Bishops of the next adjoining province as he should appoint; or ultimately, under certain circumstances, before his legates.

It is needless to add, that the cause of Cyprian, just in itself, and thus advocated, was wholly triumphant at Rome

Now, in the first place, this Sardican Council is not of universal authority; and the time was when Rome thought so too, or acted at least as if she thought so. For in the year 415, Irsinius, Bishop of Rome, rejudged the cause of Apiarius, an African priest, who had been deposed by his own Bishop, *pretending the authority of the Council of Nice* for these Sardican Canons, as if conscious that they required the authority of that greater Council; and under this pretended authority he sent his legate into Africa, to hear the cause of Apiarius. It so happened that a Synod of two hundred and seventy Bishops, among whom was the great St Augustine, was assembled at that time; and they all replied, that they knew of no such Canon among those of Nice; and after six years, during the whole of which time it should seem the imposition was attempted, they declared their final decision, that the Nicene Fathers had determined the contrary to what was pretended by the Roman legates; that delinquent Clergymen were thereby left to the judgment of their own Bishops, and Bishops to that of their Metropolitans; and that all such matters should be determined in the places where they arose: that the grace of the Holy Spirit would not be wanting in each province, for the right ordering of all such matters; and that they could find no decree of the Fathers which justified the proceedings of Rome in sending legates to them.

But, secondly, it was not without a reason that the power then given to Julius, Bishop of Rome, was limited in the Sardican Canons *to him personally*. The Council of Sardica met to restore St Athanasius, and to provide for the continued security of the orthodox. Now the Emperor had the same privilege of granting a re-hearing which is here given to Julius: and the then Emperor was Constantius, an Arian, of that very sect against whose machinations the Canons in questions were intended as safeguards. The exigency, then, arising from the heterodoxy of the *present Emperor*, was met by transferring one of his privileges, by an internal arrangement of the Church, to the *present Bishop of Rome*. The whole matter was an expedient, and fell to the ground, both according to the letter and to the spirit of the Canons in question, when the present necessity was passed.

But although that just stated is the nearest approach towards giving *to Rome* a power of hearing appeals, yet it is not the nearest approach to the like power given to another Church: the nearest approach to the power now claimed by Rome that was ever given to any Church, was given by the Fathers assembled at Chalcedon to the See of Constantinople. See Canon ix. of that Council.

In the whole matter of this note, consult Johnson's Vade Mecum; and see also Palmer's Treatise on the Church of Christ, part ii. ch. 2.

and elsewhere; indeed he tells us, that by the very fact of the ordination of Fortunatus, the faction which adhered to him was diminished almost to nothing, so that they could scarce number among their adherents, lay or cleric, so many as had joined in their condemnation:[1] for this shameless act opened the eyes of all who were hitherto deceived by the pretensions of that party, and by the hope of being readmitted into the Church by their means, the possibility of which was now precluded. I do not know that we hear anything more of this desperate faction.

The ordination of Maximus by the Novatian party at Carthage was still more obscure; and scarce gives us an opportunity of mentioning, that there were now three rival Bishops in Carthage. The only account which Cyprian deigns to give of this latter pretender is contained in the following passage of the letter so often lately quoted. "It is scarcely consistent with the majesty of the Catholic Church, to notice the impudent attempts of heretics and schismatics; I hear, however, that a party of the Novatians have lately sent as their Bishop into these parts, one Maximus, whom I had already excommunicated." The best use to make of such accounts is to collect from them the testimony even of heretics to the necessity of that discipline which the Catholic Church has ever maintained. It seems that in those days it was not thought possible to assume even the external figure of a Church, without the presence of a Bishop: and that too, a Bishop of that particular Church, where the schismatics assembled. It would have seemed monstrous then to have assumed the character of a Christian Church without a Bishop, or of a Christian Church, in London for instance, under a Bishop of Olena. But some in these wiser days seem to think otherwise.

[1] *Ep.* lv, page 87.

## CHAPTER X.

Persecution renewed on occasion of the Plague.—Cyprian's Apologetic Letter to Demetrian.—His Epistle to the Thybaritani.—The Penitent Lapsed admitted to Communion, in anticipation of Persecution.—The Exhortation to Martyrdom.—St Cyprian's Last Letter to St Cornelius.—Death of Cornelius.—Of Lucius.—How far Persecution a Test of Truth.

BEFORE Cornelius received the account of Fortunatus and his schism, a new scene of persecution had opened upon the Church; for Cyprian says, that he had been called for by the enraged populace to the lions, while he was writing the Epistle last mentioned: the blood of a Christian Bishop being required as the most acceptable libation upon the sacrifices offered to appease the wrath of Apollo the destroyer, or to propitiate Apollo the preserver.

The plague having lately raged with extraordinary fury over almost the whole of the empire, Gallus and Volusianus had struck coins with the inscription Apolloni Salutari, and had appointed sacrifices to be offered to the same deity. In these sacrifices the Christians of course refused to join; and thus they offered first to the populace, and then to the state, a specific occasion of wreaking on them the vengeance of that malicious and cruel superstition, which imputed to them every evil that afflicted this lower world.

This is a fair example of the way in which the Christian Church generally suffered under some imputation, as absurd as it was impious and malicious; and became the victim first of popular rage, and eventually of an authorised and organised persecution. Whenever the empire suffered, whether from the consequences of natural convulsions, or from the famine or disease attending on unfruitful or unhealthy seasons, or from invasion by foreign foes, or from the crimes of political incendiaries, or from the impudence or immorality of emperors, the first effect was popular discontent and commotion; and then the hated religion of Jesus was cast out to the people, that they might expend on it all their rage. If the first occasion of the discontent was such as we naturally refer to supernatural agencies, as famine or pestilence, so much the more directly did the imputation and the penalty fall upon the Christians; for they were the avowed enemies of the gods, whose vengeance was supposed to be excited against the empire for harbouring them: but if the first evil was evidently the work of man, as the burning of a city in sport; no matter, the Christians must still suffer, if the popular clamour was excited. Certainly no people had ever so deep an interest in the repose and prosperity of a nation, as the Christians had in that of the Roman Empire!

Its frequent recurrence, and its frightful effects, serve to invest this moral phenomenon with great interest, and perhaps with equally great importance. Let us see how it has been viewed by some of those who lived within its fatal influence.

Tertullian, in the second century, in his book against the Gentiles, having exclaimed against the custom of calling the assemblies of Christians, bands of lawless men, conspiracies, declares, that these titles are rather to be given to the factious crowd of people who conspire against the peace and safety of the good and peaceable, inventing against them the most absurd accusations, and then calling out for their destruction: "If the Tyber has flooded the city, or if the Nile has not flooded the fields; if the earth has trembled, or if the heavens have not fallen in showers; if there be a plague or a pestilence; presently there is a cry, 'The Christians to the lions!'"[1]

Origen, in the next age, a contemporary of Cyprian, mentions a particular instance in which an earthquake was attributed to the Church. "We know," says he, "that in our

---

[1] Tertul. adv. Gentes. §. 40, vol. iii. p. 70.

own days there was an earthquake, which in some places was very destructive; so that the impious infidels said that the Christians were the cause of the calamity, the Churches being incensed at the persecutions which they had suffered. And not the impious only, but some also, of whom better things might have been expected, said publicly, that the most terrible earthquakes happened on account of the Christians."[1] In short, so great an interest do the heathen seem to have attributed to the Christians with heaven, that it had become an old proverb in the days of Augustine, "Non pluit Deus, dic ad Christianos." Long before the time of that Father, the Gentiles had learned to associate with the Church of Christ all such occurrences as they looked on as divine interpositions; and if the gods seemed to speak in a voice of anger, the Christians were to be the sacrifice; and the destruction of their "godless superstition" the propitiation: and it mattered little whether the gods were the immediate executioners of their own sentence, or whether they employed hostile nations as their instrument; for we have it on the authority of the same Father, that a recent irruption of the barbarians was attributed to the Christian Religion.[2]

It is no wonder that the Christians should labour to free themselves as well from the odium as from the danger of such absurd imputations; and we find it a point often and most earnestly argued in their Apologetics. Arnobius even opens his work with a declaration, that he was led to compose it by the fact, that many, who seemed to fancy themselves wiser than their neighbours, declared with all the violence and fanaticism of those who pronounce an oracle, that ever since the beginning of the Christian religion the world had been manifestly declining, the human race had suffered new and terrible disasters, and that all traces of the visits of Deity to the earth, which used to be frequent, had now vanished. But it would be endless to cite all the complaints of the Christians on this head; or to recount all the arguments by which they refuted the absurdities of the heathen, and endeavoured to

[1] Orig. in Mat. cap. xxiv.     [2] Augustine De Civ. Dei, ii. 2, 3.

avert their terrible consequences. Let us confine ourselves now to a work of Cyprian, in which he touches on the same subject, and to which the above remarks may give an additional interest.

The work of Cyprian, to which we allude, is the Apologetic Epistle to Demetrian, who seems to have been a lawyer at Carthage; or, perhaps, a professor of Rhetoric, of the same grade in which Cyprian himself had been before his conversion. Some have supposed that he held a high civil station, perhaps even the Proconsulate of Africa; and that on him, therefore, personally, the execution of the penal laws, against which Cyprian argues, devolved: but I think that Mosheim [1] has sufficiently shown that this could not be; and Cyprian's character is cleared from the imputation of something almost approaching to faction, in speaking of the civil magistrate in terms of such marked disrespect as occur towards Demetrian in the work before us. That holy Bishop would never have been so far forgetful of the precepts and example of our blessed Lord and His Apostles.

Whoever and whatever Demetrian was,[2] it seems that he had been in the habit of entering into theological disputation with Cyprian; and that present circumstances had directed their discussions to the real or supposed connexion between the rise and progress of Christianity, and the anger of the gods manifested in public calamities, and those dreadful scourges of the earth, pestilence and famine. The rudeness or obstinacy of Demetrian had determined Cyprian to discontinue the verbal discussion of this interesting and important question; and to close the whole controversy, so far as he and Demetrian were concerned, with this Epistle. He himself tells us this in the opening paragraph.

"You say," says Cyprian, "that all the evils with which the

---

[1] Mosheim. de rebus ant. Const. Mag. p. 532.

[2] No one seems to suspect that Demetrian was only an imaginary person, to whom Cyprian addresses his Apology, which is intended for the heathen in general; but is not this in itself probable? And what difficulty is there in the way of such an opinion?

world is now harassed and shaken, are to be attributed to us, and to our refusing to worship your gods. But since you are ignorant of the Divine counsel and truth, you must first be told that the universe itself has already grown old. The earth has lost its pristine vigour, and can no longer put forth the energies of youth. I need not quote our Scriptures to confirm this assertion, nor enter into speculations of my own; for the world itself witnesses its own decline, by sufficient tokens. The rains of winter and the summer now maintain not their just proportion; the spring smiles not as formerly with the promise of fruitfulness, nor does autumn bend beneath so rich a burden. Less marble is dug from the exhausted quarries, less gold and silver from the impoverished mines. Husbandmen are wanting for the fields, sailors for the sea, and soldiers for the camp. Innocence and justice are banished from the Forum and the courts. Society is deprived of concord; the arts are deficient in skill; morality has relaxed her discipline. Can you suppose that all these things should retain the same vigour which they possessed when the world was yet young? Everything is necessarily attenuated as its end approaches. The sun shines more feebly in his setting; and the moon in her wane dwindles to a slender thread. The tree once green and stately in its broad shade, withers and diminishes to a stump: and the most abundant fountain is at last exhausted, and pours out drop by drop the scanty remainder of its waters. This is a law imposed upon all things by the Deity, that whatever is born must die; that whatever increases must eventually fall away: strong things must decay in strength, and large things in magnitude; and all must eventually perish. Do you attribute it to the Christians, that everything is deteriorated with the general decay and old age of the universe; or do you lay it to their charge, that life is now terminated within one hundred years, instead of extending to eight or nine hundred? . . ."

It is curious to find the Apologist confessing the premises (that is, that the world really was then in a worse condition than hitherto), and answering one false deduction from them, by another equally false in fact, though in reason and piety most just and true. But we shall find, by and by, that it was an opinion frequently expressed by Cyprian, and other great and good men, that the world was grown old, and near its end. Meanwhile we are indemnified for such false presumptions and false reasoning, by other arguments more to the purpose. For Cyprian continues :—

"Know, however, that all these things have been predicted; and know also, that they happen not as you ignorantly assume, because we worship not your gods; but because God is not worshipped by you. For since He is the Lord and Ruler of the universe, and all things obey His will, and nothing ever happens but by His hand, or His permission, when such events occur as demonstrate His indignation, they occur not because of us who worship God, but because of your iniquities, who will not seek the Lord, nor fear Him; who will not desert your vain superstitions, and acknowledge the true religion; so that God who is the same God over all, may by all be alone worshipped and supplicated." We cannot refrain from observing, with how good a grace the Christians, after they had acquired the superiority in temporal power, retorted upon the heathen their accusation, that they were the causes of evil in the world; since they had not been afraid to make the same accusation, while they were depressed and persecuted.

St Cyprian proceeds to quote several passages from the Jewish Scriptures, in which the very same judgments are denounced against those who will persist in serving false gods, as the heathens then suffered, and imputed to the vengeance of the gods against the Christians. He applies these threatenings of the prophet to the present time. He tells Demetrian, that the purpose of those judgments in the Divine counsel, was to call the heathen to repentance; yet he adds other prophecies, which intimate that the threatened judgments should fail in this purpose, and that in consequence of the obduracy of the heathen, they should still continue. This use of the Prophets was perfectly legitimate, even in argument with a heathen; for the Jewish Scriptures were of known and acknowledged antiquity; and in this instance fell upon times which supplied an external evidence of their authority and truth.[1] The conclusion of Cyprian's argument from these denunciations and their fulfilment is as follows. "Lo! scourges fall upon you from above, yet ye tremble not. If some such note of the Divine vengeance fell not upon men, encouraged by impunity, how much greater would be their boldness and impiety!"

After having at some length exposed the vices of the heathen, as calling for the vengeance of God, and amply justifying the infliction of all those calamities which were attributed to the wrath of heaven against the Church, St Cyprian proceeds to the mention of those cruelties with which the Christians were everywhere overwhelmed. "It is not enough that you yourselves serve not God; but those who do serve Him you pursue with impious rage. You neither worship God, nor suffer Him to be worshipped by others: and while you extend indulgence to the worshippers of dumb idols, and images made by the hands of men; nay even of portents and monsters; the worship of the true God is alone proscribed. The hideous gods of the Egyptians are adopted by you, and sacrifices burn on every side to apes and crocodiles; while God must be without an altar, at least in public. You disinherit, you banish, the innocent and just, and those whom God loves; you put them into chains and dungeons; you drag them to the beasts, to fire, to the sword. Nor are you satisfied with depriving us of life by a quick and simple process; you inflict the most cruel and lingering death, and are not content even with torturing us except by some new invention, and with the exercise of a savage ingenuity.

[1] Yet Lactantius, with more assumption than sound reason, says, "Non defugi hunc laborem, ut implerem materiam, quam Cyprianus non executus est in ea oratione, qua Demetrianum (sicut ipse ait) oblatrantem, atque obstrepentem veritati, redarguere conatur; qua materia non est usus, ut debuit: non enim Scriptura testimoniis, quam illi utique vanam, fictam, eorum arbitriumque putabat; sed argumentis, et ratione fuerat refellendus" v. 4.

How insatiable your cruelty! How implacable your vengeance!

"Christianity either is or is not a crime. If it be a crime, why do you not at once execute him who confesses his guilt? If it be not a crime, why do you persecute the innocent? Again: allowing it to be a crime; those who are implicated in it, but obstinately withhold a confession of their guilt, would be the proper objects of torture: but we confess, we proclaim, our adherence to the Christian cause, and our contempt of your gods. Why then are we tortured, as if we concealed our guilt? Why this attempt upon the infirmity of our bodies; upon the weakness of what is but earthly in us? Rather enter the lists with our minds; try the strength of our reason; see if you can subvert our faith with argument; and if you must conquer, conquer by an appeal to reason."

Cyprian afterwards shows, that the heathen deities were, in truth, not the patrons but the clients of their worshippers: needing their support against the power and influence of the Christians, whose exorcisms would expel them from the victims of whom they had taken possession.

But the Pagan opponents of Christianity might remark, that the Christians were not free from the same evil which afflicted the nation in general; and that the misery of persecution was an additional suffering which the Church alone endured; so that if it was indeed true that the pressure of misery was a punishment for impiety, the Christians who bore the greatest infliction at the hands of the Deity must be accounted the greatest criminals. Cyprian answers this objection thus [1]—

"He it is who experiences the whole bitterness of temporal evil, whose hopes and joys, whose very glory, is centred in this world: who hath no happy anticipations; whose very hope is but a deep despair. They, on the other hand, whose prospects, whose joys, whose ambition, are future, feel not the pains and disappointments of this life. Thus we neither despond nor murmur; but we rather rejoice in the same evils,

---

[1] To the Christians themselves Cyprian had another answer to the same observation. See his work upon the Plague.

which overwhelm you in affliction and despair: and we are taught to believe, that our very sufferings are intended to strengthen our faith. Do you reckon then, that to us and to you evils are equally evil? Do you not know from your own observation, that you and we bear not afflictions in the same way? ... Among us, hope then flourishes in its full vigour, and faith loses nothing of its confidence: our mind stands erect, and our virtue is unshaken, amid the ruins of a falling world:[1] our patience is never wearied, while our souls repose themselves still upon God. The Prophet says, 'Although the fig tree shall not blossom, neither shall fruit be in the vines; the labour of the olive shall fail, and the fields shall yield no meat; the flock shall be cut off from the fold, and there shall be no herd in the stalls: yet I will rejoice in the Lord, I will joy in the God of my salvation.' That is, the man of God, and he who worships Him, cannot be moved by the changes and miseries of this world: the vine may fail and the olive; the plain may be brown with the parched herbage; but what is this to Christians, to the servants of God, for whom Paradise stands open, for whom is prepared the fulness of grace, and the abundance of the kingdom of Heaven? They ever rejoice in the Lord, and boast and delight themselves in their God; and while they look forward to the gifts and glories of eternity, they endure manfully the wrongs and afflictions of time: for we who have set aside our natural birth, and are born again, and created anew by the Spirit, live no longer to the world, but to God."

Then Cyprian declares, that the prayers of Christians are constantly offered even for their persecutors. He sets before

---

[1] Inter ipsas sæculi labentis ruinas erecta mens est, et immobilis virtus. p. 222. Probably Cyprian had in his mind the words of Horace (*Carm.* iii. 3)—

    Justum . . . virum
    Si fractus illabatur orbis
    Impavidum ferient ruinæ.

But with Cyprian the *ruinæ* are literal, which with Horace are figurative: for Cyprian believed the end of the world to be at hand.

the heathen the necessity of repentance; and declares, that in thus doing, he most convincingly displays his charity.

This is a short summary of the contents of Cyprian's Epistle to Demetrian on the subject of the present persecution, and its occasion as pretended by the heathen. I have not thought it necessary to translate the more intemperate language of the Christian Prelate, believing it to be rather attributable to the time than to the man, or the religion which he professed: for it abounds everywhere in the controversial writings to which we shall presently arrive, among which those of Cyprian are by no means alone faulty. I hope and believe that the latter expressions of charity are more consistent with the temper of Cyprian, and a more exact transcript of his real feelings; as they certainly better agree with the precepts of Christ. Nor indeed were any of the divine injunctions of our Saviour more exactly obeyed in the early ages of the Church, than that which engages us to pray for them which despitefully use us and persecute us. Dionysius of Alexandria says of Gallus on this very occasion: "He persecuted the saints who were praying to God for his health and for his glory; and deprived himself of the benefit of their intercessions, while he drove the brethren from his dominions."[1]

And if we must give Cyprian credit for the sentiments of true charity which he professed towards the heathen; so may we be sure that the expression of firmness, and even of glorying in tribulation, which he attributes to the persecuted Christians, was really found among them: for he writes in the same strain, not only to the Gentiles, when he would set forth the evidences of the faith; but to Christians also, when he would imbue them with a proper temper, in these trying times. His exhortation to martyrdom breathes the spirit rather of an Epinicion, than of a Threnic ode: and the same spirit animates his Epistle to the Thybaritani, who had

---

[1] Eusebius, vii. 1. And see Arnobius Contra Gentes, liber i. p. 18. Da veniam Rex Summe tuos persequentibus famulos: et quod tuæ benignitatis est proprium, fugientibus ignosce tui nominis et religionis cultum. Non est mirum si ignoraris: majoris est admirationis si sciaris.

repeatedly entreated him to visit them, but to whom he excuses himself from the peculiar complexion of the times, and the necessity which lay upon him of attending his own flock with the greater care. He warns them of the coming storm; and tells them that he had received such intimations from the Lord concerning its violence, as led him to anticipate a persecution even more fierce than that under the Decii. In this he was certainly deceived; and it will follow that he either misinterpreted a real communication from heaven, or mistook for such a communication the more than ordinarily impressive emotions of an excited mind; but that he wrote under that impression is all that is needed to show the view which he took of persecution, in its extremest form, and the practical application which he made of it to those of his own faith, with the preparation which he deemed most appropriate for encountering it.

"A more fierce and dreadful conflict," says he,[1] "now awaits us, for which the soldiers of Christ ought to prepare themselves with uncorrupt faith, and a manly virtue; drinking to this end, day by day, the blood of Christ, that for Christ they may be enabled to shed their own blood. If we would manifest our willingness to be with Christ, we ought also so to walk as He walked: as St Paul tells us; 'we are sons, and if sons then heirs, heirs of God, and joint heirs with Christ, if we so suffer with Him as to be glorified with Him also.'[2] And this we should *now* bear in mind, that none of us may have his desires fixed upon this world, now ready to perish; but that all may follow Christ, who Himself liveth for ever, and giveth life to those who are established in the faith of His name."

After having quoted several warnings of our Lord and His Apostles of impending persecutions, with the accompanying promises and blessings, he proceeds, "In the midst of persecution, our Lord would have us exult and be glad; for then the crowns of faith are bestowed, then the soldiers of God are approved, then heaven is thrown open to the martyrs. Nor

[1] *Ep.* lvi. p. 90.   [2] Rom. viii. 16, 17.

did we so enrol our names in the army of the saints, as to look for a peaceable service only, and to deprecate and refuse the battle: for our Lord Himself, our example in humility and patience and long-suffering, commenced our course in actual conflict; Himself beginning that warfare which He would have us to wage; and bearing for us in His own person, that which He would have us to bear after Him. Remember that He, to whom all judgment is committed, has declared, that those who confess Him here He will confess before His Father; and that He will deny those who deny Him. . . . And let none be discouraged, dearest brethren, at seeing the company of the faithful put to flight by fear of persecution, and because he sees not the flock assembled in one place, nor hears the voice of the shepherd [Bishop]. They cannot be collected together who are appointed not to kill, but to be killed. And whithersoever, in those days, a single disciple shall be driven by necessity, being absent from the brethren in body, but present with them in spirit, let him not be cast into despondency by his flight, nor be driven to despair by the solitude of his retreat. He flies not alone, who hath Christ the companion of his flight. He is not alone, who beareth about with him everywhere the temple of God, and hath God ever within him. And if robbers, or wild beasts,[1] or any accident, cut him off in his flight, Christ still beholds His servants; and wheresoever, and under what circumstances soever, the encounter is endured, Christ bestows the reward (which He hath promised to give at the resurrection) upon each one who dies for the honour of His name, on occasion of persecution.[2] Nor is that martyrdom devoid of

[1] The number of persons thus cut off, always entered largely into the account of the havoc made among the Christians by persecution.

[2] Et persecutionis causa, pro nominis sui honore morienti præmium reddit, quod daturum se in resurrectione promisit. (P. 91.) Cyprian here avoids the promise of *immediate* glory to those who did not suffer actual martyrdom. This is worthy of remark; for if he speaks of an *immediate* crown to the martyr, but of a crown only at the resurrection to the rest of the faithful, how can he dispose of the latter except in Hades? of the Catholic doctrine of which there are no direct assertions in the

glory, which is not endured publicly: the witness and appearance of Him who crowns the martyr, being a sufficient token of the glory of the martyr.

Then having proposed to them the examples of Abel, of Abraham, of the Three Children, and of Daniel; having reminded them of the slaughter of the Innocents; but more especially having set before them the unparalleled sufferings of Jesus Christ; he warns them, that the times of Antichrist are approaching: and adapting his exhortation to their necessities, he proceeds: "Men are trained and exercised for victory in the secular games; and they account it no slight accession to their glory, if they receive the prize before a crowded assembly, in the presence of the Emperor. Lo! our great, our illustrious contest; glorious with the guerdon of a heavenly crown! Lo, how God witnesses our struggle; and looking benignantly on those whom He condescends to call His children, Himself rejoices in our victory! How great the happiness in the sight of God to contend: to be crowned by the judgment of Christ! Let us arm, my beloved brethren, let us arm for the fight! Let us prepare for the contest with a mind and a faith uncorrupted, and with devoted valour! Let those who have hitherto conquered resume their arms, lest they lose the glory which they have nobly won! Let those who have before fallen gird on their harness, that they may retrieve their former disgrace. Let honour incite the faithful, let remorse impel the fallen to the field."

In marked accordance with this last portion of his exhortation, was his own conduct in preparing his Church for the coming persecution; for besides these general exhortations to martyrdom, and other such-like obvious measures, he tells Cornelius, in a synodical letter,[1] that he had, with the concurrence of forty-one of his comprovincial Bishops, readmitted the penitent lapsed to communion. "For we are warned," said he, "by divers signs, to arm for the battle, and to summon the whole army of Christ to His banners; and at

works of St Cyprian; so that even these passing indications of his opinion are valuable. [1] *Ep.* liv.

such a time we thought it advisable to place arms in the hands of those who had before deserted their ranks, though not as incorrigible traitors or renegades: and as they had already been admitted to penance, so now to admit them to the peace of the Church. For now the communion of the brethren is as necessary to them in their perilous life, as it was heretofore at the hour of death; at which time it was always proposed to readmit them into the Church.[1] And how shall we expect those to pour out their blood for Christ, to whom we deny the cup of Christ's blood in the Supper of the Lord?"

The Epistle to Fortunatus, entitled an Exhortation to Martyrdom, is in the same strain with that just quoted. It is composed after the same manner with the Testimonies against the Jews; being little else than citations of apposite passages of Scripture, arranged under separate heads. Cyprian expresses his motive for this arrangement of the subject under the following singular figure. "The work thus performed, will be more readily adapted to every one's use. If I had presented you with a garment ready cut out, finished for myself, it would be my own garment, though for another's use, and it might be but ill fitted to his individual stature and bodily form. But now, I have sent you the fleece itself, and the purple dye from that Lamb, by whom we are redeemed, and in whom we live; and from this you can yourself form your garment according to your own will and convenience; and you will feel greater pleasure in the use of your own appropriate vesture. You will also be able to supply the like materials to others, that they too may possess the materials of a garment after their own taste; and all, throwing the robes of Christ over their former nakedness, may appear clothed with the garments of celestial grace."[2]

As Cyprian has himself prefaced this Epistle with a syllabus of its contents, I shall present this to the reader.

---

[1] The reader will remember, that on a former occasion the approach of the unhealthy season was anticipated by a similar indulgence, for a parallel reason.     [2] Page 262.

"In exhorting the brethren, and preparing them with the fortitude of virtue and of faith for the confession of their Lord, and in arming for the conflict of suffering and of death, it is necessary, in the first place, to declare, that those idols which man makes for himself are no Gods; for neither are those things that are made greater than he who designed and made them, nor can those things which perish within their very temples, unless they are preserved by the care of man, afford any protection or preservation: neither are the elements to be worshipped, which are appointed by the providence of God, for the service of man.

"When the idols have been destroyed, and the true position of the elements declared, we must show that God alone is to be worshipped.

"Then the threatenings of God against those who sacrifice to idols are to be denounced.

"And then, the difficulty with which God pardons idolaters should be shown; and that He is so indignant against the worship of idols, that He has appointed that all who are guilty of persuading others to that sin are to be put to death.

"After these things we must add, That we who are redeemed and quickened by Christ's blood, are bound to prefer Christ before all other things; because He, too, preferred nothing to us, but on our account preferred evil to good, poverty to wealth, servitude to dominion, death to immortality; that we, while we suffer, might, on the contrary, prefer the riches and delights of paradise, to the misery and vanity of the world, an eternal power and kingdom to temporal servitude, immortality to death, God and Christ to the Devil and Antichrist.

"They, too, who have been snatched from the jaws of the devil, and delivered from the snares of this world, must be warned lest, beginning to perceive themselves in difficulties and dangers, they desire to return again to the world, and so perish in their former delusion; and they must be encouraged rather to persevere in faith and virtue, and in the perfection of every grace, that they may attain to the palm and the crown of victory.

"For to this very end we are persecuted and afflicted, that is, that we may be proved; and the injuries and tortures inflicted by persecutors are not to be objects of terror; for God is more powerful to save, than the Devil to destroy.

"And lest any should be troubled above measure and affrighted by the difficulties and persecutions which surround us in this life, it ought to be proved, that it was foretold that we should be hated by the world, and persecuted; so that the truth of God may be attested by these very things, and the assurance therefore of the coming reward, which is built on the promise of the same God, may be increased: while at the same time it is apparent, that no new thing occurs in this to the Christians; since, from the beginning of the world, the good have ever suffered under the oppression and violence of the wicked.

"In the last place, we may enlarge upon the hope and the reward of the just and of martyrs, when the troubles and persecutions of this life are ended; being assured, that the reward of our sufferings hereafter will far outweigh whatever misery we endured in the martyrdom itself."[1]

Such is the strain in which Cyprian exhorts his brethren in Christ to the constancy of confessors and martyrs, and such the preparation which he made for the conflict. He was, indeed, mistaken in looking for a more fierce persecution than that from which the Church had lately emerged; but the event which happily contradicted his anticipation, diminishes not the glory of his preparation.

We are not, however, excused from the mention of confessors and martyrs under Gallus and Volusianus. For in Rome, the magistrates, intending by one deadly blow to annihilate the Church, directed their attacks against Cornelius, the Bishop of that city. But whatever might be the method of attack, the ravagers of the fold found that the flock preferred death to apostasy; and that they would rather be united in suffering, than flee from their shepherd in his danger; for not only those who had always been constant, but even many of

[1] Pp. 262, 263.

the lapsed, collected round Cornelius, now that he had borne the especial mark of the persecutors' malignity.[1] Cornelius himself was banished to Centumsellæ, whether alone, or with what number of his faithful adherents, does not appear. Cyprian wrote a congratulatory Epistle[2] to him in his banishment, greatly commending, and as a member of the same body, exulting in, his courage and constancy; and declaring the benefit which the alacrity and firmness of the Church in Rome, in baffling persecution, would afford, and indeed had afforded, to the whole body of Christians. Cyprian concludes his Epistle to his brother saint, with a pious determination and request, that whichever of them, he or Cornelius, should first be taken from the Church on earth, would continue his prayers to the Father for him who remained. An exact parallel to the affecting petition of the truly catholic martyr Ridley to Bradford, his fellow-sufferer, shortly before the execution of the latter. "Brother Bradford," says Ridley, "so long as I shall understand that thou art on thy journey," his journey, that is, to execution, "by God's grace, I shall call upon our heavenly Father, for Christ's sake, to set thee safely home; and then, good Father, speak you, and pray for the remnant that are to suffer for Christ's sake, according to what thou then shalt know more clearly."

The presentiment of Cyprian here apparent of the approaching end of his earthly intercourse with Cornelius was verified: for that Prelate died at the place of his banishment, and, as we collect with probability from some casual expressions, a martyr in the most rigorous sense of that word, as he certainly was virtually a martyr. This, however, is not quite indisputable, and at any rate the manner of his death is unknown. He died A.D. 252, and on the 14th of September; unless the Roman Breviary, being published by Papal authority and received by all the Bishops within the Roman Obedience, is to be believed before an historical testimony, in which case St Cornelius and Cyprian both suffered on the 16th of September.

[1] *Ep.* lv.      [2] *Ep.* lvii.

After an interval of a few days, Lucius was chosen Bishop of Rome in the place of Cornelius: and he too soon fell a victim to the rage of persecution; being first banished with several of his brethren, but soon after permitted or obliged to return. And we suppose with about the same degree of evidence upon which we arrive at the same conclusion respecting Cornelius, that he suffered martyrdom. Cyprian, in his Epistle to Lucius[1] after his return to Rome, while he congratulates him on his confession, intimates that it was perhaps the intention of the Lord in ordering his return, that he should be crowned with greater glory to himself, and greater benefit to the Church, in the presence of his own people. Whether this intimation had any other foundation than the pious and characteristic sentiment of St Cyprian, or whether it was justified by the event, is not certain. Mosheim says,[2] that he could make it appear that neither Cornelius nor Lucius suffered actual martyrdom; he confesses, however, that the opposite opinion is upheld by no contemptible authority.

Some expressions in Cyprian's gratulatory Epistles to Cornelius and Lucius lead us to inquire, how far he held persecution to be a test of the truth of the persecuted party. After having expressed his joy, that not only those who had before adhered to the faith, but that some also who had formerly lapsed, had joined Cornelius in his confession; so that the Church was rather united than scattered by this attack upon it; he continues: "What says Novatian to these things, dearest brother? Does he yet lay down his error? or rather, as is usual with men so infatuated as he is, does his rage increase, at the sight of our blessed prosperity: and does the madness of dissension and fanaticism gather strength among his party, in proportion as the glory of an union in faith and charity is advanced among us? . . . Does he yet perceive who is the true priest of God; which is the Church and house of Christ; who are the servants of God, against whom the Devil expends his rage; who are the Christians, whom Anti-

[1] *Ep.* lviii.   [2] De Rebus Chris. p. 529.

christ opposes? For Satan pursues not those whom he has already seduced to subjection; nor does he labour to extirpate those, whom he has made his own servants. The deadly foe of the Church passes by, as already conquered and captive, those whom he hath seduced from the pale of the Church; and directs all his efforts against those in whom he perceives that Christ dwells."[1]

And again, in the next Epistle to Lucius, "We perceive, dearest brother, and with our whole heart and understanding consent to the wisdom and goodness of the counsel of God, whence arose this sudden persecution, and to what end the whole power of the state raged against the Church of Christ, and the blessed Bishop and Martyr Cornelius, and you all; even that the Lord might confound and crush the heretics, by showing which is the Church, which is the sole Bishop chosen and appointed with the Divine sanction, who are the priests associated with the Bishops in the sacerdotal functions, which is the true flock of Christ, one in fellowship and love; who they are whom the enemy would destroy, and who are they whom the Devil would spare, as his own children. For whom doth the enemy of Christ persecute and oppose, but the army and the soldiers of Christ? Those who are already prostrate in heresy, and become his own, he passes by in contempt; but those whom he beholds erect, them he seeks to throw down."[2]

From such passages we should almost judge, that Cyprian inclined to the belief, that all heretics are exempt from persecution, that the true Church is alone subject to this expression of the Devil's enmity: in other words, that the enduring of persecution is a certain and sufficient mark of truth; which would be, to say the least, a very strong expression of a proposition, which is true only in a mitigated form. Nor are the passages just quoted the only ones in which Cyprian seems to express the same opinion; and to apply it in its practical result, as a means of separating between truth and error: for we have found him giving it as one of the

[1] *Ep.* lvii. p. 95.   [2] *Ep.* lviii. p. 97.

divine warranties of his own Episcopate, that he was obnoxious to popular and heathen fury, and more than once called for to the lions.

There is something very plausible in this method of reasoning; and it proceeds upon opinions which will always have advocates among those who find support from them, under the peculiar circumstances of their Church or sect. Nor yet are such opinions to be at once discarded; only they must be kept within due bounds, and not suffered to go quite to that length in theory, to which those who are, or fancy themselves, persecuted may be disposed to carry them; nor to be practically applied quite so unsparingly as all who find it convenient to hold them may wish. For persecution may be found sometimes, as history has evinced now, whatever it may have done in Cyprian's time, with a sect or heresy; and may even be pretended where it does not exist: and so it may be brought to bear with equal force upon opposite sides of a theological discussion, and sometimes with equal truth by both; that is, it may possess no authority at all.

It is just so with miracles, another sign of the true Church, which however may be counterfeited by the cunning and villany, and possibly by the cunning and zeal, of man; and may form a part of the illusory art even of other powers.[1] Miracles were pretended on both sides in a late controversy within the Romish pale: and the pretence to them has been revived before us, by the deluded and deluding followers of Edward Irving. Now in all these cases, *we* will not admit the miracles, real or pretended, as a test of truth; and in the former case it is a matter of demonstration, that they could not divinely approve opposing tenets. And though these were also (probably) cases of pretended miracles, there is no reason to doubt (nay rather there is the highest ground for believing) that error itself may be accompanied with the deceitful sign of lying wonders.

But I mention this only that we may return to the question of persecution with the additional light gained from a parallel

[1] See Deut xiii. and Vincentius Lirinensis, cap. xv.

case. A claim to the merit of the persecuted may be advanced by those who suffer no persecution at all; but who so confuse things that differ, as to construe even punishment for secular crimes into suffering for religion, and for theological opinions: or they may construe suffering for some dogma, which may be in itself true, but which has no connexion with religion, into suffering for an article of faith. And from the moment that any party of religionists has become involved in any sufferings, for any cause, there is a very strong temptation (a temptation which I fear has seldom been effectually resisted), to look upon and to adduce that suffering as a ground of boasting the exclusive verity of their faith, on the evidence of persecution. Even those branches of the Catholic Church which have fallen under depressing and painful circumstances, have been deceived into this erroneous judgment. In Scotland, for instance, the members of the Catholic and Apostolic Church (there to the present day, to the shame of our nation be it said, left to struggle under the difficulties and opprobrium o dissent from an adverse establishment; and, in former times to the still greater disgrace of our nation, involved in stil greater and more positive difficulties):—in Scotland, I say the members of the true Church, and the adherents of the established sect, are equally fond of adducing the persecutior which they have suffered at different times, as a plain and popular, and very exciting and effective test of the truth of their several communions. Now here again, it is demonstrative that both cannot be right, even supposing both to be persecuted, in the proper acceptation of the word, and the only acceptation in which it can be taken for anything which is a test of religious truth. But the truth is, that neither is or has been persecuted. As regards the Catholics, who have the truth on their side, by a higher evidence than they themselves could elicit from a persecution though real, it is clear, I think that what they hold to be persecution, was the rendering them obnoxious to a severe system of political pains and penalties in themselves, it is true, excessive, and continued longer thar was needful, but still directed against political opinions and practices which were associated with religion by themselves; and which the existing government was obliged, for its own security, to condemn as criminal. Admitting their high principle (which I do willingly and with admiration), still they were martyrs, if we must give them that name, to their loyalty, and not to their religion: and their suffering would go to prove, if it go to prove anything at all, not that Episcopacy is a characteristic of the Church Catholic, which is the use that they would make of it; but that the Stuarts were unjustly deprived of their kingdom, and ought at all hazard, and at any time, to be restored to it.

As for the martyrs (so called) of the Presbyterians, they are the only martyrs from the beginning of Christianity to the present day, who have died with swords in their hands. In fact, they were slaughtered insurgents, who sold their lives as dearly as they could. They were wrong in everything almost in which men can be wrong, except only that they were conscientious in their errors. The example is striking; for these, too, though not martyrs, either in patience, or in the truth of that doctrine and discipline in behalf of which (and not as its supporters, but as its inventors) they took arms and died, are yet as much vaunted to this day in Scotland, as are in England the meek and blessed martyrs and confessors in the Marian persecution, who died to witness against errors which the Scotch also have thrown off; and as our not less illustrious martyrs, King Charles and Archbishop Laud, who died for the verities which they continue to deny.

And it is farther to be remarked, that the very party which is in fact the persecuting, may be the one to complain most loudly, and to boast their sufferings for the truth. We have various forms and degrees of this self-deception in the world. There is a tendency among some to declare that they are accounted the very offscouring of all things, and to protest themselves an afflicted and despised race of men, because they and they alone among their countrymen hold the truth: but meanwhile do they not themselves put in exercise a most cruel spiritual persecution, while they declare all others reprobate, and bear themselves towards them as towards aliens and heathens. And again; at this moment, there is here a combination of all parties against the Church of England, which amounts to the spirit of persecution, and in some respects and places to the actual violence of persecution: and yet she is everywhere assailed by the very parties thus in league against her, as a persecuting Church. In a word, it is now with us as it was in the days of King Charles the Martyr, though (thank God!) in a very much mitigated degree, to whom Laud writes in the dedication of his Conference with Fisher. "One thing more let me be bold to observe to your Majesty in particular, concerning your great charge in the Church of England. She is in hard condition. She professes the ancient Catholic faith, and yet the Romanist condemns her for novelty in her doctrine. She practises Church government as it hath been in use in all ages, and all places, where the Church of Christ hath been established both in and since the days of the Apostles, and yet the separatist condemns her for Antichristianism in her discipline. The plain truth is, she is between these two factions, and unless your Majesty look to it, to whose trust she is committed, she will be ground to powder, to an irreparable dishonour and loss to this kingdom. And it is very remarkable, that while both these press hard upon the Church of England, both of them cry out against persecution, like froward children, who scratch, and kick, and bite, and yet cry out all the while as if they were killed." Of course I am not adducing this in proof of the Apostolicity or Catholicity of our Church: I thank God that we want not the testimony of the enmity of our opponents, though it may be as strong an one as *they* can bestow: but only to show the absurdity, yet possibility, of the persecutors, if either party be persecuted, making persecution the test of truth.

None of these instances, however, exactly touches the point of which Cyprian speaks, which is the suffering for the cause of Christ under the attacks of heathen assailants; and it is certainly possible that persecution may afford a more just criterion of the truth of those who suffer, when inflicted by heathens upon those who have the name and profess the faith of Christ, than when employed by one party of professed Christians against another. But in this case, too, history will not bear out the propositions of St Cyprian, if taken in their most rigid sense, and applied without limitation. Among the Arians, for instance, we find men who have suffered together with the Church Catholic; for under Julian thé Apostate, who was too hostile to the very name and pretensions of Christianity to distinguish between a sect and the true Church, the followers of Arius were involved in the common misfortune.

I think, then, that it must be admitted, that although God has employed persecution from without more frequently to purify and confirm and render illustrious the faith of the true Church, than to punish the iniquity of heretics and separatists; and that He has also, on the whole, made so marked a distinction in this respect, between the body of Christ, and all those who have broken off from that body, as to surround the former with a visible glory from above, while the latter are left in their darkness, or in their self-assumed light; yet still, the mere fact of *suffering*, under the name of *suffering for the truth as it is in Jesus*, is not sufficient to prove one a member of the Church of Christ, any more than the fact of suffering for the dogmas of a sect is sufficient to confirm the truth of those dogmas.

And this was, I imagine, the more solid conviction of Cyprian himself; for he seems to me to lay much more stress upon his sound reasoning, that there is *no confession* or *martyrdom* out of the Church, though there may be those *who suffer and die;* than upon his more oratorical assumption, that none but the faithful would be put to the test, or none but they would endure it. Indeed, so far from collecting from a broad view of Cyprian's works, that none but Catholics ever did, or in his opinion ever could, suffer and die for the name of Christ; we shall rather collect from such passages as those which I shall presently adduce, that some at least, if not many, had actually thus suffered and died; and that his repeated and earnest references to the position in which such persons stood in respect of the Church, arose out of the necessity which their existence at least, and their pretensions, if not their number, produced.

Thus, speaking of Nicostratus, he says,[1] "This deserter and renegade boasts himself a confessor: whereas he can neither be nor be called a confessor, who has denied the Church of Christ." Again, at the conclusion of the Epistle to Antonianus: "Apostates and deserters, or the adversaries of Christ, who sow discord in His Church, cannot be admitted by any Apostolic rule to the peace of the Church, no not though they be slain for the name of Christ, while they are yet without: since they have maintained neither the spirit nor the unity of the Church."[2] And even in the passage immediately following that before quoted, in which he exults over Novatian as having escaped persecution, Cyprian says, "Even if one of such a party should fall into the hands of the enemy, there is still no sufficient ground for his boasting himself a confessor of the Christian name; since it is plain, that if such persons are ever put to death out of the Church, they receive not the crown of their fidelity, but the meet reward of their perfidy; nor can they, whom we behold separated from the household of faith by their reckless discord, be accounted among those who continue of one mind in the house of God."[3] The very event which Cyprian here admits as possible, and against the pernicious effects of which he provides an antidote, did actually occur; for Socrates tells us in his Ecclesiastical History,[4] that Novatian, who escaped, indeed, the persecution in which Cornelius and Lucius perished, suffered death under Valerian.

In a word (for we are forced to take refuge at last in this safe harbour), no popular test of the truth—such as the endurance of persecution, though it may appeal ever so strongly to man's affections; or pretended miracles, though they may take his reason almost by storm—no such test can be safely

[1] *Ep.* xlix. p. 63.
[2] *Ep.* lii. p. 75.
[3] *Ep.* lvii. p. 95.
[4] Lib. iv. 28.

trusted alone, however valuable it may be in its right place, and however fascinating its use but after all we must apply a more severe rule of judging between catholic verity and the fancies and vagaries of sectaries and fanatics. We must listen to no reasoning, however supported, which tends to shake our faith in that which has been the doctrine of the first days of the Church, and has been ever held as the faith of the Apostles: our eyes must be closed against all portents, our ears must be stopped against all boastings and lamentations, which would subvert that primitive doctrine; or else we shall be in danger of falling victims to those delusions, by which Satan would deceive, if it were possible, the very elect; and from which it is only possible that they can be saved by the application of those means which God has committed to them, to prove all things, that they may hold fast that which is good.

It can scarcely be necessary to remark, that the questions here touched are all and altogether different from that which relates to persecution as a sign of the truth of Christianity itself, in opposition to heathenism and infidelity. Upon this subject St Cyprian expresses himself most excellently at the close of his tract on the Vanity of Idols, wher 'ie is stating the evidences of his religion to the Gentiles. "The followers of Jesus," says he,[1] "are put to the torture, are crucified, and suffer all manner of indignities, that their sincerity may be tried to the uttermost. Suffering, which is the test of truth, is inflicted on them, that Christ the Son of God, on whom they believe as the Author of eternal life to man, may be proclaimed not only with the voice of the preacher, but with the testimony also of martyrs." This reasoning has all the force of demonstration, when it is considered, that those who first suffered as Christians, could not possibly be deceived as to the truth of those events, in attestation of which they shed their blood: nor would it so much as shake this evidence, if some few isolated individuals had been found willing to maintain an obstinate adherence to known falsehood before the

[1] De Idoli Van. p. 228.

face of torture and of death: such single exceptions of a general rule may afford psychological phenomena of great interest and importance; but can never shake those foundations of human testimony, on which we may and must build as unquestionably secure.

Thus in a history of these times, and of the persecution under Gallus, we have found leisure to speculate upon those subjects which persecution naturally suggests: as Cyprian himself, though he had anticipated a more violent attack upon the Church than that which they had experienced from the Decii, found himself now, however, at liberty to continue among his people, and to encourage them with many works, and constant pastoral care; whereas in the former case he had been driven from his charge by the more violent rage of the persecutors. In writing of the Decian persecution, we were chiefly occupied in detailing instances of suffering and constancy; but now we have found time and opportunity to turn our eyes to the attendants of persecution, to its usual causes and consequences: to the feelings, doctrines, and encouragements, rather than the actual sufferings, of martyrs and confessors: and to the calm reasoning of Christians upon the passing events: to the way in which men were prepared for the conflict, rather than the way in which they actually endured it: to the crown of martyrdom, towards which their hopes were directed, rather than the instruments of torture and of death.

## CHAPTER XI.

The Plague rages at Carthage.—Cyprian's Tract *De Mortalitate.*—The Expectation of the Last Day in the early Church :—Gibbon's use of it.—Cyprian's Opinion on the Time, Person, and Character of Antichrist.

THE persecution at length ceased, but the plague, which had afforded to the heathen the first pretence of persecution, still remained ; a more destructive, but a less cruel, enemy ; for certainly the Christians must have felt that it was better to fall into the hands of the Lord, than into the hands of men. This scourge of the nations afforded an additional and most important and interesting occasion of the display of the character of St Cyprian, as a Christian and as a Bishop.

The symptoms of this terrible disease Cyprian has himself described ; they seem to have included a fearful state of exhaustion, with fever, and mortifying and putrid sores :[1] and Pontius tells us, that this terrible pestilence swept away numbers daily, sometimes carrying off whole households. The carcases of men lay in the streets, and there were none to bury them ; the uninfected deserted their sick relatives, or even turned them out to die unattended in the streets. Yet

[1] Quod nunc corporis vires solutus in fluxum venter eviscerat, quod in faucium vulnera conceptus medullitus ignis exæstuat, quod assiduo vomitu intestina quatiuntur, quod oculi vi sanguinis inardescunt, quod quorundam vel pedes vel aliquæ membrorum partes contagio morbidæ putredinis amputantur, quod per jacturas et damna corporum prorumpente languore vel debilitatur incessus, vel auditus obstruitur, vel cœcatur aspectus. *De Mortalitate,* p. 232.

those who had not courage to attend the living, or to bury the dead, summoned resolution to rob those who were in the extremity of sickness; and the fears of the Gentile inhabitants of the great city of Carthage were only surpassed by their cupidity. In short, all was consternation, misery, and crime. There is no reason to suspect Pontius of exaggeration here; indeed, exaggeration of such horrors would scarce be possible. Gibbon gives an appalling account of the miseries of these times. "Our habits of thinking," says he, "so fondly connect the order of the universe with the fate of man, that this gloomy period of history has been decorated with inundations, earthquakes, uncommon meteors, preternatural darkness, and a crowd of prodigies, fictitious or exaggerated. But a long and general famine was a calamity of a more serious kind. It was the inevitable consequence of rapine and oppression, which extirpated the produce of the present, and the hope of future, harvests. Famine is always followed by epidemical diseases, the effect of scanty and unwholesome food. Other causes must, however, have contributed to the furious plague, which from the year 250, to the year 265, raged without intermission in every province, every city, and almost every family of the Roman empire. During some time five thousand persons died daily in Rome; and many towns that had escaped the hands of barbarians, were entirely depopulated.

"We have the knowledge of a very curious circumstance, of some use, perhaps, in the melancholy calculation of human calamities. An exact register was kept at Alexandria of all the citizens entitled to receive the distribution of corn. It was found, that the ancient number of those comprised between the ages of forty and seventy, had been equal to the whole sum of claimants, from fourteen to fourscore years of age, who remained alive after the reign of Gallus. Applying this authentic fact to the most correct tables of mortality, it evidently proves, that above half the people of Alexandria had perished; and could we venture to extend the analogy to the other provinces, we might suspect, that war, pestilence, and famine, had consumed, in a few years, the moiety of the human species." [1]

The courage and the charity of Cyprian shone with resplendent lustre, in this gloom of misery and vice. Assembling his people as heretofore, he inculcated, with the authority of a Bishop, the highest moral lesson, enforced with the most powerful and religious motives. He exhorted them to a proper care of the sick, and to a pious sepulture of the dead; and that, not only of their own numbers, but even of the very Gentiles who were taking occasion of the plague to persecute them: thus did he illustrate the divine precept of our Lord, by which we are taught to love our enemies, to repay evil with good, and to bless those who persecute us; and thus did he exhort them to imitate the mercy of God, who maketh His sun to rise on the evil and on the good, and sendeth rain on the just and on the unjust. If the heathen had heard him addressing such lessons to his people, says Pontius, surely they must have been converted.

The consequence of this care on the part of the pastor, was manifested in the conduct of the flock. Provision was made for the visiting of the sick, and for the burying of the dead; and those who had no money to give, gave their labour. That pious care of the Christians for their departed brethren, which so forcibly struck the Apostate Julian, was here extended, under the most distressing and appalling circumstances, not to their brethren only, but to their very enemies. How great effect does this give to the severity with which Cyprian upbraids the heathen, in his Epistle to Demetrian, with their desertion of the dead and of the dying! "You cry out," says he, "against the plague and the pestilence, while by that very plague and pestilence the crimes of individuals are either detected or increased; while pity is withheld from the infected, and avarice and robbery gloat over the dead. The very persons who dare not perform the pious obsequies of the departed, are rash in their schemes of plunder: they flee from funerals, that they may rush upon the spoil; and it would

[1] Gibbon's Decline and Fall, vol. i. p. 455, end of chap. x.

almost seem that the wretched sufferers are left alone in their sickness, lest perchance they should escape death, if they were attended. For he surely manifests a desire for another's death, who scarce waits for it, that he may seize upon his wealth." [1]

There were other considerations, however, to be urged upon his people by Cyprian at this juncture, besides those which excited them to charity and good works: they were to be fortified against personal afflictions; against the fear of death, and against immoderate sorrow for departed friends. Accordingly, the watchful Bishop prepared a discourse on the present mortality, which was probably delivered from his own lips to his assembled people, as well as distributed among them as a written tract: and he expressly declares, that this was done in obedience to repeated warnings from Heaven. In this discourse he urges much at length, and with characteristic eloquence, the Scriptural encouragement to patience in suffering, and the reasons which a Christian has to look on death as a blessing, though it come in the most terrible form. To that which is equally applicable to all times of affliction in this discourse, I will not advert: but I may mention, that among the causes of the impatience which Cyprian had to contend against, was the fear of some, that they might be deprived, by the progress of the plague, of the honour of martyrdom. He reminds such persons, that martyrdom is not to be accounted as a property even of the best and most courageous Christians, nor to be reckoned upon as if in every man's power; since it is in a double sense a free gift of God, Who both places us in the way to it, and enables us to endure it; and both by an exercise of His free grace. He encourages them to believe, moreover, that God, who trieth the hearts and reins, would, if they were really prepared for martyrdom, bestow on them the reward of martyrs, though they died not under the sword of the magistrate, but beneath His own fatherly visitation: for if, in vengeance, He rejected Cain's offering, anticipating the crime not yet perpetrated; much more could He, in

[1] Page 219.

mercy, accept them, though the noble act which they meditated was not yet accomplished, and might perchance be placed out of their power.

He relates an anecdote of a brother Bishop, who was at the point of death, and clinging still tenaciously to life, prayed earnestly for a short respite. While he was thus praying, and while death was closing upon him, a youth stood beside him, of an aspect noble and heavenly, and such as mortal eyes could scarce behold, except those that were about to open upon another world. With an indignant voice and manner, he cried aloud to the dying man; DO YE SHRINK FROM SUFFERING; ARE YE UNWILLING TO DEPART; WHAT WOULD YE THAT I SHOULD DO FOR YOU?[1] This rebuke, says Cyprian, could not have been intended chiefly for the dying Bishop, to whom it had already ceased to be of use as a practical admonition; but it was uttered that he might publish it to those whom he should leave behind, and that we might apply it to our spiritual benefit.

There is another topic often touched by St Cyprian, in this and other works, to which I shall advert at greater length; because the prevalence of the opinion which we shall find him expressing, is made by Gibbon one of the *natural* causes of the rapid increase of Christianity, in a discussion which is so conducted as to interpose secondary causes to our perception of the first divine cause, to which rather they ought to direct our attention.

We have already seen Cyprian reasoning with Demetrian, from a presumption that the world was rapidly approaching its end: and this belief, from which he there gathered topics of reproof to the heathen, he here employs to animate and encourage his brethren in Christ, in their present transitory struggle with afflictions. "The kingdom of God, brethren most beloved, has begun its nearer approaches. The reward of life, the fruition of eternal bliss, perpetual security, and the enjoyment of paradise lately forfeited, are dawning upon us,

[1] Pati timetis, exire non vultis, quid faciam vobis? *De Mortalitate*, p. 234.

as the world passes away. What place, then, is there left, for fear and trepidation."[1] And again, having inculcated the general lesson of resignation at the death of friends, he adds: "this submission, which ought always to be the temper of the servants of God, is now much more incumbent on them, while the world is hastening to destruction, in the midst of accumulated evils. We who have seen terrible events, and know that yet more terrible are impending, should reckon it our privilege and happiness to escape the more quickly. If your house shook, and threatened every moment to bury you beneath its trembling walls, would you not rush out of it as soon as possible? If you were on a voyage, and the winds and the swelling waves threatened destruction to your vessel, would you not hasten to the port? Behold, then, the world, nodding to its fall, and affording every indication not only of an age past maturity, but of its approaching end: and dost thou not give God thanks: dost thou not congratulate thine own felicity, that thou art snatched by an earlier deliverance from impending wreck and ruin?"[2]

It is scarcely necessary to transcribe other passages to the same purpose; though we may make several references, to show how habitually the notion of which we are speaking pervaded Cyprian's mind. In his Treatise on the Unity of the Church, he refers the heresies and divisions which gave occasion to that work to the prophecy of St Paul to Timothy, that *in the last days* perilous times should come, and divisions arising from the wilful and insubordinate temper of many in the Church.[3] In his book on the Vanity of Idols, he connects the calling of the Gentiles with the end of the world, in such terms as to prove that he imagined the prophecies which he adduces, spoke of his own days, as the fulness of times, and the approaching end.[4] In his Epistle to the people of Thybaris, before quoted, he draws the same conclusion from the afflictions which the Church was then suffering:[5] and in his Epistle to Cornelius, he refers the schisms in the Church

[1] De Mort. p. 229.   [2] Page 236.   [3] Page 200.
[4] Page 227.   [5] *Ep.* lvi.

to the last days spoken of by St Paul, with the Apostle's warning, that such evils should precede them.[1] Thus, whether he had to rebuke the wilfulness of sectaries, or to meet the arguments of the heathen, or to exhort the brethren to meet martyrdom with courage, or the terrible death by pestilence with patience, or the loss of friends with resignation; whether he had to support the faith of the Church against heresies, or its order against schism, he still referred to that overwhelming consideration, that the end of all things was at hand.

Nor does Cyprian stand alone in this mistaken conviction. St Chrysostom says, "the end is no longer to be delayed; for these things are even at the door. We know not, whether even in this our generation, the death of all things temporal may not arrive, and that dreadful day dawn, the day of judgment. For the greater part of the signs of that day are before us: the Gospel is preached in all lands; we have had wars, and earthquakes, and famine; and what besides is there to intervene? But you do not recognise these signs. Learn, however, that this blindness of yours is among the greatest of them; for so it was in the days of Noe, and of Sodom,"[2] &c. And not to accumulate instances unnecessarily, Gregory, Bishop of Rome, at the close of the fifth century, writes: "As when night is ending and day beginning, before the sun rises there is a sort of twilight, while the remains of the departing darkness are changing perfectly into the radiance of the day which succeeds; so the end of this world is already mingling with the commencement of the next, and the very gloom of what remains has begun to be illuminated with the incoming of things spiritual." And again: "Why is it, I ask, that in these last times so many things begin to be clear about souls which before were hidden; so that by open revelations and disclosures the age to come seems forcing itself on us and dawning?"

[1] *Ep.* lv.
[2] Chrysostomi Hom. xx. al. xxi. in Matt. last paragraph, vol. vii. p. 304, new Edition of Paris.

Indeed, as the learned author of the tract on Purgatory, in the "Tracts for the Times," from which the quotations from Gregory are borrowed, observes, "Nothing has been more common in every age, than to think the day of judgment approaching; and perhaps it was intended that the Church should ever so suppose. Perhaps so to suppose is even a mark of a Christian mind; which at least will ever be on its watch-tower to see whether it be coming or no, from desire of its Saviour's return." [1]

Now it is not to be doubted, that this prevailing expectation of the end of the world would materially influence the character of Christians; and that for the better: and thus indirectly it would be influential in the propagation of the faith; since the purity of the Church was one of the great moral elements of its influence over the heathen, and one which we as Christians can never be ashamed to recognise. I confess that Gibbon does *verbally* ascribe to this opinion its appropriate effect *in* the primitive Church : but let us remember that it is his main object in the fifteenth chapter of his work, to which we are referring, to state the causes of the *rapid growth* of the Christian Church; the second of which he makes "the doctrine of a future life, improved by every additional circumstance which could give weight and efficacy to that important truth." Having this his object in mind, and taking his words in their proper connexion, we shall see that he would represent the heathen as frightened into Christianity by that expectation which purified the character of Christians; and not as being won over to the Church, by the beauty of the Christian character thus purified.

It is thus that he expresses himself. "When the promise of eternal happiness was proposed to mankind, on condition of adopting the faith, and of observing the precepts of the Gospel, it is no wonder that so advantageous an offer *should have been accepted by great numbers of every religion, of every rank, and of every province in the Roman empire.* The ancient

[1] Tracts for the Times, No. 79, p. 46.

Christians were animated by a contempt for their present existence, and by a just confidence of immortality, of which the doubtful and imperfect faith of modern ages cannot give us any adequate notion. In the primitive Church, the influence of truth was very powerfully strengthened by an opinion, which, however it may deserve respect for its usefulness and antiquity, has not been found agreeable to experience. It was universally believed, that the end of the world, and the kingdom of heaven, were at hand. The near approach of this wonderful event had been predicted by the Apostles; the tradition of it was preserved by their earliest disciples, and those who understood in their literal sense the discourses of Christ Himself, were obliged to expect the second and glorious coming of the Son of Man in the clouds, before that generation was totally extinguished, which had beheld His humble condition upon earth, and which might still witness of the calamities of the Jews under Vespasian or Hadrian. The revolution of seventeen centuries has instructed us not to press too closely the mysterious language of prophecy and revelation; but as long as, for wise purposes, the error was permitted to subsist in the Church, it was productive of the most salutary effects on the faith and practice of Christians, who lived in the awful expectation of that moment, when the globe itself, and all the various races of mankind, should tremble at the appearance of their divine Judge."

Now not to mention the malicious tone of this passage, and the temerity with which its infidel author has ventured so to interpret prophecy as to make it false (surely his unhallowed hand might have refrained at least from touching the ark itself!); is it not manifest, that as concerns the expectation of the coming of Christ, and that also of the Millennium, to which he next adverts, and in short every expectation founded on the reception and belief of what was revealed by Christ, and propagated among His disciples, with or without some mixture of human error; is it not manifest, that such an expectation could only produce an effect on those who had believed already; that is, on those who had embraced the revelation of the truth? But if so, this expectation was not among the direct causes of the growth of Christianity, by directing towards it, or frightening into it, those who were without: and if it was, and was by God Himself intended to be a means of purifying the lives and affections of Christians, and so indirectly working upon the heathen, who saw their good works, and glorified Our Father which is in Heaven, little will be gained to the cause of infidelity, from this ground of a Christian's rejoicing and humble boast.

And here some other remarks are suggested, upon the Christian's hope of his Lord's speedy coming. The expectation of a rapid period of the world was never a matter of faith in the Church, nor imposed as such by any body of Christians, nor by any individual. It was at most an opinion of many great and good men, which had in it nothing contrary to true piety; and which gave a high and noble tone to the applied theology of each passing age. It is in vain therefore to argue from their mistake in this matter, which was not a matter of faith, against the authority of the Fathers, as witnessing to the rule of faith. It is equally in vain to argue from hence against the importance of the unanimous judgment of the doctors of the Church, in its earliest and best days: for in the first place it is not clear that the unanimous judgment of the Fathers, at any one time, was ever recorded upon this subject;[1] and moreover, the expectation of the end of the world as imme-

[1] The author of the *Advent Sermons on Antichrist* (No. 83 of Tracts for the Times) says, after having quoted some prophecies of impending persecution from the Scriptures, "These passages were understood by the early Christians to relate to the persecution, which was to come in the last times; and they seem evidently to bear upon them that meaning. Our Saviour's words, indeed, about the fiery trial which was coming, might seem at first sight to refer to the early persecutions, those to which the first Christians were exposed; and doubtless so they do. Yet, violent as these persecutions were, *they were not considered by those who suffered them, to be the proper fulfilment of the prophecy*" (p. 44). Now if they looked for a farther fulfilment of these prophecies, they looked for a time in which they might be fulfilled; and so those to whom the learned author refers, did not expect the end of the world as immediately approaching.

diately impending at any particular time, could never, in the very nature of things, become catholic; for it must always want the *semper* of catholicity, though at any one time it might have had (which however I deny in fact) the *ubique*, and the *ab omnibus*. For example, those only who lived before and during the time of Cyprian, could possibly agree with him in supposing that *in his day* the end was at hand. This is, indeed, self-evident, and may appear like solemn trifling; but it has really its importance derived from the misrepresentations of those who deride the appeal to antiquity in theological discussions: for such opinions of particular times, or of individual persons, are often adduced against us, as weakening the authority of tradition, or of the recorded universal judgment of all ages and Churches, in attestation of doctrinal truth. But we of the Anglican Church receive not as conclusive the testimony of one man or of one age; therefore to weaken the authority of one man or one age, is not to weaken the support of our system: and again, we distinguish between doctrine and opinion; and should distinguish between catholic doctrine, and pious and probable opinion, even if it should happen to be catholic: in the latter *it is conceivable*, that the whole Church *might* err, and yet the promise of Christ not fail; in the former we know not how to believe that this could be the case, and therefore we believe Christ and the Church.

Besides which it is to be remembered, that whatever weight the judgment of individuals, or even of Churches, may have on such a subject as the times of the end of the world, it must have as an interpretation of prophecy, as yet unfulfilled: and even those among us who place the authority of tradition at the highest, plainly declare, that "the Fathers do not convey to us the interpretation of prophecy, with the same certainty as they convey doctrine." Even, therefore, should it be admitted, for argument's sake, that the Fathers have here as a body, interpreted wrongly, our confidence in their authority, where they ought to be appealed to, is not a whit shaken. But let me remit the reader to the Tract last quoted; the three first pages of which will convince all who know what is the doctrine of Rome on the Authority of Tradition, that that doctrine is not the doctrine of those who wish to remember that, our Church was once stigmatized as the "Church of the Traditioners,"[1] and to convert the imputation into a badge of honour and a pledge of fidelity and truth. As for persuading those who know *not* what the doctrine of Rome is, that is out of the question; they want one of the things to be compared, and cannot therefore judge of their disparity. It would be well if they could be persuaded to hold their tongues, until they have qualified themselves to speak.

Here, too, I cannot withhold a comparison of the modesty of the general expressions of Cyprian, and the rest of the Fathers here quoted, with the temerity of those *interpreters* (shall I call them?) of sacred Scripture in these days, who would fix the very year and the very day, at which we are to look for the end of the present system of things. In nothing does Antiquity rebuke modern speculators more severely, though silently, than by the reverence, the holy fear, with which she was wont to touch whatever is sacred, to inquire into whatever is hidden.

Of Cyprian's belief that the end of the world was at hand, it was an almost necessary part, that Antichrist was also already come, or very soon to be revealed: and accordingly he states most clearly that he looked for the revelation of that mystery of iniquity, as preceding the coming of Christ. "Let it not move you," says he to the brethren of Legio and Asturia,[2] "that in these latter days the faith of some has been wavering; that the fear of God has diminished among them, and the bonds of union broken. These things have been foretold as the attendants of the end of the world; and our Lord and His Apostles have agreed in predicting, that *at the close of the world*, and *at the coming of Antichrist*, all good things should appear to fail, and all evil things, and all things hostile to the Church, should increase." And again, "Anti-

[1] See note B of the Appendix to Dr Hook's Call to Union on the Principles of the English Reformation.
[2] *Ep.* lxviii. p. 120.

christ is at hand, but Christ also cometh immediately after. The enemy advances in his rage, but the Lord delays not His coming, to avenge our sufferings and afflictions."[1]

That Antichrist was very near at hand, was evidently, then, a part of Cyprian's belief; but when we come to inquire what was his notion concerning the character of Antichrist, and his personality, so to speak, we shall find the same vagueness in him, that we must find in all who cannot avoid the mention of such things as are vaguely set before us in Scripture to excite us to piety and to watchfulness, because the mysterious annunciations have become deeply impressed upon their feelings; but who dare not take such liberties with Holy Writ, as to erect for themselves a figure of full proportions, out of a few striking lineaments. It should seem, however, that Cyprian believed Antichrist to be a man, an individual, as opposed to a sect or party, to a prevailing tone of ethics or divinity, to a system of philosophy, or a spirit of philosophising, or to a vague accession of evils, whether persecution, or moral or religious evil, in which light Antichrist seems to be viewed by different persons at present. For in his testimonies against the Jews, having referred to the prophecy in the fourteenth chapter of Isaiah, especially to the words, "Is this the man that made the earth to tremble, that did shake kingdoms, that made the world as a wilderness?" he speaks of Antichrist as of him who shall come as a man.[2] And the following passage may seem to tend the same way: "those virgins (who are cut off in the plague) leave the world in peace, and with an untarnished reputation, and have not to dread the threat, the seductiones et lupanaria, of the approaching Antichrist."[3] Here, besides the person of Antichrist, we have also one feature of his character, a heartless and shameless debauchery; in a word, a total moral degradation.

The assertion that Antiochus, in the very act of persecution

---

[1] *Ep.* lvi. p. 92.
[2] De Antichristo, quod in hominem veniat. Test. Jud. lib. iii. § 118. p. 329.
[3] De Mort. p. 233.

mentioned in the historical book of the Maccabees, was an impersonation, or at least a precursive figure, of Antichrist,[1] also leads to the conclusion, that Cyprian made that mystery of iniquity an individual; and intimates another part of his expected character and actions, that he should be a savage persecutor. And yet another character of that coming pest is indicated by the assertion of Cyprian, that those who separate the Church, imitate his character, and are actuated by his spirit. "Their perversion," says he, in his Epistle to Cornelius on the schism of Fortunatus and Felicissimus, "is to be lamented even to tears, whom the Devil so thoroughly blinds, that, disregarding the eternal pains of hell, they dare to imitate the approach of the coming Antichrist."[2] And again:[3] "If we set aside the errors for which men contend, and revert religiously and faithfully to the authority of the Gospel, and to the tradition of Apostolical principles, we shall perceive, that no portion of the grace of the Church, and of salvation, remains at their disposal, who scatter and oppose the Church of Christ; and who are called adversaries by Christ Himself, but by His Apostles *Antichrist*." Hence we may collect, I think, as from no obscure hints, that Antichrist was, in Cyprian's judgment, to be not only a persecutor and an alien from all the hopes and blessings of Christianity, but that he was to be also an apostate; ravaging that fold to which he had once belonged.

I have only to add, that there has nothing intervened, that I know of, which should prevent our having the same notions of Antichrist, and the same feelings about his coming, that St Cyprian had: and so long as the end shall be yet future, the words of Cyprian may well express the feelings of those who are on their post as watchmen, and convey a timely warning to the careless. As an appropriate precept and encouragement to those who deeply feel these things, he reminds Lucius, that he has returned to his Episcopal throne, "that

---

[1] Rex Antiochus infestus, immo in Antiocho Antichristus expressus. Ad Fort. p. 270.

[2] *Ep.* lv. p. 89.   [3] *Ep.* lxxiii p. 134.

the Bishop may stand at the Altar of God, to exhort his flock to take up the arms which shall prepare them for confession and martyrdom, and to second his precepts with his actions; and thus to prepare his soldiers for the battle, while Antichrist is approaching, with the incitements not only of his voice and of his exhortations, but by the example also of his faith and firmness."[1]

[1] *Ep.* lviii. p. 96.

## CHAPTER XII.

Weakness of the Roman Empire.—Numidian Christians carried captive by Barbarians.—Collections made in Carthage to redeem them.—Cyprian's Epistle to Cæcilius on the Mixed Cup.—His Doctrine applied to Half Communion, and other Errors in the present day.

SUCH was the state of the Roman Empire in this age, that while its very centre was subject to the incursions of the Goths, the confines were exposed to the ravages of the several barbarian nations on whose territories they bordered: and Numidia, with the rest of the frontier provinces, was subject to this kind of border warfare. On one occasion, in the beginning of the year 253, a descent having been made on their territory, a number of Christians were carried off, together with other Numidian captives, by their barbarian invaders,[1] and the brethren of their own province being too

[1] It is difficult, if not impossible, to determine who were the barbarians, into whose hands the Numidian brethren had fallen. Some have supposed that they were Persians; but it should seem to be sufficient to set aside this notion, that their victorious invasion of the Roman Empire was not till the year 260, seven years after the events of which we are speaking; and yet this opinion must be mentioned, because it has had its influence in determining or rather in rendering indeterminable, the date of the Epistle of Cyprian to the Numidian Bishops. Bishop Pearson, in his *Annales Cyprianici*, argues with great learning, from St Augustine and others, that the invaders in this instance were some warrior nations bordering on Numidia to the south. The Franks seem about this time to have pushed their successes through Spain into Mauritania, and may well have reached Numidia also, in their rapid foray: but perhaps it may be difficult to determine whether this irruption of the Franks exactly synchronises with the Epistle of Cyprian. See Gibbon's Decline and Fall, vol. i. p. 415.

poor to redeem them from captivity, the Church in Carthage took advantage of the opportunity of relieving the distressed members of a sister Church; and of acting upon that Christian communion, which binds together all the members of Christ's body, first, individuals with their particular Church, and then, in those Churches, with the whole body. On this occasion, a collection was made in Carthage, at the instance of St Cyprian, to whom the Numidians had applied for assistance; and notwithstanding the large demands on their charity which had already arisen during the plague, no less than a hundred thousand sesterces (nearly eight hundred pounds) was transmitted from the Carthaginians to the distressed Church of the Numidians.

The Epistle with which Cyprian accompanied this charitable collection, is replete with the expressions of those sentiments of Christian benevolence, and of those principles of Christian fellowship, which alone entitles even liberality to the name of *Charity*, and to the reward of a Christian grace. "I read your letter," says he to the Numidian Bishops, "with much emotion, and not without tears at the sad account which you gave of our brethren in Christ. For who can help grieving in such a case, or refuse to look on their calamity as his own; since St Paul says, *if one member suffer, all the members suffer with it:* and again, *who is weak, and I am not weak?* The peril therefore and the captivity of our brethren should be felt as if it were our own; since we are one body with them, and not only natural affection, but religious principle, should incite us to relieve them. Moreover, since we are told, that they who are baptised have put on Christ; we should behold Christ Himself in these our suffering members: and He who redeemed us from death, should in them be by us redeemed from danger: He who delivered us from the jaws of the Devil, and is now in the power of the barbarians, should by us be delivered thence: and He who paid for us the ransom of His blood, should now be ransomed by our pecuniary aid. Doubtless He now suffers these events, that our faith may be put to the test; that it may be seen, whether each of us is willing to do that for others, which he would wish to have done for himself,"[1] &c. . . . He afterwards says, that the brethren in Carthage, though they hoped that no such need would occur, yet desired to be acquainted with it, if their help should be again required in a like case.

In return for this supply, which was the act of fellowship which Cyprian and his Church were enabled to afford, they request the prayers of the poor Numidians, which would be on their part an equal reciprocation of Christian fellowship. "That you may be enabled to return the benefit which you receive from the contributors, by your prayers, and by Eucharistic commemorations, I have subjoined their names," says Cyprian, "together with those of the other Bishops, who, happening to be in Carthage, have contributed according to their ability. We bid you farewell, brethren, and desire your constant remembrance."

I need not remind the reader, that this fraternal intercourse of giving and receiving between distant Churches, united in one faith, is accordant with the Apostolical precepts and practice. It is also perfectly in the spirit of primitive Christianity, and probably existed in the earlier ages of the Church, to a much greater extent than we are aware. The Church of Rome, distinguished from the earliest ages for its wealth, was also honourably distinguished for its diffusive benevolence; and it became an established custom to make collections in Rome for the poorer, but more ancient and mother Church at Jerusalem. "Dionysius, Bishop of Corinth, writing to the Roman Church in the time of Soter, eleventh Bishop of Rome, about the middle of the second century, says, that 'it had been customary with them from the beginning to benefit all the brethren in various ways; and to send assistance to many Churches in all cities, thus relieving the poverty of the needy; and to supply aid to the brethren condemned to the mines, by the gifts which they had sent even from the beginning; that they preserved as Romans the customs of the Romans, delivered to them from their fathers; and that their

[1] *Ep.* lx. p. 99.

blessed Bishop Soter had not only observed this custom, but had increased it by supplying abundantly the provision allotted to the saints, and by comforting with blessed words the brethren who came to him, even as a loving father acts towards his children.' The same mercy and charity of the Roman Church is mentioned by Dionysius Alexandrinus, in the following century, in an Epistle to Stephen, where he states that all Syria and Arabia had received supplies from Rome."[1]

Perhaps it would be well if this practice of making collections for poor Churches with which we are in communion, as well as for the poor under any other name, were more frequent; for it would be a constantly recurring memorial and exercise of that communion which exists (and ought not to be a dormant or forgotten privilege), as truly between Catholic Churches as corporate bodies, as between Catholic Christians as individuals; and even more truly than between Christians with all men whoever, as of the same blood with them, and children of the same heavenly Father. And as the poor shall never cease out of the land; so that we shall never lack the privilege of doing unto Christ the good which they require and receive at our hand; so also between particular and national Churches there will always be a sufficient disparity to enjoin the duty, and to afford the privilege of communicating in giving and receiving.

The next Epistle (the sixty-third), written to Cæcilius to enforce the necessity of using wine in the Eucharistic cup, is most instructive on the subject of the primitive doctrine of the Holy Communion. A passing indication that it was written during persecution enables us with sufficient accuracy to refer this Epistle to the spring of the year 253. Its first occasion and object are soon related; but it affords so many indications of Cyprian's opinion upon the doctrine of the Eucharist, that we shall be obliged to examine it at considerable length.

At the time of which we are writing, a very frequent,

[1] Palmer's Treatise on the Church of Christ, vol. ii. p. 498.

perhaps a daily, participation in the Eucharistic feast was the universal custom among Christians : but there were men, who were induced from a fear that their religion would be betrayed by the smell of the wine, taken in the morning, to consecrate the cup only with water; and thus to avoid an involuntary confession, and the consequent persecution. These persons are to be distinguished from the *Aquarii* or *Encratites*;[1] a pernicious sect, who refused to consecrate wine at the Eucharist, because, forsooth, they thought it wrong to use either wine or flesh, and would be more holy than Christ Himself. Had he been refuting the error of such persons, Cyprian would have been more indignantly severe: as it is, he exposes the danger and impropriety of the practice in question firmly, indeed, but with much patience and forbearance; and the hardest things that he says of those who were Aquarii from timidity, is, that they seem ashamed of Christ's blood, and that, therefore, they cannot hope to be worthy to pour out their own blood for His sake. And he maintains, with arguments only too abundantly conclusive, that wine must at all hazards and at all events be mingled with the cup, and taken by the people, or that the communicants are deprived of the blood of Christ in the Eucharist.

And his expressions in this Epistle are such, and his arguments are so conducted, as to afford the most convincing proof, that in two things at least he was most decidedly opposed to the modern Romish system, in that (1) he could never have consented to take the cup from the laity; and (2) he cannot have held the dogma of transubstantiation.

It would be absurd to make a parade of the evidence which we derive from Cyprian's works, that the laity in his days received the Eucharist in both kinds; since the custom of the Church for several centuries is confessed on all hands; and since the only question is, not whether Rome took away the cup from the laity, but whether she did not, in so doing, act presumptuously, tyrannically, and sacrilegiously : *presumptuously*, in contradicting our Lord's intention, as collected

[1] For an account of these Aquarii, see Bingham's Orig. Ecc. xv. ii. 7.

from the method of His institution, handed down and interpreted in and by the Apostolical method of administering these most solemn mysteries of our faith: *tyrannically*, in thus curtailing the people's privileges in this blessed Sacrament: and *sacrilegiously*, in depriving the people of grace, when she took away from them one of the means of its conveyance. I maintain, upon grounds which I proceed to adduce, that Cyprian would have held that Rome has fallen under the whole of this censure.

"Although," says he, "I know that almost all the Bishops by divine appointment set over the Churches of the Lord throughout the world maintain the order of Gospel truth and divine tradition, and do not depart from that which Christ our Master taught and did, to follow a new invention; yet since some, either through ignorance or simplicity, do *not* do that which Jesus Christ our Lord and Saviour did and taught, in the consecration of the cup of the Lord, and in the administering it to the people; I have thought it as well necessary as religious, to write this Epistle to you, that if any one be still involved in that error, he may receive the light of truth, and return to the root and original of the divine tradition."[1] Let it be borne in mind, as we read this passage, what it is that Cyprian calls a novel invention, an error; and in what sort of things he holds the divine tradition, the Gospel truth, the teaching and example of our Lord and Master, to be imperative; what are the desertions of it which he attributes to ignorance or simplicity at the best; and what he judges it a matter of religious necessity to set right: and I think it will be sufficiently clear, that he would have pronounced precisely the same judgment on the actual taking away the cup from the laity, which he pronounced on the virtual taking it away from the Eucharist altogether by a fancied consecration of that which could not become the blood of Christ.

But let us again hear the words of Cyprian. "We ought to follow the truth of God, not the custom of men: for God

[1] P. 104.

saith by the mouth of Isaiah, *In vain do they worship Me, teaching the commandments and doctrines of men* (Is. xxix. 13, see vers. LXX). And again the Lord Himself repeats this rebuke in the Gospel, saying, *Ye reject the commandment of God, that ye may establish your own traditions;* and again in another place he says, *He who shall break one of the least of these commandments, and shall teach men so, shall be called the least in the kingdom of heaven.* Now if it is not lawful to break *even the least* of the Lord's commandments, how much less is it permitted to change or infringe by any human tradition, a divine rule concerning that which is so great, so important, and so essentially connected with the very Sacrament of our Lord's passion, and our redemption. For if Jesus Christ our Lord and our God is Himself the High Priest of God the Father, and first offered Himself as a sacrifice to the Father, and commanded us to do this in the remembrance of Him; surely that priest truly discharges the office in the room of Christ, who imitates the actions of Christ; and he *then* offers a full and true sacrifice in the Church to God the Father, *when* he so enters upon the offering, as Christ also seems to have done," [1] &c.

I do not adduce these passages, nor any of those presently quoted, as if they were an expression of his *avowed* judgment, upon a point which was never discussed in the Church, till he had long gone to his crown. He does *not* here afford an actual and specific condemnation of the practice of Rome in withholding the cup from the laity: such a condemnation, preceding the times in which it was to be applied, could only be expected from our divine Lord, who could foresee its future necessity: and such a condemnation we actually have in His words DRINK *ye* ALL *of it:* and again, *Except ye eat the flesh of the Son of man,* AND DRINK HIS BLOOD, *ye have no life in you.* But such expressions as those just quoted from St Cyprian indicate his mind sufficiently to make us *morally certain,* that he would at once have protested against the breach of a rule (not sanctified, for it was already divine, but) handed down and

[1] Pp. 108, 109.

attested by inspired Apostles, and holy Bishops, and martyrs and saints, in short, by the whole Church of the living God, the pillar and ground of the truth, from the first time that the Eucharist was ever celebrated with lay communicants. Surely Cyprian would have judged, that in this Rome acted most *presumptuously:* and perhaps his opinion would not have been altered, if he had known that the Council of Constance, which first enjoined half communion, would venture to do so expressly, notwithstanding our Lord did appoint it in both kinds.

But I maintain farther, that there is every reason to believe, that Cyprian would have judged that Rome acted *tyrannically* and *sacrilegiously*, as well as rashly, in thus mutilating the feast of the Eucharist, and curtailing the privilege of the people, so as to leave it doubtful at the least whether he did not deprive them of grace, in taking from them one of the means by which it is conveyed. For I observe, that in his argument to enforce the necessary presence of wine in the cup, he distinguishes the meaning of each portion of the mixed cup, telling us that the water signifies the people, that the wine signifies the blood of Christ:[1] and that he reasons thus; that if but one be offered, it will be without the people, or without the blood of Christ respectively. Now if he thus distinguishes between the separate portions of the mixed cup, in one part of the Eucharist; much more surely would he have distinguished between the separate elements of the

---

[1] See p. 108. It is worth noting, that this reasoning, does not touch the validity of our oblation, and communion without *water* in the cup: for though it were most *desirable* that we should have every possible figure of communion with the brethren in the Eucharistic cup, it is only *essential* that we have the New Testament in Christ's blood. It may be *desirable*, that is, that we have the *water*, but is only *essential* that we *have the wine*. By all participating in the same cup, we have the actual communion with the brethren, and may therefore dispense with the figure: but if all do not partake of the cup, they receive neither the figure nor the reality of Christ's blood; neither the figure nor the reality of communion, either with Christ, or with the Church. Palmer, in his Origines Liturgicæ, has shown how strong our position is in this matter against the cavils of Rome.

Eucharist themselves: especially, since for thus doing he would have had ample authority in the words of the Apostle; *the cup of blessing which we bless, is it not the communion of the blood of Christ? The bread which we break, is it not the communion of the body of Christ?*[1] and since the whole body of the Church has ever attested the same thing, in the formulary of administering; where the bread is ever called the body of Christ, and the cup the blood of Christ.[2] But if there is a distinct *meaning in*, according to the very lowest view of the Sacraments, there is a distinct *instruction conveyed by* each portion of the Eucharist: and surely to deprive the people of either portion of the instruction, can consist with no proper respect to the institution of God; with no sound exercise of the Church's love, as the mother of the faithful; with no common care for the spiritual advantage of the people: and still less can such an act consist with any right view of the dignity and efficacy of the Eucharist, of the duty of the Church, of the privilege of the people, if the Eucharist be more than a means of instruction, even a conveyance of grace.

But it is not a mere matter of probable deduction that Cyprian *would* make, he actually *does* make the cup the instrument of particular blessings, so as to convey the complement of the Eucharistic grace, as it certainly forms the complement of the Eucharistic oblation and feast. For he quotes the Psalmist, [saying, Thy exhilarating cup is very good (calix tuus inebrians perquam optimus); and spiritualises this into an assertion of the graces conveyed by the Eucharistic cup, in a manner which would be wholly inapposite,

[1] 1 Cor. x. 16.
[2] This is true even of the Romish Liturgy of the mass, for in receiving the *host* the priest says, CORPUS *Domini nostri Jesu Christi custodiat animam meum in vitam æternam:* and in receiving the *chalice* he says, SANGUIS *Domini, &c.* But this is not the only instance in which the Liturgy of the mass, which is, as a whole, more ancient than the doctrines of Rome on the subject of the Eucharist, is very inconveniently adapted to the service of that Church.

as applied to the Eucharistic feast without the cup, as much so indeed as applied to the cup without the wine: and I especially speak here of the *feast* of the Eucharist, as well as the sacrifice; because the Romanists also make the cup a part of the sacrifice, though they take it away from the people in the feast. Let this be borne in mind, while we observe that the whole force of Cyprian's reasoning, when he thus applies the Psalmist's words to the matter in hand, is derived from the particular properties of wine, *with its effects upon him who drinks it*, so as to display his notion of that forming a part of the Eucharistic feast; and this is all that we want, whether or no his illustration is the happiest that might be imagined. "That exhilaration," says he, "produced by the cup of the Lord and His blood, not being like that which is produced by common wine, the Psalmist declares the exhilarating cup to be very good: for the cup of the Lord so exhilarates those who drink it, as to make them sober."[1] These few words are sufficient to indicate the drift of his reasoning here; and to show also, that it would be absurd, if no especial grace was conveyed to the recipients by means of the cup; or if the whole efficacy of the Eucharist resided in either kind. Indeed, if this latter figment of Rome were true, the practice which Cyprian condemns was quite as absurd, as it was erroneous. Why did not the *Aquarii*, who feared detection from the smell of wine, receive the bread only? As in the Church of Rome now, the single Priest or Bishop who was required to officiate, might consecrate and offer, and himself receive of the wine, for he had no occasion, his duties and avocations being all clerical, to endanger his safety by mixing with the heathen: and the many of the laity, whose occupation would not permit seclusion, would have been just as safe, as upon the Aquarian plan. There was more reason then to refrain from the wine at the Lord's Supper, if it were both lawful and equally beneficial, than there has ever been since: and if it be in itself unlawful, nothing

---

[1] P. 107.

can make it lawful; if it be any thing short of *quite* as beneficial to the communicant, none without tyranny and sacrilege can deprive the Church, or any member of the Church, of the greater benefit.

But I go even farther. The pretence of the Roman Church, that the laity in receiving the body of Christ, receive also His blood, would at once have overturned Cyprian's whole argument in this Epistle. A Romanist now could not, without exposing himself to the recoil of his own weapon, refute the very error which Cyprian exposes, upon the same grounds which Cyprian takes, who was unshackled by a future invention of the Church. And herein, whether he is right or wrong, Cyprian is intensely Anti-Romish.

One or two more extracts from the Epistle before us will enforce this assertion. "In Baptism the Holy Spirit is received; and so those who have been baptised, and have received the Holy Spirit, come to the drinking of the cup of the Lord. . . . Baptism is once for all received; but, on the contrary, there is *always* a thirst for the cup of the Lord, and it is constantly drank [Calix Domini in Ecclesiæ semper et sititur et bibitur]."[1] Now who are they who always thirst for the cup of the Lord but the baptised? And who has, or can have, a right to take away from them that for which they have always thirsted, and which they have always received?

Again: if it be reasonable to ask, and it is highly reasonable, "How shall we drink new wine of the fruit of the vine with Christ in the kingdom of His Father, if in the sacrifice we offer not the wine of God the Father, and of Christ; nor mix the cup of Lord according to the divine tradition?"[2]— Is it not equally reasonable, and even more natural, to ask, How shall we drink of the fruit of the vine new with Christ in His kingdom, unless we drink of the cup of His blood in the Eucharist? Would not he who asked the first question, most probably have asked the second, if occasion served? And would he not have held it a spiritual tyranny and sacrilege, to deprive the people of the privilege spoken of in those

[1] Page 106.   [2] Page 107.

mystical words of Scripture; or even to have laid them under a reasonable doubt, whether they were deprived of it or no?

These remarks having been suggested directly from what Cyprian says, as deducible from his reasoning, by the addition of such steps only as are wholly in accordance both with his tone of argument, and with his known opinions; I conceive that we might well suppose him to speak thus, if he could be called upon to give his judgment on the depriving the laity of the cup in the blessed Eucharist.

'There is, then,[1] no excuse for following the practice of any, who may have hitherto administered the Lord's Supper to the people in one kind only, withholding from them the cup, which is the blood of our Lord. For we must ask, whom do they follow? If in the Sacrament which Christ ordained, Christ alone is to be followed, surely this is our sufficient rule. We must hold to the truth of God, though particular customs of men be against it. Does not Isaiah say, *In vain do they worship Me, teaching the doctrines and commandments of men?* And does not the Lord say, *Ye reject the commandment of God, that ye may establish your own traditions?* And again: *Whoever shall break one of the least of these commandments, and teach men so, the same shall be called the least in the kingdom of heaven?* And if one of the least of Christ's commandments cannot be broken with impunity, how much less may any of those institutions which we have from Christ Himself, handed down by the Church in all ages hitherto, by Apostles and all holy men, and which form a part of His own appointed method of celebrating those tremendous mysteries of His body and blood? The priest then only performs his proper office, when he does as Christ did, the great High Priest of our calling: and all religion and sound discipline will be overthrown, if that which was divinely appointed in such a matter is to be broken through or not, at the will of men.

'Nor yet are we to view this question as if it concerned

[1] Non est ergo, etc. p. 108. I am not here making a translation, but running a parallel.

obedience to God alone; since something is due in all such matters to the Church and to the people of God. And how can you, without tyranny, take away from the people that which is theirs of right? and since it is so theirs as to be the instrument of grace to them, how can you deprive them of it, without lowering the Church's holiness? If they receive not the blood of Christ poured out for them, how can they be expected, if occasion should call for it, to pour out their blood for the truth? If they drink not into Christ's death, how can they be expected to live in newness of life? No. Let not this reproach remain any longer on the Church, or on any party in it; but do you return to, and let us all hold, the divine, the Apostolical custom and tradition: and maintain in those sacred mysteries a due reverence to God, and a due charity to all men.'

We proceed to show, in the second place, that the author of the Epistle under consideration could not have held the doctrine of Transubstantiation.

Here, again, let us first see the ground on which Cyprian stood in respect of the question before us; lest we should on the one hand expect too much from his testimony, or on the other make too light of that which we have.

The question last discussed is one of custom; or rather it is so represented by those who must so represent it, to place it within the bounds even of that exaggerated spiritual power before which they bow. They, with us, confess that the *custom* was otherwise in Cyprian's days; yet hold that it has been rightly altered before our own. But the question of Transubstantiation is one of doctrine; and must have been the same, therefore, through all ages, in all orthodox Churches. Although, therefore, we are just as well able to point out the actual rise and growth of this doctrine, as of the former practice, this is denied by the Romanists, who claim the Church in all ages, and all orthodox Christians, Cyprian of course among the rest, as maintaining their present doctrine. Their claim, however, will not subvert the truth of history; and they are in vain challenged to prove from ancient and authentic records, that the doctrine of Transubstantiation was held by the ancient Church, or even by any one divine, through many centuries.

But this fact of the novelty of the doctrine, which makes it impossible for the Romanists to prove their point from the Fathers, makes it also more difficult to find an express condemnation of their view of the question by the same Fathers. For who would, who *could*, except with the spirit of prophecy, condemn a doctrine in express terms, which was not taught till ages after he entered into his rest? And because Cyprian could never have dreamt that a question should be discussed, which was first mooted in the eighth century;[1] because he could never by anticipation imagine, that a determination of that question should be imposed as a matter of faith necessary to salvation; it would be unreasonable to look in Cyprian for any express denial or refutation of that doctrine; or any actual protest against the spiritual tyranny which decreed such a monstrous opinion as necessary to be believed. This, as in the former case, could only be expected from divine inspiration, or from our Lord Himself; and there in fact we find it, *totidem verbis:* for He who said, *Drink ye* ALL *of this*, also said, by His Apostle Paul, "As often as ye eat this bread, and drink

[1] There are, however, polemical miracles related as having been wrought in proof of the doctrine in question before this time. For instance, Gregory the Great, seeing a woman laugh at the celebration of the Eucharist, asked her why she laughed; and was answered, "Because you call the bread which I myself made, the body of our Lord." And at the prayers of the saint the consecrated bread appeared as flesh. Of course this miracle is an after invention; for, indeed, both the sneer of the woman and the miraculous answer to it, are in the spirit of a much later age. But I mention this miracle as suggesting a remark on others of the like kind; that *they*, as well as the writings of the doctors of the Church, bear testimony to the changes which have been made in the doctrine of Transubstantiation. So long as portions of Christ's body were all that was required for the establishment of the then doctrine of Rome, the bread was in the habit of miraculously assuming the appearance of divided flesh: but when "*whole Christ*" was wanted to attest an improvement of the doctrine "*whole Christ*," a little babe in the cradle, or the like appeared. Romish inventions, not to say the Roman Church, makes Heaven most accommodating in its miraculous tokens.

this cup, ye do show the Lord's death till He come. Wherefore whosoever shall eat this bread, and drink *this* cup of the Lord, unworthily, shall be guilty of the body and blood of the Lord. But let a man examine himself, and so let him eat of *that* bread, and drink of *that* cup." And again, "the bread which we break, is it not the communion of the body of Christ?"[1]

All that we must *expect* then in Cyprian, touching the figment of transubstantiation, is what we find also in him touching the reveries of Emmanuel Swedenborg, or the inspirations of the Quakers or of the Irvingites; that is, such a manner of expression as can be accounted for only by his profound ignorance of the doctrine in question. If we find any thing (which in fact we shall not) which may be distorted into a verdict in favour of that doctrine, we shall not be much staggered; because it is natural to fall into a manner of expression not rigidly correct, when error, on either hand, has not yet called for precision: but if it should happen (as it will) that we find something literally adverse to it, its effect will be great in proportion. Any one who will find in a writer so early as St Cyprian *a specific condemnation* of the doctrine of transubstantiation, will do Rome a great favour, however paradoxical the assertion may appear; for he will be producing historical evidence of its existence, such as she has never yet been able to find.

But now, that we may know what it is that we are to compare with Cyprian's doctrine, we must state where it is that we are obliged to dissent from Rome; and how far we should or may go along with her.

That the bread and wine, then, in the blessed Eucharist, are verily and indeed the body and blood of Christ, we must hold, or desert the Catholic faith, and the doctrine of our own Church, as stated even in her elementary Catechism. Wherein consists the presence of the body and blood of Christ; that is, how it is present, and how we are to reconcile the verity of its presence with the substance of the bread and wine still

---

[1] 1 Cor. xi. 26-28, and x. 16.

before us; we do not absolutely define. We may leave even the Romanist to hold his own view of this (I mean *this* specifically; the presence of Christ, not the absence of the bread), so he hold it only as a pious opinion, not to be imposed on others as a matter of faith: nay, so far, we may even allow him greater liberty in his faith than the ultraprotestant, who altogether denies, or explains away, the presence of Christ in the Eucharist. But that the bread and wine are no longer present in the Lord's Supper, *that* we cannot admit; nay, we may not; for we cannot if we do receive Christ's words, and those of the Apostles, in their simplicity.

Perhaps I ought to apologise for all this preparation: but few who have not turned their minds to the subject polemically, are aware of the importance of bearing in mind the position of those whose judgment they would apply to the question, and of forming a precise notion of the matter in dispute.

But now to the immediate subject.

What did Melchisedec offer? Bread and wine. In this Melchisedec typified the Eucharist, as Cyprian tells us, with the consent, as I believe, of all the Fathers who have touched upon the subject, and with perfect truth. But how does Cyprian express this? Christ "offered *the very same thing* which Melchisedec had offered, that is, *bread and wine;* that is, in very truth, His own body and blood," [panem et vinum, suum scilicet corpus et sanguinem].[1] These words are equally strong against the Romish and the Zuinglian doctrine of the Eucharist. The Romanist could not consistently say that Christ offered *bread and wine:* the Zuinglian will not endure to hear that He offered *His own body and blood* in the Eucharist.

Cyprian quotes Genesis xlix. 10. He shall wash his garments in wine, and his clothes in the blood of the grape: and asks,[1] when the blood of the grape is mentioned, what is signified but *the wine* of the cup of our Lord's blood? Here the last remark may be repeated.

[1] Page 105.

But the following passage is one of the most remarkable incidental testimonies against the Romish doctrine of transubstantiation, that all antiquity affords.

"That waters signify people, holy Scripture tells us in the Apocalypse, when saying, *The waters which thou sawest, upon which that harlot sitteth, are peoples, and multitudes, and nations of the heathen, and tongues.* And the like figure we see is contained in the Sacrament of the cup : for since Christ bare us all, who also bare our sins, we perceive that the people is to be understood in the water, while the blood of Christ is shown in the wine. When, therefore, water is mingled with wine in the cup, the people is made one with Christ, and the host of the believing is associated and joined with Him, in whom they have believed. Which association and conjunction of water and of wine is so made in the cup of the Lord, that there can be no separation of either from the commixture. Whence it cometh, that nothing can separate the Church, that is, the multitude constituting the Church, and maintaining faithfully and with unmoved constancy, that faith which it hath received, from Christ, so as to shake their inseparable love, or to put an end to it. Therefore on no account can water be offered alone, in the consecration of the cup, nor wine alone : for if any one offers only wine, the blood of Christ begins to exist without us, but if the water be alone, the people begins to be without Christ : but when both are mixed together, and combined by a perfect union, then is the spiritual and heavenly Sacrament perfected. And so neither water alone, nor wine alone, is the cup of the Lord, unless each be mingled with the other ; just as neither flour alone, nor water alone, can be the body of the Lord ; but both must be joined together, and united in the substance of one loaf. In which Sacrament also the people is displayed united ; for as many grains collected together, and mingled and joined one with another, make one loaf; so in Christ, who is the heavenly bread, we know that there is but one body, with which the whole number of the faithful is conjoined and made one."

Now here, either both are transubstantiated, the water and the wine, or neither is: but if the water is transubstantiated, it is into the whole body of Christ's people: that is, water[1] no longer remains in the cup, but the whole body of Christ's people is there bodily in its stead: but this is absurd: therefore the wine is not transubstantiated according to the opinion of Cyprian here expressed.

Or again: either both are represented, Christ's blood and the people, or neither is. But the people are represented; for Cyprian says so (as he does indeed of Christ's blood, though I would overlook for a moment the actual assertion), and therefore according to Cyprian, Christ's blood is represented. But this is not the doctrine of Rome.[2]

There are also in the same Epistle, from which we have been now quoting, several passing expressions decidedly anti-Romish; and which we should have adduced as affording no vague intimation of Cyprian's judgment, if we had not had the above-mentioned stronger passages to rest our argument upon. Such are, for instance, "Non potest *videri* sanguis ejus, quo redempti et vivificati sumus, esse in calice quando vinum desit,"[3] instead of non potest *esse* or *fieri* sanguis ejus —in calice. And again, " Quia passionis ejus intentionem in sacrificiis omnibus facimus (*passio est* enim *Domini* sacrificium quod offerimus) [instead of, *Dominus* est enim hostia quam offerimus, or the like,] nihil aliud quam quod ille fecit facere debemus."[4]

---

[1] Aquas, &c., p. 108.

[2] In fact, the Romanists do away with the sacramental nature of the Eucharist altogether, by removing wholly the thing signifying: so that there is no outward sign. Moreover in making a *miracle* of their transubstantiation, they deprive the presence of Christ in the Eucharist of all *mystery*: and the solemn name of the Sacrament of the Altar, so common in the old Fathers, *the stupendous mysteries*, is really inapplicable to that Sacrament according to their view of it. Nor should it be forgotten, that they thus lower a mystery into a miracle, which is spiritually a much inferior thing (*greater things than these shall he do; because I go unto My Father*; John xiv. 12; see also John v. 20 and i. 50) in order to provide that which we are expressly told profiteth nothing; for *it is the Spirit that quickeneth, the flesh profiteth nothing*.

[3] Page 104.

[4] Page 109.

Surely we have here stronger evidence than we could have expected, under the circumstances, of Cyprian's judgment against Rome, in her innovations in the doctrine of the Eucharist: and were it not that it would extend this chapter unduly, I should show, that we have equally strong, and most express testimony against those who deny the real presence of Christ in the Lord's Supper, and the spiritual virtual change of the elements in that solemn feast. On a review of the whole Epistle to Cæcilius, we arrive (as it seems to me) at the following doctrines concerning the Eucharist, as taught by St Cyprian: doctrines of the Catholic Church every one of them, and of the Church of England, because she is Catholic; but not doctrines of those who actually or virtually dissent from Catholic truth and communion; not doctrines of those who embrace the additional and superinduced dogmas of the Church of Rome.

'In the holy Eucharist, there is a commemorative celebration of Christ's death; for therein we ever mention Christ's passion, which is indeed the sum of our offering. But there is not a commemorative celebration only, but also an oblation to God; and a feast upon the sacrifice of Christ: wherein we not only express our faith and thankfulness in and for, but receive the benefits of, His death and passion: such as remission of our sins, and grace and strength, according as our need may be. And since our need is daily, daily we should receive this means of grace; or, at least, as often as may be, as our Lord hath taught us to pray, Give us this day our daily bread. And in this heavenly feast we eat and drink Christ's body and blood virtually, while we eat and drink bread and wine actually; the one being pressed with our teeth, the other being fed upon by our faith: and so that we receive not the benefit merely as being engaged in a solemn service, or merely as being in general, and by the whole ceremony, excited to a higher devotion, and so blessed with a more singular grace;— but we receive an appropriate and especial grace in the very act of receiving the consecrated elements; perhaps even a peculiar blessing with each part of the Sacrament. Nor is it right to separate any essential part of the Eucharist from the rest; and the cup is essential, both in the consecration, and in the communion or receiving: therefore the cup may not be taken away, either from the Eucharist, or from the communicant; and those who should take it away from the people would be guilty of an awful boldness in disturbing a divine institution, and an apostolic tradition and custom; and of sacrilege against the sacrament and the Church; and of tyranny and injustice towards those whom they should deprive of any portion of the Sacrament, with its appropriate graces and blessings.

'As for those who leave the Church, they deprive themselves of all sacramental benefit in the Eucharist, which can only be validly administered in the Church. We need not much care if some of them teach a lower tone of doctrine concerning these tremendous mysteries, which they imagine that they celebrate; since it is certain that they cannot descend in their doctrinal views, below the efficacy of their own ceremonial: for the Holy Ghost doth not animate a schismatical body; and where the Holy Ghost is not, the Eucharist can receive no valid consecration, and convey no spiritual benefit. But though viewed relatively to themselves only, the doctrine of the schismatic may not deserve a refutation; yet if a time should come at which a spirit of liberalism should give importance in the eyes of those who maintain the Catholic communion, with too little of the Catholic spirit, to the reasonings which would disturb our doctrine, and subvert our discipline (and since Cyprian's day perhaps such a time has come), then it may be necessary to reply specifically to the objections of heretics, and to vindicate the mystery and dignity of the Holy Eucharist from their carnal reasoning, and from their irreverence.'

If I have added a few light touches to complete this sketch, those who are best able to judge will confess that they are in total harmony with Cyprian's own hand: nay, were it not for the fear of extending this study over a yet more disproportionate part of the work, I believe I could fill up every part of the picture with the lineaments and colours of St Cyprian himself.

## CHAPTER XIII.

Revolutions in the Roman Empire.—Questions of Fidus touching a lapsed Bishop, and the Case of Infant Baptism.—The Case of Fortunianus:—Of Basilides and Martialis:—Of Marcianus of Arles.—The Insolence of Pupianus.

MEANWHILE revolutions succeeded one another in the Roman empire, which materially benefited the external condition of the Church. We have already mentioned the loss of the Decii in the autumn of 251, and the renewal of the persecution by Gallus. The Goths, before whom the Decii had fallen, *though*, or rather *because*, their retreat had been purchased at a great price, still remained formidable enemies of the Roman crown and empire: and while Gallus was reposing in the luxuries of his capital, Æmilianus, the governor of Pannonia and Mæsia, had advanced against the Barbarians in Illyria, and repulsed them. The money collected for a tribute to the Goths, was converted by the victorious general to a more popular and more politic use; distributing it as a donation to the legions, he was proclaimed Emperor on the field. Gallus, who went to meet the usurper, was deserted by his army, and murdered; and Æmilianus was confirmed by the senate in the dignity conferred on him by the army. This was in the April of 253.

But the avenger of Gallus tarried not long. Valerian had been sent to bring the legions of Gaul to Germany, to the aid of Gallus: and though too late to save his master, he arrived in time to receive the fruits of his deposition and murder, without the guilt of either. At the approach of Valerian,

Æmilianus was slain by his army, and Valerian was acknowledged emperor by the Roman world, with more of unanimity than usually appeared on such occasions.

The disturbances in the empire following the revolt of Æmilianus, had occasioned a partial repose in the Church: and Valerian seems to have made it one of the earliest acts of his government, to confirm the security of the Christians. In the first dawn of a less troubled day, the chair of Lucius, at Rome, had been filled by the election and consecration of Stephen, on the thirteenth of May (253), after it had been vacant eight days. And now that a serene day had fully opened upon the Church, Cyprian took the earliest opportunity to convoke a provincial synod of the African Bishops. At this synod sixty-six Bishops were assembled; and from their consistory an answer was returned to an Epistle of one Fidus (of whom we know nothing), in which two questions had been submitted to Cyprian, the answers to both of which are important, as affording the synodical judgment of a provincial council of those days, with the important concurrence of Cyprian, upon two points of primitive discipline and order.

Victor, a Presbyter, had lapsed; and Therapius, Bishop of Bulla, had received him to communion, before he had fulfilled the appointed penitential course. Of this Fidus wrote to acquaint Cyprian; and he, with his associates at the Synod, proceeded to reprimand Therapius, who was one of their number; but determined that Victor should retain the privilege improperly, though with a Bishop's authority, extended to him.

Here we have the important rule recognised, that the act of a Bishop (and by parity of reasoning of any other ecclesiastical Minister) may be valid, though it be improper and irregular; that is of course, provided that the act itself, supposing it to be done with every circumstance of propriety, is within the limits of his office. For the judgment of the Bishops proceeded upon the principle, that the peace of the Church once given, in whatever manner, by a Bishop, ought not to be recalled.[1]

[1] *Ep.* lix. p. 98.

The second question of Fidus related to the Baptism of new-born infants. He had declared his opinion, that they ought not to be baptised within the second or third days from their birth; with a doubt whether they ought not to be kept unbaptised even till the eighth day: arguing for the first delay, that children at their birth were in such a sense unclean, as to present a repulsive appearance, and to make us naturally unwilling to impart to them the kiss of peace, which was in those days a part of the ceremonial of Baptism:[1] and grounding his preference for the still longer interval on the analogy of Baptism with the Jewish rite of Circumcision. The issue of this appeal to Cyprian is conclusive against the doctrine and practice of Antipædobaptists; and the question of Fidus, both from the answer which it elicited, and from the form in which it is proposed, is almost as important in its results, as it is in itself unsound and absurd. For it is inconceivable that Fidus should have grounded his objection against baptising until after the second or third day on such a whimsical reason, if there had been the shadow of an argument in his favour from the practice of the Church. And as for his reason for deferring Baptism until the eighth day, because of the analogy between Baptism and Circumcision, this argument, which is neither absurd nor fanciful, but in itself pious and reasonable enough, must *on that very account* have already prevailed with the Church, unless the point had been otherwise settled by Apostolic and Catholic usage. So that by a singular infelicity, the reasonableness of the arguments of Fidus, where they are reasonable, tells as much against his cause, as their absurdity, where they are absurd.

It is to be observed, moreover, that the reasoning of Fidus from the analogy of Baptism with Circumcision, for delaying Baptism for eight days, is precisely opposed to the reasoning of the Antipædobaptists of later ages, who will not admit any analogy at all, extending to the age of the recipients, between the initiatory rites of Judaism and Christianity.

I have anticipated the answer to the question proposed by

[1] See Bingham, *Orig. Ecc.* xii. iv. 5.

Fidus: it was simply, that Baptism is to be denied to none, on account of their youth or age. As for the strange fancies of Fidus, St Cyprian reminds him (and the allusion contains a hidden rebuke), that to the pure all things are pure; and that since God fashioneth us even in the womb, the new-born babe coming more immediately from the hands of God, rather claims our more affectionate and reverential embrace. When Elisha raised the widow's son, he put his own mouth and each of his limbs on the mouth and corresponding members of the child; a thing not to be understood literally, or, at least, not without a spiritual meaning; for the different dimensions of the man and of the child seem to forbid such a contact: herein then we are taught, that when once fashioned by the hand of God, all men are in a spiritual and divine sense equal. As for Circumcision, the type was done away, when the antitype appeared; and Christ rising on the eighth day, or the day after the Sabbath, procured for us a spiritual circumcision, into which we may be baptised at any time; and, in a word, if there be a difficulty in the admission of any to the laver of regeneration and the sacrament of remission, it should rather seem to affect those old and hardened offenders, who have added to their original corruption, many and long offences; and not infants, who are personally guiltless, and bear the sin and death only of the race from which they spring.

In the too hasty admission of Victor to communion, we have already seen an instance of the usual attendants upon a temporary repose in the Church, after persecution. We are now called on to notice several other instances of a like kind, though of much greater importance; for the attention of Cyprian was now variously occupied by the return of Bishops in Africa, in Spain, and in Gaul, to the exercise of the spiritual functions from which they had been justly and canonically deposed for apostasy. The first case, which is also the simplest, and the least important in itself and in its results, is that of Fortunianus, Bishop of Assuri. It may be told in a few words.

Fortunianus had fallen in the late persecution into the most grievous form of apostasy, having sacrificed to idols, and incurred the extreme penalty of the Sacrificati.[1] But after the persecution had ceased, he looked back with regret on the forfeited honours and emoluments of his Episcopal functions,[2] and endeavoured again to obtrude himself into the office which he had thus voluntarily rejected; and of which, so far as we are able to judge from the slight notices that we have of him, he had never been worthy. It seems probable, that, on the defection of Fortunianus, Epictetus had been chosen to succeed him; for it is to him by name, together with the Assuritani in general, that Cyprian directs his Epistle; and to whom he declares the necessity of maintaining in this, as in every instance, the discipline of the Church; which appointed, that persons in the situation to which Fortunianus had degraded himself, should never, even after long penance, rise to any station above that of the lay communicants. As for Fortunianus, he says that he had better have spent his time in the appointed and appropriate penance, than sought to approach the Altar of God, after having sacrificed to Devils; or to exhort others to fidelity and courage, having proved himself a coward and an apostate. If any man worship the beast and his image, he shall be tormented in the presence of the holy Angels; and shall he who is thus marked out for eternal wrath venture to approach God in so sacred a character, wherein not he only, but the people also are concerned? Without the Holy Ghost is no Eucharist; and how can he who has denied his Lord, and despises the discipline of the Church, to which the Holy Ghost is promised, look for that Spirit to sanctify his ministrations? Fortunianus, then, was on no account to be restored to his forfeited Episcopate.

I know not that we have any farther account of Fortunianus in ecclesiastical history, and suppose therefore that the judgment of Cyprian was held conclusive by all parties.

[1] " Post gravem lapsum." *Ep.* lxiv. p. 110. " Quasi post aras diaboli accedere ad altare Dei fas sit." P. 111.
[2] " Stipes, et oblationes, et lucra desiderant." P. 111.

A greater complication of circumstances, and the bearing of the whole on the claims of the Church and Bishop of Rome, make the next instance in which the judgment of Cyprian was sought on a like occasion far more important. Basilides and Martialis, two Spanish Bishops, had fallen into many very heinous offences, in the greater part of which they were equally implicated: they had incurred the guilt of the *Libellatici*, one of those classes into which the lapsed were distributed for the purpose of apportioning their ecclesiastical penance. The separate offences of these two delinquents Cyprian himself enumerates in the following order: Basilides, besides his apostasy, had blasphemed God in sickness, a crime which he himself confessed; Martialis had often sat with the college of the heathen priests, at the gross and obscene feasts of the Gentiles; and had followed also the heathen rites of sepulture for his sons, depositing their remains with the bodies of aliens and idolaters: besides which, both had been guilty of other offences.

Basilides, conscience stricken at the complication of guilt with which he was overwhelmed, had voluntarily confessed his unworthiness to retain his Episcopal functions, and had retreated into the rank of penitents; confessing that he could justly look for no greater lenity, than to be received in due time as a lay-communicant. Martialis has left no record of his repentance even for a time; and there is no hint that he ever abdicated his Episcopal chair, or concurred in the justice of the sentence by which he was deprived: both however were judicially deposed from the Order which they had disgraced; I say both, for I conceive that the voluntary secession of Basilides would not have so voided his chair as to make the appointment of his successor canonical, which however Cyprian declares it to have been: or perhaps his secession was coetaneous with the sentence of the Bishops; and, like Uzziah, "they thrust him out from thence; yea, himself hasted also to go out, because the Lord had smitten him." However, though it is not actually mentioned, I can only suppose that a synod of Bishops, having adjudged the case of both delinquents, declared their seats void, and proceeded to consecrate other Bishops as their successors. This would have been according to the universal custom of the Church; it is not too much, therefore, thus to fill up the blank in the history.

However this was, Martialis determined, if possible, to maintain the dignity by cunning,[1] which he had forfeited by crime: and Basilides also, repenting of his repentance, and lamenting not his sins but his degradation, when it kept him from the high station which he had held, in a Church no longer persecuted; endeavoured also by a bold and nefarious policy, to regain his Episcopate. He sent, therefore, a false statement of the whole affair to Stephen, Bishop of Rome, entreating that he would communicate with him as with a Bishop of the Church; and hoping to deceive the distant Prelate into such a measure, and thus to obtain the powerful countenance of his support. The fraud of Basilides succeeded to his heart's content. Stephen was deceived, and endeavoured to restore him to his forfeited dignity. But the principles of Catholic polity were not to be so readily surmounted; and though he succeeded in the means, Basilides wholly failed in the end which he had in view.

Yet for a while he seemed to triumph; and Martialis shared in the temporary advantage of his scheme. The important sanction of Stephen's support induced many to receive Basilides again, as if he had been duly restored to his forfeited dignity, and to the Episcopal communion: and the similarity of their cases probably induced them to associate Martialis with Basilides, as equally worthy of the same lenity.[2] But those who duly respected the sanctity of the Episcopate and the Apostolic order of the Church, still adhered to the

---

[1] Nec Martiali potest profuisse *fallacia* quo minus ipse quoque elictis gravibus involutus, &c.   *Ep.* lxviii. p. 119.

[2] I have found it impossible to separate exactly between the acts of those two delinquents, and to give a clear history of Martialis, without sometimes associating him with Basilides (where history does not speak explicitly), whose case is more fully narrated.

communion of Felix and Sabinus, who had been consecrated to fill the chairs of the two apostates, in spite of the declared or inferred judgment of the Bishop of Rome.

These virtuous and wise Christians, however, sought farther support in the concurrence of Cyprian, and accordingly wrote to him an account of what had passed, asking his advice. He wrote therefore the Epistle, from which we derive all our information on this subject, to the people of Legio, Asturia, and Emerita, who were chiefly concerned in the decision of the question. In this Epistle he most clearly and unhesitatingly declares that the favourable judgment of Rome in such a case was nothing worth: that Basilides had added to the catalogue of his offences, already sufficiently numerous, by venturing to appeal to Rome: that they who retained his communion on the ground of a favourable judgment from Rome were mistaken in their principle, and wrong in their conduct: and that those who neglected in this case the decree of Pope Stephen, and maintained the Catholic discipline of the Church, were worthy of all praise. And now this Epistle of Cyprian is a standing record of Catholic principles, in direct opposition to more than one branch of the usurped authority of the Bishop of Rome.[1]

Another event occurred about this time, in which the interference of St Cyprian was earnestly sought, after an ineffectual appeal to Stephen, Bishop of Rome; and in which the conduct of Cyprian admirably exemplifies his principle of the equal and concurrent jurisdiction of Bishops; while the whole affair greatly magnifies his importance in the Church of that age, and displays at the same time his practical wisdom, and his decision of character.

It will be remembered how decidedly the schism of Nova-

---

[1] Whatever concerns the Papal supremacy, I have viewed in the light of Cyprian's history and writings in a former work: "*The testimony of St Cyprian against Rome; an Essay towards determining the judgment of St Cyprian, touching Papal Supremacy.*" To this I shall take the liberty of referring, when that particular branch of our controversy with Rome is in question.

tian in the Church of Rome had been repudiated, and how promptly his errors had been condemned by the whole body of Catholic Bishops. But Marcianus, Bishop of Arles, had joined the party of Novatian, and embraced those erroneous principles of discipline, according to which those who had once fallen were refused the privilege of penance, and cut off from all hope of being received again into Church communion. Upon this, Faustinus, Bishop of Lyons, a neighbouring see, wrote to Stephen of Rome; who, both for the importance of his see, and for the especial degree in which that Church had been affected by the schism and error of Novatian, was the Bishop most concerned, and whose judgment should naturally have the greatest weight; beseeching him to interfere in this extremity, for the maintenance of the Catholic faith and unity. This request of Faustinus had been accompanied with the like appeal from other Bishops in the Gallican Provinces; but at present Stephen had not been moved to give any attention to the case.

In this supineness of Stephen, Faustinus once and again applied to Cyprian; who was next to Stephen in adventitious importance, whether in general from the greatness of his see, or in the present question from his having been much engaged with proceedings touching the case of Novatian; and whose Episcopate gave him an equal right to interfere (unless he himself greatly mistook the principles of the Catholic Church); while his personal character, and his greater experience in the Episcopate, elevated him in moral influence even above the Bishop of Rome, lately elected, and a man, as his after history proves, scarce worthy to sustain the dignity which descended upon him from Saint Cornelius.

Cyprian, then, bearing in mind the duty of the Episcopal office, to sustain the sound part of the Church at all times against the encroachments of heresy and schism, having been thus twice appealed to, wrote to Stephen,[1] to move him to exertion on this occasion, and to suggest (unless one who reads the Epistle will rather say to dictate) the course which he should

[1] *Ep.* lxvii. p. 115.

pursue. Having briefly mentioned the circumstances before related, and touched upon the duty of Bishops in such a case, he proceeds: "You ought therefore to write very ample letters to our fellow-Bishops in Gaul, that they may no longer suffer Marcianus, in his pride and obstinacy, and in his enmity against true piety and the peace of the Church, to insult over our whole college, as one not excommunicated by us, but as one who has long boasted, that following in the steps of Novatian, he has voluntarily seceded from our fellowship; whereas in fact Novatian, whom he follows, has been long ago decreed excommunicate, and an enemy to the Church."
. . . . "How absurd is it, then, dearest brother, that in spite of the excommunication and total repudiation of Novatian by the Bishops of the whole world, we should now suffer his satellites to make a jest of us, and to erect themselves into judges of the true majesty and dignity of the Church! Let letters be directed by you to the province and people of Arles,[1] that when Marcianus has been excommunicated, they may proceed to elect another in his place; and that the flock of Christ, which is at present scattered and wounded by him, and cast under reproach, may be again collected together."

Cyprian proceeds through the rest of the Epistle to state and apply the principles of ecclesiastical polity, on which his interference was grounded, and to urge Stephen by every inducement to make the necessary exertions: "The numerous body of Bishops," says he, "is compacted with the cement of mutual agreement, and by the bond of unity; that if any one of our number should endeavour to introduce heresy, and to tear and scatter the flock of Christ, the rest may interfere, and like good shepherds gather the Lord's sheep into one flock.

[1] *In provinciam et ad plebem Arelate consistantem:* and before, *Ad coepiscopos nostros.* The letters directed to the Bishops of Gaul probably respected the judicial sentence against Marcianus, which they alone could pronounce, and the consequent excommunication, of which they were the proper ministers. The letters to the people of Arles respected, doubtless, the election of a successor to the deprived delinquent, in which they were not without a voice.

For what, if some port has become unsafe by the destruction of its breakwaters; do not the sailors run into other neighbouring ports, where they may enter without danger, and ride in safety? Or if some inn on the road be infested and occupied by brigands, so that whoever enters it is in danger of being robbed; do not travellers, so soon as this is known, seek safer inns on their journey, where they may lodge in security and peace? And so it should be now with us, that we may receive our brethren, who are driven against the rocks of Marcianus, and seek the safe harbour of the Church, and that we may afford to them admission into such a safe inn as that which is mentioned in the Gospel, where those who have fallen among thieves and been wounded, may be hospitably received and attended to."

And afterwards: "Let him not pronounce but receive sentence; nor let him act as if it were his part to judge the College of Bishops, when he is himself condemned by their whole number. For the glorious reputation of our predecessors, the blessed martyrs Cornelius and Lucius, is to be maintained; whose memory since we honour, much more should *you*, who are their vicar and successor, exalt and maintain it by the weight of your authority. For they, when they were full of the Spirit of God, and were going to martyrdom, thought, with the consent of us all, that the lapsed should be restored to the peace of the Church." . . . "Signify to me in plain terms, who is substituted in the place of Marcianus at Arles, that I may know to whom to refer our brethren, and to whom to write."

We may suppose that this Epistle of Cyprian to Pope Stephen had the desired effect; we hear not, that I know of, any thing more of Marcianus. However, whatever may have been its use then, it is now one of our most valuable monuments of antiquity, towards a just estimate of the authority of the Bishop of Rome: the substance of this letter, and still more its tone, and the circumstances out of which it arose, where an appeal was made to a Bishop of Carthage, subsequent to a similar appeal to the Bishop of Rome, cannot be fairly reconciled with the present system of Papal Supremacy.[1]

There is something of interest in the character and practices of such men as Novatian; whose name survives in a party which they originate, and in which their erroneous principles are embodied; while such men as Fortunianus, Marcianus, Basilides, and Martialis, remembered only for some single scene in which they bore a disgraceful part, would swell the pages of history to worse than no purpose, but that their very vices, calling for the interference of better men, serve as occasions for the practical application of principles which are never antiquated, and never useless. One Pupianus, of whom we have next to speak, falls even into a lower rank than these latter; and without exciting a tinge of interest, or giving occasion for any thing more than the display of patience and forbearance, by his impertinence and conceit, obliges us to record his name and his folly: and yet even to him we owe something; for the marvellous condescension of Cyprian in affording a circumstantial refutation of his charges, and a full vindication of his own character, has supplied us with many facts, of which we have availed ourselves in the former portions of this work.

The very salutation of the Epistle of Cyprian, to which we allude, has been supposed to afford an indication of one of the impertinences of Pupianus: "Cyprian, who is also called Thascius, to his brother Florentius, who is also called Pupianus, health!" Thus writes Cyprian, and the most probable reason for this strange address is, that Pupianus had insolently addressed him by his heathen appellation Thascius, as if to deny his worthiness of the Christian name; an unrighteous taunt, which Cyprian merely retorts, by reminding him also of his Gentile cognomen.

Not to take up too much time in repeating either the accusation of Pupianus, or the vindication of St Cyprian, we may gather, that in general Pupianus, who had held com-

[1] See *Barrow on the Pope's Supremacy*, p. 346, Ed. Oxon. 1836; or *the Testimony of St Cyprian against Rome*, pp. 110, *et seq.*

munion with Cyprian before the Decian persecution, and had even admired his singular virtue and humility, had been so much puffed up by his own confession, while Cyprian had discreetly used his freedom to retire till the heat of the persecution was past, that he not only judged himself exalted far beyond Cyprian in dignity, but even erected himself into a judge of his character, and a reprover of his actions. Nor yet did he content himself with a harsh judgment upon this particular act; but making his own inferences from the past occurrences, he attributed all those unhappy dissensions which had divided the Church on occasion of Novatian's schism, to the injudicious and haughty conduct of the Bishop of Carthage: and forgetting what was due to the office and dignity of a Bishop, he believed without farther inquisition, whatever base report the enemies of Cyprian invented, though they were some of them such as it is shameful to mention, and the very Gentiles abhor. Actuated by such shameless reports, Pupianus ventured to declare Cyprian unworthy of the Episcopate, and to renounce his communion.

Cyprian does not evade any of these charges, nor hesitate to commend himself, as the Apostle Paul had done, when circumstances made it necessary. He reminds Pupianus, that the pains of persecution had not fallen on him alone, saying with something of irony, "The approaching persecution lifted you up, indeed, to the very highest dignity of martyrdom; but me it degraded with the oppressive weight of a proscription, when it was publicly proclaimed, *If any one possesses or retains any of the goods of Cæcilius Cyprian, a Bishop of the Christians ;*—that those who would not believe me to be a Bishop, by the choice of God, might at least afford credit to the proscription of the Devil." The accusation of pride, Cyprian refutes from the testimony of the Gentiles, and from the former admission of Pupianus himself; and most justly retorts it upon the insolent assailant. The general charges he repudiates by the witness of the whole Church, both of the Clergy, and of the laity; of holy widows and virgins; of martyrs, and of confessors from their prisons. But after all, the burden of his vindication against the report of aliens and schismatics, rests on the higher ground of his sacred office: and he pleads the dignity and sanctity of his Episcopate in a tone, which could not be assumed in a parallel case with any effect in these days, when we have learned to look on sanctity without reverence, and on dignity without fear.

"Is it to be supposed," he asks, "that God, who suffereth not a sparrow to fall to the ground without His knowledge, should suffer Bishops to be ordained without His providence? If you believe such revolting reports against me, what is it but to believe, that neither by God, nor through Him, Bishops are appointed? Is my own testimony of myself greater than the witness of God? And yet now I am called to answer the accusations of men ungodly, cut off from the Church, and deprived of the Holy Ghost, though the witness of God is and has been with me, in my Episcopate.[1] Is there no force still in the example and precepts of Christ and of the Apostle, who would not insult and revile God's High Priest; but taught us not to speak evil of the ruler of the people of God?"

"What pride! what arrogance! That rulers and Bishops should be called before your tribunal; and that, unless we are acquitted before *you*, and absolved by *your* sentence, Lo! for these six years past the brethren have had no Bishop, the people no leader, the flock no pastor, the Church no ruler, Christ no representative, and God no priest! Let Pupianus, forsooth, be brought in, to ratify the judgment of God and of Christ, lest so great a number of the faithful, who have been gathered into the Church under our Episcopate, should seem

---

[1] This principle is preserved in the Scottish Episcopal Church; or, as I should rather speak, in the Church Catholic in Scotland; which declares in one of its Canons (XXXVI.), "No accusation shall be received against a Deacon, or Presbyter, or Bishop, unless proceeding from and supported by the testimony of credible persons, *who are regular communicants in the Scottish Episcopal Church.*" I take this opportunity of observing, that the constitution and state of a Church which we hold to be Catholic, and with which, therefore, we maintain communion, is not the most unappropriate part of the information of an Anglican Churchman.

to have departed without the hope of salvation: lest the multitude of converts should be adjudged to have received, through us, a baptism void of grace, and of the Holy Spirit: lest peace and communion, extended to so many penitents, should be null, without your confirmation! Deign, then, now at least, to pronounce your sentence upon us, and to ratify our Episcopate by your recognition; that God and Christ may be at liberty to acknowledge with thanks, that by you a Priest has been restored to their altar, and a ruler to their people!"

In such a strain does Cyprian continue his letter, which he closes in these words: "Such is the answer which I have made in the innocency of my conscience, and in my full trust in my Lord and my God. You have my letter, I have yours. At the last day both will be read over before the judgment-seat of Christ."[1]

[1] *Ep.* lxix. p. 124.

## CHAPTER XIV.

The Question of the Baptism of Heretics, and the Controversy arising out of it.—Its origin in Asia Minor :—It is discussed in a Synod at Carthage.—Cyprian's Letter to the Bishops of Numidia.—The Character of several Objections against his Rule.—A Synod of Seventy-Two Bishops assembled at Carthage to determine the question.—Cyprian's account to Stephen of the proceedings of the Synod.—Cyprian's Letter to Jubaianus.

THE great controversy concerning the rebaptising of heretics, which is certainly the most remarkable event that has engaged our attention, both in its conduct and in its consequences, had already excited internal commotion in the Church, and was now to embroil the province over which Cyprian presided, in the general discord.

There is some difficulty in determining the exact dates of the events to which this controversy gave rise, and the sequence of the several minor occurrences is often obscure. The long and learned note appended to Sect. xviii. Sæc. III. of Mosheim's Commentaries of the Affairs of the Church before Constantine, seems to me to present the most judicious arrangement of the several events; I shall take that historian therefore as my guide. Mosheim, however, is no guide in theology: and it is well, that though the records of those times have left the dates and order of certain occurrences obscure, they speak clearly enough on the theological questions which we are about to touch.

The broader features of the controversy are readily traced in the Epistles of Cyprian and Firmilian, which afford also some indications of personal character, in the several actors in the busy scene, which may give interest to the repulsive but most important story of theological disputation. The character of Stephen, Bishop of Rome, must be allowed to suffer under the lash of his opponents' satire and arguments, almost as much as the subsequent claims of the Church over which he presided suffer from the development of truly catholic principles in the conduct of the controversy. If the Epistles of Stephen, which are lost, would have placed the conduct and character of that Prelate in a better light, than that in which they appear in the accounts of his opponents, I sincerely wish that they were forthcoming. His conduct must have been outrageous indeed, to exceed the picture of him which the historian is obliged to present, from existing records; and yet the Church of Rome has been suspected of suppressing his Epistles, that the character of the Pontiff might not suffer by the additional light which they would throw upon the history of those times. Perhaps, too, the historians of the Roman obedience have needlessly confused the occurrences in which Stephen took so prominent and heartless a part: for this is certainly a page of history on which they can engage with no great complacency; and they might have rejoiced if Raymond Missorius[1] had succeeded in his attempt to prove, that the Epistles relating to this controversy, attributed to Cyprian and Firmilian, were forged by the Donatists of Africa, whose error sought support from those records.

The question agitated was really one of vital importance. Whether or no those who had received baptism from the hands of an heretic, should be admitted into the Church by a second baptism: or rather (for this is the more correct way of stating the question, though the other is the more common and popular), whether the sprinkling by a heretic should be accounted any baptism at all; and therefore, whether one who had received such a sprinkling should be baptised. This question had never been authoritatively determined in the Church of Christ. The usage of Rome was indeed clear; but

[1] A Franciscan of the last century.

yet no Church at that time imagined the local custom of
Rome a rule for the conduct of all Christendom.  It had been
debated on several occasions; and perhaps it had received
several solutions in different provinces, each particular Church
obeying the decision of its several Bishop, or of the synod of
the province of which it formed a part.  Meanwhile all agreed,
if not in the particular rule or discipline, yet in the much more
important matter, that the Bishop was the centre of authority
in such matters to his own Church, or the synod of provincial
Bishops to each province; and that they did right who followed the determination of the Bishop or the synod respectively, until the paramount authority of the Universal Church
should determine the question.[1]

In Asia, synods had been held at Synnada and Iconium,
and some other places, in which it had been determined, that
heretical baptism was invalid.  In Africa, Agrippinus of Carthage had presided in a Council, at which the same determination was adopted:[2] but the Council was not held to be binding on the whole African Church; for we shall find a smaller
synod of Bishops presently consulting Cyprian on the question,
as if it had not been set at rest.  In Rome, and in the dio-
ceses in its provinces, the opinion seems always to have been,
that they who came over from heresy, and had received
baptism in their separation from the Church, should be
received, nevertheless, without a second baptism; at least
Stephen, who advocated that rule, appeals to the tradition of
his own Church in support of his opinion.

The region in which this difference first created dissension
with Rome, was in Asia Minor; Cappadocia, Cilicia, and the
neighbouring provinces.  Perhaps some Asiatic Christians
may have expressed their opinion upon the subject at Rome;

---

[1] St Augustine to Januarius, *Ep.* liv. vol. ii. p. 167, thus states the
principle which should be adhered to in such matters.  "Faciat quisque
quod in ea ecclesia, in quam venit, invenerit."  In the same Epistle
Augustine gives the celebrated rule of St Ambrose, "ad quam forte
ecclesiam veneris, ejus morem serva, si cuiquam non vis esse scandalo,
nec quemquam tibi."

[2] *Epistles* lxxi. and lxxiii.

and if they did this imprudently, still more if they did it intemperately, they were highly culpable. Perhaps some converted heretics, who had been received into the Church at Rome without baptism, may have been rejected on their return to Asia: or some who had been rejected in Asia may have been received at Rome; and in either case, the discipline of a particular Church, which every other Church ought to respect, was dishonoured. But, from whatever causes, Stephen became all at once highly indignant at the error, as he thought it, of the Asiatic Churches, and wrote to Asia concerning Helenus and Firmilian, and the rest of the Bishops of those parts, threatening to withdraw from their communion, because they repeated the baptism of heretics.[1] The letter of Firmilian, of which we shall presently have much to say, and of which we are all along making great use, shows, that this threat was carried into execution.

While affairs were in this posture between Asia and Rome, Cyprian little thought of the storm which was gathering around him, and was soon to burst over his head. He was settling the state of his own Church and province, after the persecution, with the assistance of thirty-two Bishops assembled with him at Carthage. During their session, a question was put to Cyprian by some Numidian Bishops (eighteen in number) upon the very matter which was then embroiling the Eastern Church with Rome. The letter of the Numidians is lost, but Cyprian's answer will afford a sufficient indication of its contents, and will put us in possession of his own judgment upon the disputed question, with that of the thirty-two Bishops assembled with him in council.

This letter contains a very careful and comprehensive statement of the principle upon which Cyprian and his adherents determined the question touching heretical baptism. St Cyprian himself evidently views it in that light, for he again and again refers to it, as containing a clear statement of his opinions, and of the ground on which they rested. As it is very short, as compared with its importance, I shall give it entire.

[1] Eusebius vii. 5.

"Cyprian and thirty-one others, to Januarius and the other Bishops of Numidia.

"When we were all assembled in council, we read, dearest brethren, your Epistle to us, on the matter of those who *seem* to have been baptised[1] among heretics and schismatics, whether, when they came into the Catholic Church, which is one and true, they ought to be baptised? And although you yourselves maintain, in constancy and purity, the Catholic rule upon that point; yet, since you have thought good out of our mutual charity to consult us, we send you our opinion, which is not new, but the same which was established long since by our predecessors, and which we have observed ourselves, with as great unanimity as that which you have evinced; for this we believe, and hold as an undoubted verity, that no one can be baptised out of the Church, since there is but one baptism appointed, and that in the holy Church; and since it is written, *They have left Me, the fountain of living water, and have hewn out for themselves broken fountains, which can hold no water.*[2] And again, another Scripture speaks in a voice of warning: *Abstain from strange water, and of a fountain of strange water drink not.*[3] The water, therefore, should first be cleansed and sanctified by the Priest, that it may avail by its use in baptism to wash away the sins of him who is immersed in it: wherefore saith the Lord by the prophet Ezekiel, *and I will sprinkle clear water upon you, and ye shall be clear from all your filthiness; and from all your idols will I cleanse you; a new heart also will I give you, and a new spirit will I put within you.*[4] But how can he cleanse and sanctify the water, who is himself unclean, and upon whom the Holy Ghost is not; for the Lord saith, *Whatsoever the*

---

[1] "Baptizati videntur." Cyprian constantly makes the distinction between a real and a seeming baptism: and thus he, quite as truly as Stephen, taught, that none could be *re*baptised. St Cyril says, "none but heretics are rebaptised, since their former baptism was not baptism." Catechesis, Introductory Lecture, p. 7, in the translation in the Library of Fathers, Oxon., 1838.

[2] Jer. ii. 13.  
[3] Prov. vi. 24.  
[4] Ezekiel xxxvi. 25, 26.

unclean person toucheth shall be unclean?[1]  Or how can one give to another remission of sins in baptism, who cannot himself lay down his own sins, being without the Church?

"Besides, the very intercession which is made at Baptism is a witness of the truth. For when we say, '*Dost thou believe in eternal life, and in the remission of sins by the holy Church?*' we mean that remission of sins is not given except in the Church; but that among the heretics, where the Church is not, sins cannot be remitted. They then who assert that heretics can baptise, must either change the interrogation, or must vindicate the truth against their own opinion, by the very use of it; unless, indeed, they contend, that even those have a Church whose baptism they admit.

"Moreover, he who is baptised must also be anointed, that when he has received the chrism, that is the unction, he may be indeed the anointed of God, and have in him the grace of Christ. Now there is a Eucharistic oblation of oil, from the matter of which the baptised are anointed, after the oil has been consecrated on the altar; but he cannot have consecrated the creature of oil, who had neither an altar nor a church. Whence, again, there can be no spiritual unction among heretics, since it is quite clear that oil cannot be consecrated, and made an Eucharistic oblation, by them.[2] And

---

[1] Numb. xix. 22.

[2] This passage is difficult, and I have seen no explanation which removes the difficulty; I have therefore ventured to render it paraphrastically, conveying an explanation together with a translation; yet by no means positively asserting that my explanation is the right one. The words in the original are as follows. "*Porro autem Eucharistia est, unde baptizati unguuntur oleo in altari sanctificato. Sanctificare autem non potuit olei creaturam qui nec altare habuit nec ecclesiam. Unde nec unctio spiritualis apud hæreticos potest esse, quando constet oleum sanctificari et Eucharistiam fieri apud illos omnino non posse.*" The word *Eucharistia* here, has been always, so far as I know, made to refer to *the* Eucharist, or the Supper of the Lord, administered to the newly baptised. But though chrism and confirmation were held to be necessary to the completion of Baptism, I know not that *the* Eucharist ever was: and at any rate, if he had then been speaking of the Supper of the Lord, Cyprian would have made it another member of the argument, and not confused it with the

we ought to bear in mind the Scripture, *Let not the oil of a sinner anoint mine head*.[1] And this warning the Holy Spirit mention of the oil; when he had already separated the mention of the oil from that of the water, which are much more on a par, and much more nearly connected theologically speaking. He would have reasoned thus: The heretic cannot consecrate water, *ergo* he cannot baptise. He cannot consecrate oil, *ergo* he cannot baptise. Neither can he consecrate the Eucharist, *ergo* he cannot baptise. But as the reasoning of Cyprian stands, that third proof of his position is sadly confused with the second, to the great detriment of both; that is, *if*, which I question, he accepted the third at all, as a part of his reasoning, or *if* he is there speaking at all of that oblation which is κατ' ἐξοχὴν, *the* Eucharist. This reasoning will be *seen* in its full force by those who will observe in how orderly a manner Cyprian advances, in this Epistle, from one step of his argument to another, closing each with a reference to Scripture. It will be *felt* by those who know how the Christians of that time were accustomed to speak of the tremendous mysteries of the Christian altar; and who know how very improbable it is, that such an one as St Cyprian should thus speak of those mysteries, as it were, by the way, while the oil of chrism is the real and immediate subject of his reasoning. Thus, neither as an orderly reasoner, nor as a theologian, can Cyprian be supposed to make any reference to the Eucharistic sacrifice in this passage. To speak, too, of *the creature of oil*, is quite analogous to speaking of *the creatures of bread and wine*; which is a usual way of designating those elements, when they were about to be sanctified by an Eucharistic oblation, and invocation of the Holy Ghost. Nor is the analogy between the consecrations of the oil and of the bread and wine too obscure to afford propriety to such a similarity of phrases. St Cyril of Jerusalem says (Cat. Myst. iii. 3 p. 268, of Church's translation), in a passage, by the way, which renders it absolutely impossible that Cyril can have held the doctrine of transubstantiation. "Beware of supposing this to be plain ointment. For as the bread of the Eucharist, after the invocation of the Holy Ghost, is mere bread no longer, but the body of Christ; so also this holy ointment is no more simple ointment, nor (so to say) common, after the invocation, but the gift of Christ; and by the presence of His Godhead, it causes in us the Holy Ghost." And in the title of a prayer in the Apostolical constitution we find the very word *Eucharist*, as applied to a part of the ceremonial of unction; ΕΥΧΑΡΙΣΤΙΑ περὶ τοῦ μυστικοῦ μύρου.

I think I have said enough to show, that the *Eucharistia* of which Cyprian speaks *may* be connected with the oil of chrism, and not with the Sacrament of the Lord's Supper: and if it *may* be, some respect to Cyprian's reasoning will bring us to the conclusion, that it *is* connected with the oil.

[1] Ps. clxi. 5, LXX. and Vulgate.

gave beforehand in the Psalms, lest any, leaving his proper course, and wandering from the path of truth, should be anointed by heretics, and the enemies of Christ.

"And, yet again, what sort of prayer can a sacrilegious and sinful priest offer for the baptised, since it is said, *God heareth not a sinner; but if any one worshippeth Him, and doeth His will, him He heareth?*[1]

"But who can give that which he hath not? or how can he, who has himself lost the Holy Spirit, minister spiritual gifts?

"On the whole then we conclude, that he is to be baptised and renewed, who comes as a novice to the Church; and that he ought to be sanctified within her pale, by those who are themselves holy; since it is written, *Be ye holy, for I am holy, saith the Lord:*[2] so, then, he who has been led into an error, and been baptised without the Church, let him put off this, among his other offences, in the true and Catholic baptism,—that when he would have come to God, while he sought a true priest, he fell into the hands of a sacrilegious one, through deceit and error.

"Finally, to consent to the validity of the baptism of heretics and schismatics is in effect to approve of it. For in this case, either all or none is validly performed. If the heretic could baptise, he could also give the Holy Ghost. But if he who is without the Church cannot give the Holy Ghost, because he is himself without the Holy Ghost, neither can he baptise the convert: for there is one baptism, and one Holy Spirit, and one Church, founded by the Lord Christ upon Peter [or upon a rock[3]], so that in its very foundation it may bear the mark of unity. Hence it follows, that since among them everything is false and empty, nothing of their doing in such matters ought to be acknowledged by us. For what can

---

[1] John ix. 13.      [2] Lev. xix. 2.

[3] See the note of the Benedictine Editors. I have no objection to admit that the Church is founded on Peter: but since there can have been no temptation to convert *Petrum* into *petram;* while there has been such strong temptation to convert *petram* into *Petrum;* various readings in such passages really *do* look suspicious. However, the Romanists must be allowed the benefit of their character for integrity in such matters.

be ratified and confirmed by God which they do who are called His enemies in the Gospel? *He who is not with Me is against Me; he who gathereth not with Me scattereth.*[1] And the blessed Apostle Saint John also, guarding the commandments and precepts of his Lord, has written in his Epistle, *Ye have heard that Antichrist shall come; even now are there many Antichrists, whereby we know that it is the last time. They went out from us, but they were not of us; for if they had been of us, they would no doubt have continued with us.*[2] And from hence we ought to consider, whether they who are enemies of the Lord, and who are called Antichrists, can confer the grace of Christ. Wherefore we, who remain with the Lord, and maintain His unity, and administer the priesthood in His Church according as He has put us in charge, ought to repudiate and reject whatever His adversaries and Antichrists do, and to account it as mere profanation. And to those who escape from error and pravity, and acknowledge the true faith of the one Church, we ought to communicate in all the sacraments of divine grace, and in the verity of unity and faith.

"Dearest brethren, we wish you continued health."[3]

Having given this Epistle entire, we have once for all put the reader in possession of Cyprian's judgment on the point at issue, from which he never swerved. As we follow the controversy, however, in its several turns, we shall mark such new arguments as were elicited by the circumstances of the contest, and were adduced from time to time in answer to new objections.

Though the Council from which the above Epistle was sent, thus confirming the determination of a Numidian Synod, and following the steps of a former Synod in Carthage, may be supposed to have settled the question to the satisfaction of all Catholics in those provinces; yet there were other parts of Africa which were as yet unsupplied with any authoritative rule for the admission of heretics into the Church; and whose

---

[1] Luke xi. 23.  [2] 1 John ii. 18, 19.
[3] *Ep.* lxx. pp. 124, 152, 126.

Bishops, therefore, being left to their private judgment in this matter, might innocently differ in opinion and practice, one from another, and from the Numidian and Carthaginian Churches. Under such circumstances they would gladly obtain the advice of a Bishop, so eminent, both in character and station, as St Cyprian; especially after he had presided in a Council where the question had been debated and determined. Hence we find Cyprian writing to a Bishop in Mauritania, named Quintus, in answer to a request made through one Lucius, a Presbyter, that he would give him his opinion on that subject. "Lucius, our brother Presbyter, has informed me, dearest brother, of your wish," says Cyprian, "that I should send you my judgment concerning those who have received the semblance of Baptism among heretics and schismatics."[1] He sends therefore to Quintus a copy of the letter to the Numidians before given; adding an answer to the objection, that there is but one baptism. "Some will say," says he, "that there is but one baptism. True, but that one must be in the one Catholic Church. But those who admit the baptism of heretics, as well as that of the Church, make two baptisms; or else, which is still worse, prefer the profane and contaminating sprinkling of the heretics, to the one true and lawful baptism of the Church Catholic. Or at any rate, to make but one baptism, yet to recognise the baptism of heretics, is to admit that heretics may truly baptise, and to allow them the power of washing, cleansing, and sanctifying the spiritual man. But this is to grant too much to them; for how can they give that which they have not themselves? We do not say, then, that converts from them to the Church are to be *re*baptised, but that they are to be baptised."

Another objection, which Cyprian discusses in this Epistle, shows that the trick of meeting arguments by reasoning perfectly irrelevant, is by no means peculiar to these days. If the adversaries of truth can find something in ancient custom which looks like a support of their cause on the most superficial view, they are not deterred from adducing it,

[1] *Ep.* lxxi. p. 126.

though if it be examined more deeply, it tells altogether against them. They know that the mass of the people is taken only by the first aspect of things; so that the desired effect will be already produced, before a more candid instructor can teach them to look below the surface.

It had been a primitive and catholic custom, to receive those back again into the Church who had been baptised therein, but had left it, for a time, for the communion of heretics, by penance only and imposition of hands, without a second baptism. This custom respects a case utterly different from that which was now agitated; and if it could be applied at all to the question, it would rather go to support the peculiar sanctity of Baptism administered in the Catholic Church: yet it was adduced, as establishing their point, by those who were for receiving without baptism schismatics, who had not been baptised in the Church. The fair statement of this argument is sufficient for its refutation, without the reasoning of Cyprian; and I almost wonder (especially since he opposes the misapplication of custom more than sufficiently by the mention of the true custom of Africa, founded on the decision of the Council which met under Agrippinus), that he should condescend to meet it by showing that custom against reason is not to be followed. However, he was right in prudence to argue with men according to their folly: and in a future Epistle (to Jubaianus), with equal condescension, and practical wisdom, we find him refuting two other arguments equally irrelevant, which were adduced by the opponents of his opinion, that heretics should be received into the Church by Baptism. The two arguments to which I allude are, (1) That the Church denied not a martyr's crown to them, who died in the true faith, though before Baptism: and, (2) that those who had been baptised by Philip in Samaria were not rebaptised by Peter and John, but only received imposition of hands. Such are some of the arguments against which Cyprian had to contend. I shall not mention them again in their proper order: they deserve to be strung together for their absurdity, and not to form a link in the historical sequence of events.

Cyprian's anxiety to determine this question with the greatest possible authority, seems most plainly to indicate, that he was aware of the full extent of the violence with which Stephen, Bishop of Rome, was likely to proceed against those who differed from him in opinion and practice. The anticipation of a future difference would make him in no degree disposed to submit his judgment to another, or to yield upon any other ground than conclusive reasoning; for he was certainly no slave to foreign influence, and no moral coward: but the coming struggle which could neither shake nor frighten him, would and should make him very desirous to determine the question, with the full concurrence of his comprovincial Bishops; both that the question might be discussed with greater opportunities of arriving at the truth; and that the decision, when made, might carry with it the greater weight.

Urged by these motives, he assembled, shortly after the last Synod had dispersed, a second Synod of seventy-two Bishops; some being present from Numidia, in which province the question had been already determined in an assembly of eighteen Bishops, in accordance with the views of Cyprian, and his comprovincials. In this second Council the decision of the former was confirmed; and a decree was also made upon another matter of discipline, whereby it was ordered, that those who had been ordained by schismatics, and even those who had received Orders in the Church, but had afterwards seceded, should be received, on their return to the Catholic Church, only to lay communion.

Of the proceedings of this second Synod, Cyprian informs Stephen of Rome in the seventy-second of the Cyprianic Epistles. It will be interesting to the reader to observe the tone in which Cyprian speaks to the Roman Pontiff; and that upon a subject of such vital importance, as to justify, at least in Stephen's opinion, the breach of communion with those who ventured to oppose his views.

"I found it necessary, for the discussion and determination of many points, to collect a Synod of several Bishops; in which many things were canvassed and determined: and having decreed that those who have been washed without the Church, and stained with the contaminating touch of the water used by heretics and schismatics, ought to be baptised, when they come over to us, and to the one Church;' we thought it right to communicate this decree especially to you, that we might confer with your gravity and wisdom on a point which so nearly touches the authority of the priesthood, and the unity and dignity with which the Church Catholic is divinely appointed. We hold it insufficient to lay hands upon them for the receiving of the Holy Ghost, unless they also received the Baptism of the Church: for they can only be accounted sons of God fully sanctified, when they have been born again of both sacraments,[1] since it is written, *unless a*

[1] That is, of the sacrament of water for the remission of sins; and of imposition of hands for the receiving of the Holy Ghost: which latter is a sacrament in no other sense than the sign of the cross used in Baptism by us may be called a sacrament; and is not at all a sacrament in the limited polemical sense, in which *we* say that there are but two Sacraments, and in which *the Romanist* says that there are seven. Imposition of hands was held a part and complement of the Sacrament of Baptism.

To the learned it is sufficiently plain, that instances of the application of the term "*sacramentum*," to any ordinance or other subject by the Fathers of the Church, are quite irrelevant in our controversy with Rome touching the number of the Sacraments; for we admit in every other than the limited sense in which the word is used in this controversy, that there are other Sacraments: whereas the Romanist will not admit, that in all those things called "*sacramenta*," by the writers in question, are Sacraments in the same polemical sense. We need not hesitate to speak of *the sacrament* of unity, of *the Lord's Prayer* as *a sacrament*, of *the sacrament* of imposition of hands or *confirmation*, if only we be rightly understood to mean just so much as the Fathers meant, and no more: and if more be necessarily intended, then the Romanist will be as little able to employ the terms "*sacramentum unitatis*," as we to speak of the *sacrament of confirmation*. I know nothing that can better express our view of the matter, than the words of St Augustine, "Sacramentis numero paucissimis, observatione facillimis, significatione præstantissimis, societatem novi populi [Dominus] colligavit; sicut est Baptismus Trinitatis nomine consecratus, communicatio corporis et sanguinis ipsius, et si quid aliud in Scripturis canonicis commendatur." [*Ep*. liv. vol. ii. p. 164.] Thus does this great Father clearly distinguish between the higher mysteries of Baptism and the Lord's Supper, and those which to avoid misconception we may call rather sacramentals than sacraments.

*man be born of water and of the Spirit, he cannot enter the kingdom of God.* We find it recorded too, in the Acts of the Apostles, that this principle was fully recognised and preserved by the Apostles: so that, when the Holy Spirit had descended upon Gentiles in the house of Cornelius the centurion, who were there present, warm in faith, and believing in the Lord with their whole heart, so that they blessed God in divers tongues, through the divine inspiration; yet St Peter, mindful of the divine ordinance, and of the Gospel, commanded that *they* should be baptised, who were already full of the Holy Ghost, that nothing should seem wanting to the perfect observance of the divine ordinance, in the conduct of the Apostles."[1]

Then telling Stephen that he sends copies of his letters to Quintus and to the Bishops of Numidia, in which the grounds of this decision were discussed, Cyprian proceeds to mention the decree before alluded to, concerning the reception of lapsed ecclesiastics to lay communion; and, finally, anticipating Stephen's rejection of the decision of the Council touching the baptism of heretics, he thus concludes: "These things we have made known to you, dearest brother, from regard to our mutual respect, and as befits my sincere regard for you; trusting that your own piety and soundness in the faith will sufficiently commend to you what is itself religious and orthodox. We know, however, that some men are unwilling to lay down opinions which they have once taken up, and are not easily persuaded to confess a change in their sentiments; yet they can retain the opinions which they have once adopted as their own, without sacrificing the peace and unity of their colleagues. And so we, in the matter before us, neither impose restraint, nor dictate a rule of proceeding to any man, since every Bishop has full right to administer the affairs of his own Church according to his own judgment, rendering to the Lord an account of his deeds."

Another Epistle of Cyprian, written about the same time to Jubaianus, an African Prelate, puts us more fully in possession

[1] *Ep.* lxxii. p. 128.

of the topics of controversy on this question, than any other of the records of these times. Jubaianus had proposed to Cyprian his own objections to his opinion; and had sent also a letter from some nameless person, in which other difficulties were proposed. This double attack upon his opinion Cyprian fully meets. He first mentions the two Synods which had been held, and also his letter to Quintus, in which the rule was stated, with the principles on which it was founded. He then proceeds to answer objections. Some it seems argued, that since Novatian affected to baptise those who deserted to him from the Church, therefore the Church ought to receive heretics without baptism, lest Catholics should seem so far to symbolise with Novatian, and to have borrowed his custom.

In answer to this notable argument, St Cyprian shows, that, to be consistent, Novatian should have been baptised into his own heresy. He insinuates, that it would be as reasonable to put off the proper conduct of humanity, because in some things apes have imitated men; as for the Church to desert her customs, because they had been aped by Novatian. And he argues, *ad hominem* (and the argument is of very general application, and well worth repeating), "Is it really to be held a sufficient reason for not doing this, that Novatian has done it? What then? since Novatian usurps the honour of an Episcopate, are we to renounce our Episcopacy? Or, because Novatian endeavours to erect an altar, and against all right to offer sacrifice, are we to desert our altar, and to relinquish our sacrifice?"[1]

An argument more worthy of Cyprian's attention occurs next: one, indeed, which hinged on the very principle on which the Church Catholic afterwards determined the present question. I find, says Cyprian, in the letter which you transmitted to me, a notion, that we ought not to inquire who was the minister of Baptism in any particular case; since the baptised may receive remission of sins, according to that which he believed: as that Marcionites, for instance, need

[1] *Ep.* lxxiii. p. 130.

not to be baptised, since they have received a semblance of Baptism, in the name of Jesus Christ.

Let us take Cyprian's solution of this difficulty in his own words.

"We ought therefore to examine the faith of those who believe, out of the Church, to determine whether it be such as that they can on account of it obtain any grace. For if there be but one faith common to us and to heretics, there may be one grace also. If the Patripassians, for instance, the Valentiniani, the Ophitæ, the Marcionites, and other pestilent sects, the very poison and dagger of the truth, confess the same Father, the same Son, ths same Holy Spirit, the same Church, that we confess, they may share with us in our Baptism, since their faith also is one with ours. But, not to run through all the heretics, and all their follies and blasphemies (since it is painful to speak of that, at the very knowledge of which one shudders and is ashamed), let us examine the case of Marcion alone, of whom mention was made in the Epistle which you sent to me, whether the validity of his baptism can be reasonably admitted.

Now the Lord, when He sent forth His disciples after His resurrection, taught them in what form they ought to baptise, saying, *All power is given to Me in heaven and in earth. Go ye therefore, and teach all nations, baptising them in the name of the Father, and of the Son, and of the Holy Ghost.* In these words Christ involves the doctrine of the Trinity, and in the mystery of the Trinity were the nations to be baptised. Now does Marcion hold the doctrine of the Trinity? Does he ascribe creation to the same Father with us? Does he recognise the same Son, Christ born of the Virgin Mary, who is the Word made flesh, who bare our sins, who by His death conquered death, who was the first-fruits and the promise of the resurrection to us, in His flesh, so as to assure His disciples that they also should rise in the same flesh? Far different is the faith of Marcion, and of the rest of the heretics! Yea, among them is nothing but error and blasphemy and contention, the foes of holiness and truth. How, therefore, can it be made to appear, that they who are baptised among them can receive remission of sins, and the grace of God, on account of their faith, when their very faith itself is a lie? For if, as some imagine, one who is without the Church, can receive anything according to his faith; surely he must receive that which he believes; he then who believes a lie cannot receive the truth; but rather, according to his faith, he receives impurity and profanation."[1]

Cyprian also argues, that if the faith of a heretic might avail to his receiving the grace of Baptism, it would also avail to the receiving of the grace of imposition of hands; with which rite however all were for receiving them; and after a long interval he proceeds: "There is no pretence for setting up the name of Christ against the truth in this matter, and for saying that they who are baptised in the name of Jesus Christ, wherever and however, have received the grace of Baptism: whereas Christ Himself says, *Not every one that saith unto Me Lord, Lord, shall enter into the kingdom of heaven;* and since He also warns us against being deceived by false prophets, and false Christs, coming in His name; *Many shall come in My name,* saith He, *saying, I am Christ, and shall deceive many;* but He adds, *beware; lo! I have foretold you all.* Whence we learn, that we are not to receive and vindicate what arrogates the name of Christ, but only what is done according to the truth of Christ. It is true that the Apostles taught much of the name of Christ for the remission of sins; but this was not as if the Son could profit any without or in opposition to the Father; but that they might evince to the Jews, who boasted that they had the Father, that the Father would profit them nothing, unless they believed in the Son, whom He sent. . . . Finally, since after the resurrection the Apostles were sent forth to baptise the Gentiles in the name of the Father and of the Son and of the Holy Ghost, how can some venture to say, that a Gentile baptised without the Church, yea, against the Church, anywhere, and in whatever form, so that it be only in the name of Jesus Christ, can

[1] *Ep.* lxxiii. pp. 130, 131.

obtain remission of sins; when Christ Himself commands that the nations be baptised in the Trinity in Unity: unless, indeed, he who denies Christ is denied by Christ; yet he who denies the Father, whom Christ Himself confessed, is not denied by Him; and unless he who blasphemes Him, whom Christ called His Lord and His God, shall be rewarded by Christ with remission of sins, and the sanctification of Baptism."[1] And again: "if one could be baptised among heretics, he might also receive remission of sins: and with remission of sins, sanctification; and he is made the temple of God. But, I ask, of what God? Not of the Creator; for in Him he believes not. Not of Christ; for he denies that Christ is God. Not of the Holy Ghost; for since the Three are One God, how can the Holy Ghost be propitiated by him, who is the enemy either of the Father or of the Son?"[2]

These passages, long as they are, are but extracts from the reasoning of Cyprian against the notion, that heretics might receive grace, according to their faith, in their own mockery of the Baptismal rite. But such expressions were of course open to the imputation of bigotry, from those who could not understand, that the most energetic maintenance of the truth, the utmost hatred of error, is not inconsistent with true love, and personal forbearance. Against the pseudo-charity, therefore, or liberalism of some, he presents the following admirable exposition of a passage from the Epistle to the Philippians, which had been claimed then, as it is continually now, as favouring such principles.

"As for the fancy of some, that the words of St Paul, *Notwithstanding every way, whether in pretence or truth, let Christ be preached*, afford any sanction to the proceedings of heretics, we are convinced that they give no support either to heretics or to their abettors. For in truth St Paul was not speaking of heretics, or of anything concerning them. The two classes of persons whose preaching he mentions, were both of the brethren; though some were disorderly in their conduct, and regardless of the laws of the Church, while the rest preserved

[1] Pages 134, 135.    [2] Page 133.

the truth of the Gospel with a due reverence and fear. Now while some of these constantly and boldly preached the word of the Lord, and some of envy and ill will; while some maintained a sincere love for His person, but others were filled with hatred and malevolence; he patiently endured all, since, whether in pretence or in truth, the name of Christ, which he also preached, came to the knowledge of many; and the preaching of all, though perhaps some were novices and imperfectly taught, yet prevailed to the spread of truth. Now surely it is one thing for those who are within the Church to speak of Christ; and another for those who are without the Church, and its enemies, to baptise in the name of Christ. Let not those then who would vindicate the proceedings *of heretics*, adduce the expressions of St Paul *concerning brethren:* but let them point out some place in which he grants that anything is to be conceded to heretics, in which he approves their faith and baptism, in which he has taught that they who are in schism, and are blasphemers, can obtain remission of their sins, without the pale of the Church."[1] He then proceeds to note what St Paul does say of heretics, and of the zeal with which we should oppose their errors, and the fear with which we should renounce their fellowship.

The argument of expediency was also pressed against St Cyprian's rule; it was objected, that the necessity of being baptised would repel heretics from the Church, and that it would bring on the Church unnecessary odium. These objections St Cyprian answers with characteristic courage and decision, plainly declaring, that in such cases the boldest way, that of the highest principle is the best. As for the heretics, if their baptism be admitted, it will tend to make them think, from the very testimony of the Church, that they in their separation are not cut off from the privilege of true Christians; but if they find that their baptism is disallowed, they will, perhaps at least, be startled by a more serious view of their position, and make the greater haste to regain the privileges which they have lost. As for the dreaded odium

[1] Page 133.

of rebaptising: if we dare not incur this, shall we not involve ourselves in a greater difficulty? for if we grant a true baptism to heretics, we grant that not right and presumptive, but mere and usurped possession, is the only title to this privilege: and thus one of the noblest parts of the appanage of the Church is not only seized by others, but yielded by ourselves: but how perilous it may be to surrender our rights in spiritual matters, we are divinely taught by the example of Esau; who found no place for repentance, having sold his birthright.

Let us take the conclusion of this Epistle, for the conclusion also of the present chapter; to which it is very appropriate, forming as it does a sort of transition from the amicable discussion to the violent agitation of this great question. Reverting to the calm, already ruffled, with regret; yet looking forward to the storm with the confidence of moral rectitude and courage; Cyprian appears before the world protesting his love of harmony, and his desire to maintain unity as well as truth; and desiring for his own part not to be moved from the advantages of a patient continuance in well-doing, whatever may occur.

"I have written, dearest brother, as briefly as I could, dictating to none, nor daring to condemn those beforehand, who may use their liberty of judging and of acting, to the best of their judgment. If it be possible to avoid it, I will not quarrel *on account of heretics* with any who are united with me *in the bonds of truth* and *by the peace of the Lord:* especially since the Apostle says, *if anyone wanteth to be contentious, we have no such custom, neither the Church of God.* I hold fast, in patience and meekness, the love of the Christians, the honour of our college, the bond of faith, the unity of the Episcopate: and to this end I have exercised myself in the composition of a book *on the advantages of patience,* which I have now finished to the best of my weak ability, and with the grace and help of the Lord. Of this book I send you a copy, as a token of our mutual affection." [1]

[1] Page 137.

## CHAPTER XV.

Stephen, Bishop of Rome, interferes in the Controversy about the Baptism of Heretics.—Cyprian's Epistle to Pompeius.—The last Council assembled at Carthage to determine the Question;—St Cyprian's opening Address;—And several of the more remarkable Suffrages.—The Unanimity of the Council against the Judgment of Stephen, and the Custom of Rome.—Irenæus and Victor.—Dionysius and Stephen.

HENCEFORWARD Stephen occupies a place in the foreground of the picture, and the whole scene is troubled.

About this time, that arrogant and violent Prelate addressed an Epistle to Cyprian, in which he expressed the opinion of his own Church, with something less of humility and temper than became the character of a Bishop. This Epistle is lost; but Cyprian has himself preserved several parts of it, and these we may suppose the most important parts, since they are selected by Cyprian as most requiring an answer. These detached fragments of Stephen's letter occur in an Epistle of Cyprian to Pompeius, who had requested Cyprian to furnish him with a copy of it.

"I send you," says Cyprian, "a transcript of Stephen's letter; and when you read it, you will abundantly discover his error, in labouring to establish the cause of heretics against Christians, and against the Church of God. For among other things which he advances, either arrogantly or impertinently, or which he so states as to be even inconsistent with himself, he has gone so far as to write thus: '*If, then, any are come over to you from any heresy whatever* [a quacumque hæresi], *let no new rule be followed, but according to traditional usage let* him be received by imposition of hands and penance; for even heretics themselves follow in this instance the legitimate custom, and baptise, not their proselytes, but communicate them only.'"[1]

Cyprian's answer to this judgment and reasoning of Stephen, will throw some light on the estimation in which the decree of the Roman Pontiff, and the tradition and custom of the Roman Church, were held in the Church Catholic.

St Cyprian reasons thus:

He has forbidden that converts from any heresy should be baptised; that is, he has determined that the baptism of all heretics is lawful and valid. And forasmuch as each heresy has its own baptism, and its distinctive crimes, he has accumulated upon himself the baptism and the crimes of all.

As for the tradition of which he speaks, whence is it? Does it descend from divine and evangelical authority? Have we it from the commands and Epistles of the Apostles? Divine traditions, divine commands, are to be obeyed. If, then, either in the Gospels, or in the Acts, or in the Apostolical Epistles, we are forbidden to baptise converts from heresy, and required to receive them at once to penance with imposition of hands;—be it so. But if heretics have no other name and character in the sacred Scriptures but that of enemies and antichrists,—if we are taught to avoid them,—if they are said to be perverse, and self-condemned; why are we not to condemn those, who, as the Apostle tells us, have condemned themselves? And now there are even worse heresies in the Church, than in the Apostles' days; as that of Marcion, for instance. As for those who set up the traditions of men against the divine word, the Apostle teaches us to withdraw ourselves from all such, for they are proud, knowing nothing.[2] Again:

"Neither ought the custom which has crept in unawares among some, to stand in the way of the universal prevalence of truth; for custom without truth, is but the rust of error. . . . Nor is the cause obscure which is to be followed by those who desire, religiously and in simplicity, to set aside error

[1] *Ep.* lxxiv. p. 138.　　[2] 1 Tim. iv.

and to discover the truth, and bring it to light. For when we return to the fountain and origin of divine tradition, human error ceases; and when we have looked into the intention of the heavenly mysteries, whatever before lay hid beneath the obscurity and cloud of darkness, is brought into the full light of truth. If a water-course, which used to flow copiously, suddenly dries up, do we not go to the well-head to discover the cause of the interruption; whether the spring itself has failed, or whether the stream which flows freely from thence has been diverted in some part of its course: so that if the defect arise from a broken channel, the proper repairs may restore the stream to its accustomed uses, in the same plenty in which it issues from the spring? And such is the course which the Priests of God should pursue, in the maintaining of the divine precepts. If the truth has been lost or obscured in any matter, we should trace it back to its divine origin, and to the tradition of the Apostles, and we then should gather our rules and frame our conduct according to the divine original. Now we find it recorded, that there is one God, and one Christ, and one hope, and one faith, and one Church, and one Baptism appointed in that one Church only; and whosoever departs from the unity of these things, necessarily has his part with heretics,"[1] &c. . . . The application of this rule to the particular question of Baptism we have already seen; but it is interesting to find Cyprian arguing against the positions of the Roman Church and Pontiff of that day, on precisely the same Catholic ground that our Church now occupies, and is learning to vindicate to herself once again, after the noble example of her early reformers.

Cyprian proceeds to declare against the reasoning of Stephen:

That to adduce the custom of heretics is indeed a notable device.

That if the name of Christ was sufficient in Baptism, then it would be sufficient in imposition of hands also; and the heretics who confer the one, according to Stephen, might also confer the other.

[1] *Ep.* lxxiv. pp. 141, 142.

That a Bishop ought not only to teach, but also to learn; for he becomes more fit to teach, as he adds daily to his stock of true knowledge.

Such is the tone (though not the exact words and order) of some of the remarks of Cyprian upon Stephen's authority and reasoning. Among others the following striking passage occurs: "Doth *he* give glory to God, who communicates with the Baptism of Marcion? Doth *he* give glory to God, who thinks that remission of sins can be given among those who blaspheme God? Doth *he* give glory to God, who asserts that children of God may be born without the Church of an adulteress and fornicator? Doth *he* give honour to God, who vindicates the cause of heresy against the Church; forsaking the unity and truth which came from the law of God? Doth *he* give glory to God, who, the friend of heretics, the enemy of Christ, judges those priests of God worthy of excommunication who defend the truth of Christ and the unity of the Church? If *this* be to honour God, if the fear and discipline of God be thus guarded by His priest, let us throw down our arms, let us submit our hands to captivity, let us surrender the administration of the Gospel, the ordinances of Christ, the majesty of God, to the Devil: let the oath of our divine warfare be dissolved, let the standard of the armies of heaven be betrayed: let the Church yield to heretics, light to darkness, faith to perfidy, hope to despair, reason to error, immortality to death, love to hatred, truth to a lie, Christ to Antichrist. No wonder that schisms and heresies thus arise day after day, and grow with a strange rapidity and strength, and erect their scaly heads against the Church of God, injecting the poison of their error more and more fatally, while both authority and stability is given to them by the advocacy of some; while their baptism is defended; while faith and truth are betrayed; while that which is done against the Church without her pale, is vindicated in the Church itself. But if, dearest brother, we have any love of God, any faith and regard for the truth; if we keep the law of Christ, if we guard inviolate the purity of His spouse, if the words of the Lord are written in our hearts,

*When the Son of man cometh shall He find faith on the earth?* As faithful soldiers of God, let us fight for a true faith and a pure religion; with the courage of tried fidelity, let us guard the camp divinely committed to our keeping."

The Epistle of Stephen to Cyprian was answered, as we collect with probability at least, by the African Church; which seems with Cyprian to have maintained a far better temper than Stephen, and to have sought his concurrence, so long as it could be hoped for, and his continued communion, until it was denied by himself.[1] This was expressly declared in the first Epistle to him before cited; and Cyprian continues to call Stephen "brother," which he would not do, unless he still retained him, and wished to retain him, in the unity of the Church.

The last effort[2] which the Africans made to retain peace with Rome, seems to have been after Stephen had so scandalously abused Cyprian, as to call him a false Christ, a false Apostle, a deceitful worker: and after he had fulminated his excommunications against the whole Church of Carthage. Even after this the Africans sent messengers to Rome to bring things to a better state if possible; but their message was rejected, and their legates treated with disrespect and contumely.

Things being now in such a deplorable condition, Cyprian, seeking countenance in the consent of good and great men in the Church, communicated the whole affair to Firmilian, one of those Asiatic Bishops who were already in the same condemnation with himself, and for the same cause. Firmilian had been a pupil of Origen; he was Bishop of Cesaræa, in Cappadocia, and was a Prelate of great note in his day: and

---

[1] Need I remind the reader, that the Church of England at the Reformation pursued precisely the same Catholic course with Rome, and met with precisely the same uncharitable and schismatical return? We are accused of having left the Church of Rome: the truth is, that the Church of Rome thrust us out against our will, and with the utmost contumely and cruelty.

See Mosheim, p. 544.

his long reply to Cyprian's communication amply sustains his character with posterity. It is certainly a masterly production, or rather the production of a master mind; for it was written in so great haste, that he himself apologises for its defects on that score. But it is chiefly valuable to us, not as attesting the genius of its author, but as supplying indications which were else wanting of some minor incidents of this controversy; and as affording irrefragable proofs that Rome and its Bishop had not *then* those *exclusive* claims to respect and obedience, which she arrogates *now* over all Bishops and all Churches. In this latter point of view I have considered the Epistle of Firmilian in another work;[1] and I have made continual use of his historical hints, in the present view of this controversy.

But the most important step which Cyprian took, was the calling a Council of eighty-five Bishops, the last, and the most celebrated of all those that met under his Episcopate, for the discussion of this question. We have no records remaining of the other Councils, but the mention of them in the several Epistles before cited: but of this Council the synodal acts still remain.

When the far greater part of the Bishops of Africa, Numidia, and Mauritania had assembled,[2] with the Priests and Deacons (much people being also present), and when the letter of Jubaianus to Cyprian concerning the baptising of heretics, with the answer of Cyprian, and also a reply of Jubaianus, expressing his concurrence, had been read, Cyprian rose, and thus addressed the Synod.

"You have heard, most beloved colleagues, what my fellow Bishop Jubaianus wrote to me, desiring my poor judgment upon the unlawful and profane baptism of heretics: you have heard, too, my reply; that I thought, as I have always thought and still think, that heretics, on their return to the Church, ought to be baptised and sanctified with the Church's baptism. You have also heard the second Epistle of Jubaianus, in

[1] Testimony of St Cyprian against Rome, pp. 170-178.
[2] On the first of September, 256.

which he not only expresses his assent to my judgment, but declares himself thankful also for the information which I had been able to afford him. It remains that we declare, each of us, what we think upon this subject, neither judging any one, nor forbidding any, if he judge otherwise, to communicate his opinion. For neither has any one of us constituted himself a Bishop of Bishops, nor reduced his colleagues to the necessity of conforming to his judgment, by a tyrannical display of terrors; since every Bishop has a right to judge for himself, and is at liberty to use his own authority, and can no more be judged by another, than he can judge another. But let us all expect the judgment of our Lord Jesus Christ, who alone hath the power, both to constitute us governors in His Church, and to pronounce judgment upon our conduct."[1]

The modesty and forbearance of the opening of the Council by the insulted Cyprian, has the especial praise of Augustine; who differed from him in his judgment, but could not help admiring the manner in which it was enforced. And indeed it is remarkable, that not only in Cyprian, but in the whole Synod assembled with him, so far as we collect from the several suffrages, the merits of the question were discussed without any undue reference to those feelings which must have been excited by the unwarrantable and rash severity of Stephen.

Some few of the more remarkable of those suffrages I shall transcribe.

Cæcilius of Bilta, whose suffrage is first in order, seems to have resembled Cyprian as much in his diffuse and oratorical style, as in his judgment. "I acknowledge," says he, "but one baptism within the Church, and without the Church none. That one baptism is only where there is a true hope, and an assured faith. For so it is written: *One faith, one hope, one baptism;* not among heretics, where hope there is none, and where faith is falsehood; where all things are carried on with lying; where a demoniac exercises, a profane man puts the baptismal interrogatories, his words eating as a cancer; when

---

[1] Page 329.

an infidel imposes the faith, the wicked man remits sins, Anti-Christ sprinkles in the name of Christ, he who is cursed of God blesses, the dead promises life, the broiler gives peace, the blasphemer invokes God, the profane man administers the sacred functions, and the sacrilegious consecrates the altar. To all these evils yet another is added, that the chief ministers of Satan dare to offer the Eucharist. Or if these things be not so, let those who join the heretics in their mockeries deny them if they can. Behold, to what iniquities the Church is now compelled to consent, while she is forced to receive such men to communion, without baptism, and without pardon. Surely, my brethren, we ought to flee from such wickedness, and to separate ourselves from such iniquity; and to hold that one baptism, which is committed to the Church alone."

Polycarp of Adrumettium spoke third: "They who approve the baptism of heretics, invalidate our own."

Nicomedes of Segurnæ said, "I hold that heretics should be received into the Church by baptism, because they can receive no remission of sins without the Church, and from sinners."

The suffrage of Mummulus of Galba. "The verity of our mother, the Church Catholic, hath always remained, and yet remains among us, my brethren; and even more especially in the recognition of the Trinity in Baptism, since our Lord said, *Go ye, and baptise the nations in the name of the Father, and of the Son, and of the Holy Spirit.* Since then we are certain that the heretics have neither the Father, nor the Son, nor the Holy Spirit, they who come to the Church our mother, ought to be truly regenerated and baptised: that they may, by the holy and heavenly laver, be delivered from the canker which is destroying them, and from the wrath of damnation, and from the sulliage of error."

Fortunatus of Tuchaboris said, "Jesus Christ our Lord and God, and the Son of God the Father and Creator, founded His Church on a rock, not upon heresy; and gave the privilege of Baptism to Bishops, not to heretics. Wherefore they who are without the Church, and opposing themselves to

CHRIST scatter the sheep of His flock, cannot baptise without the Church."

Secundinus of Carpi spoke thus. "Are heretics Christians, or are they not? If they be Christians, why are they not in the Church of Christ? If they be *not* Christians, how can they make men Christians? Or whither tends that word of the Lord, *He that is not with Me is against Me, and he who gathereth not with Me scattereth?* Whence it follows, that the Holy Spirit cannot descend, by imposition of hands, upon strange children, and the progeny of Antichrist: since it is clear that heretics have no baptism."

Adelphius of Thasbalte. "The report that we *re*baptise, is false, and as malicious as it is untrue: for the Church does not *re*baptise heretics, but baptise them."

Pelagianus of Luperciana. "It is written, *Either the Lord is your God, or Baal is your God;* and now, in like manner, either the Church is the Church, or heresy is the Church. But if heresy be not the Church, how can heretics have at their disposal the Baptism of the Church?"

Marcellus of Zama. "Since there is no remission of sins, except in the Baptism of the Church, he who baptises not a heretic holds communion with a sinner."

Zosimus of Tharassa said, "When truth has been revealed, let error yield to truth: for even Peter, who before enjoined circumcision, yielded to the truth which Paul preached."

The suffrage of Therapius of Bulla. "Who so betrays the Baptism of the Church to heretics, what is he but a Judas to the spouse of Christ?"

Verulus of Rusiccas. "A man that is an heretic cannot impart that which himself hath not; much less a schismatic, who hath lost that which he had."

Clarus of Massula said, "The intention of our Lord Jesus Christ is clear, from His sending His Apostles, and committing to them alone the authority which was given to Him by the Father; to which Apostles we succeed, governing the Church of the Lord with the same authority, and baptising those who rightly believe. On the other hand, heretics, who have neither authority being without, nor the Church of Christ, can baptise none with the Baptism of Christ."

Natalis of Oëa delivered the proxies of Pompeius and Dioga with his own suffrage, saying, "As well I myself, as Pompeius of Sabra, and Dioga of Leftis-Magna, who have delegated their authority to me, and though absent in body are present in spirit, agree in the judgment of our colleagues, that heretics cannot communicate with us, until they have received the Church's Baptism."

And last of all spoke Cyprian of Carthage. "My Epistle to Jubaianus declares my opinion at large: That heretics, who are declared by the terms of the Gospel, and by the declaration of the Apostle, to be both adversaries of Christ, and Antichrists, when they come into the Church, ought to be baptised with the one Baptism of the Church; that of adversaries they may be made friends, and of Antichrists Christians."

Thus the eighty-five Bishops assembled at this Council, with two others who voted therein by proxy, unanimously agreed, that heretics ought to be baptised on their conversion to the Church: and thus by their Synodical act, they deliberately chose the condemnation of Stephen and his Church, (with whatever penalty of right attended it,) before a submission to that authority, when their consciences were opposed to its dictates.

They were already, indeed, excommunicated by Stephen; unless we rather hold with Firmilian, that Stephen, by his excommunication of the African Churches, had cut himself off from the Church of Christ. But in thus voluntarily binding the burden of his anathema upon themselves, rather than bending beneath the weight of a new custom imposed by his Church, surely the African Bishops in the Council spoke volumes, as to their judgment of Rome as an infallible Church, and of her Bishop as the centre of unity.

With this Council ended the controversy upon the baptism of heretics, so far as Africa was concerned; and henceforth we hear of no farther discussions upon the subject; though there is no shadow of evidence that either Cyprian, and the

Churches who adhered to his opinion, or Stephen and his party, ever came into a different judgment from that which we have seen them maintaining respectively. Mosheim suggests, that the unanimity of the Africans upon this subject, and the consent of the Asiatics in their judgment, wrought so far at least with Stephen, as to moderate the *expression* of his anger. The Africans themselves, always disposed to peace, and to holding their own opinions, and maintaining their own customs, while they conceded the same licence to others, were not likely to move the question with needless or untimely violence. That they were cut off from all external fellowship with Rome they must have regretted; but not imagining that this was tantamount to being cast into a lower hell than is opened for any other but delinquents against the Church of Rome, they needed not to sink the dignity of an independent Church by an idle clamour. Nor yet were they forced by the law of charity, to proselytise their opponents, as if they could so only deliver them from eternal wrath; for neither was Carthage any more than Rome to be accounted infallible, nor Cyprian, any more than Stephen, to be made *the* centre of necessary unity to all Christendom. Eventually the evil cured itself, and that peace succeeded, which could never have returned, had the violence of Stephen long irritated the Church, or had it been borne with less patience than that which arose from conscious rectitude, and an absence of all fear. In St Augustine's time, we find the Africans agreeing against the Donatists in the judgment of the Catholic Church, (which was not however the judgment of Stephen, though *verbally* more near to it than to that of Cyprian,) to which they probably conformed insensibly.

Besides, as Victor, a former Bishop of Rome, had found in Saint Irenæus one to advise more moderate measures than he was disposed to adopt, in the controversy concerning the keeping of Easter; so did Pope Stephen find in Dionysius of Alexandria, one not less disposed nor less able than Irenæus to take the same fraternal part. For Eusebius[1] preserves a

[1] Lib. VII. cap. v.

portion of a letter from Dionysius to Sixtus of Rome, Stephen's successor, concerning Baptism. Stephen, says the historian, had signified to Helenus and Firmilian, with the other Bishops of Cilicia, Cappadocia, and the neighbouring provinces, that he had henceforth withdrawn his communion from them, because they baptised heretics. "But," says Dionysius to Sixtus, "consider, I beseech you, the importance of this affair. For it has been determined even in great Councils, that those heretics who return to the Catholic Church shall be received into the rank of Catechumens, and that they shall afterwards be cleansed from the impurities which they have contracted with the waters of Baptism. I myself," continues Dionysius, "wrote to Stephen, entreating for them his indulgence."

Of the precise opinion of Dionysius himself in this important question we are not able to speak positively. The last citation, from one of his Epistles, seems to favour the views of Cyprian; perhaps what he says to Sixtus on a subsequent occasion, looks the other way. "I have need," says he, "of your counsel, to guard me from error in a question on which I have been consulted. One of the brethren, who had always been reputed among the faithful, and who had always communicated not only before my Episcopate, but even before that of the blessed Heraclas, was present one day at the celebration of Baptism, and heard the interrogations put to the candidates, and their answers. This man came to me, and throwing himself at my feet, bewailed his unhappy lot, saying, that the Baptism which he had received at the hand of heretics, was not like ours, nor had any thing in common with it: that the Baptism of which he had partaken was full of impiety and blasphemy; and that he was grievously afflicted on that account, not daring to raise his eyes to heaven for very shame and remorse. In a word, he besought me to give him the true Baptism, and to confer on him the grace of adoption. I have hitherto ventured to do nothing in this matter, and have told him, that the long time that he has been in communion with the true Church ought to satisfy him; that he had often been present at the prayers of the faithful, and answered Amen; that he had stretched forth his hand to receive the consecrated bread; that he had again and again partaken of the Body and Blood of our Lord Jesus Christ. I exhorted him on these grounds to be of good courage, and to continue still to communicate in faith and hope: yet he will not be comforted; he dare not approach the holy table, and we can hardly persuade him to join in the prayers of the Church."[1]

Now though this relation seems rather to favour the view of Stephen than that of Cyprian, yet it is only at first sight; for Dionysius does not ground the propriety of the old man's communicating on the validity of his Baptism, but on the length of time that he had been received to a participation with the Church even in her higher mysteries. I do not mean that Cyprian would have agreed with Dionysius (though I cannot deny it), but I say, and that without hesitation, that Stephen would not have reasoned as he did. But whatever might have been the opinion of Dionysius on the abstract question, nothing can be more clear than his condemnation of the way in which one side of it was enforced by Rome. "Of this at least," says he, "I am sure, that the Africans have not now introduced this custom, but that it has the sanction of the practice of ancient Bishops, and the authority of many Councils held as well at Iconium and Synnada as at other places. For my own part, I should be loth to combat their opinions, to oppose their decisions, or to contest the point with them in any way; for it is written, *Thou shalt not remove thy neighbour's landmark.*"[2]

[1] Eusebius VII. ix.
[2] Letter of Dionysius to Philemon, a priest of the Church of Rome, *apud Euseb.* VII. vii.

## CHAPTER XVI.

A General View of the Principles involved in the Controversy Concerning the Baptism of Heretics.

THE custom of the Church, established on the authority of General Councils, has subsequently determined the question of the baptism of heretics; so that the Council of Carthage has now no authority, nor is there any place in the Church for the controversy out of which it arose: but it must always be a matter of interest to enter into the merits of a question, which divided the Church so remarkably, and which was so vigorously disputed in distant parts of the world; and besides, there are principles recognised throughout the discussion, at least on St Cyprian's part, and in every suffrage in the Council, which can never be antiquated. I propose, therefore, shortly to review the opinions of the parties here opposed, and to elicit some of the general principles which are involved in the grounds on which the question was discussed.

This was no contest about terms: the opinions of the contending parties were quite incompatible; nor did any friendly mediator, of sufficient weight to be heard, propose the middle course afterwards approved by the Church; a course which doubtless either of them would have pursued, had it been *previously* pointed out by such paramount authority; but which nevertheless would have found an advocate, neither in Stephen nor in Cyprian, had it been proposed for the first time during the heat of the debate.

Those who adhered to Cyprian, without all doubt denied utterly, not the lawfulness only, but the *validity*, actual or possible, present or latent, of the sprinklings and lustrations of heretics and schismatics. We have this position so avowedly occupied, so carefully and zealously defended, that we cannot doubt that it was maintained in all its prominence and with all its consequences. Of Stephen's expressions and reasonings we have no original documents; and we receive what little we possess through his enemies: hence the exact opinion of Stephen on this point admits a doubt, though I think hardly; for in the Epistle from Cyprian to Pompeius before cited, it seems probable that we have his very words; and if so, it is certain that their plain meaning must prevail against any deductions from the Epistle of Firmilian, which the learned Bingham[1] quotes as evidence, that Stephen held the very doctrine which was afterwards sanctioned by the Council of Arles: viz., that the baptism of those heretics only who baptised in the name and in the faith of the Trinity, should be so far recognised as not to be repeated.

Firmilian, it is true, brings in the opponents of Cyprian, saying, "No enquiry need be made who was the baptiser, since he who was baptized may receive grace on the invocation of the Trinity of Names, Father, Son, and Holy Ghost." But if I mistake not, it is more probable that Firmilian here groups together all the objectors and all the objections (in which case some things which are not his will seem to be attributed to Stephen personally, if he be taken as the representative of the whole body), than that Cyprian misrepresents Stephen in a letter which was accompanied with a copy of the very Epistle from which he takes his quotations. Cyprian himself has to answer those who were for allowing a baptism in the name of

[1] In his scholastic History of Lay Baptism appended to vol. iii. of his Works, Ed. 1836, chap. i. p. 56. Milner also makes the judgment of Stephen the same with that of the Catholic Church afterwards. "Stephen, Bishop of Rome, maintained," says he, "that, if persons had been baptized in the name of the Father, the Son, and the Holy Ghost, imposition of hands would then be sufficient for their reception into the Church: the point was left undecided, because no party had power to compel others; most Christians, however, have long since agreed with Stephen." Cent. III. chap. xiii.

Christ only, as well as those who were for admitting every Baptism in the name of the Trinity: so that if such indications were sufficient to determine the judgment of Stephen personally, it must be determined different ways. Moreover, it must be observed, that Cyprian not only quotes Stephen as allowing the broadest recognition of the baptism of all heretics; but that in refuting Stephen, he refutes the positions of one who held that extreme opinion. Cyprian, then, who surely knew pretty well how the matter stood, took Stephen for the advocate of every heretical baptism: and on the whole, I think, we must conclude, that Stephen took in this case the extreme opposite from the opinion of Cyprian, and that neither the one nor the other held precisely, as the Church afterwards determined, either at Arles, or at Constantinople.[1]

Nor did either party, nor does the decision of the Catholic Church, hold with the modern doctrine of Rome, which falls as much below the lowest depths of Stephen's opinion as Stephen fell below the uncompromising doctrine of Cyprian: and which is quite as much at variance with the subsequent judgment of the Church, as that judgment is at variance with either Stephen or Cyprian. The Church's judgment in few words was this: That all who had been baptised by schismatics,

[1] I must not, however, withhold the unqualified praise with which Vincentius Lirinensis views the proceedings of Stephen, which would look as if the opinion of Stephen was that of the Catholic Church. But the question recurs in this form, are not we as well able to judge of the history of these events as Vincentius himself was? And though *in the absence of records* Vincentius would be received as the best authority, yet *having the same records to consult as he had*, are we not equally able to form a history from them? In fact, Vincentius is not quite correct in his historical notice of this question; for Agrippinus was not, as he states, the originator of the African custom, unless both Cyprian and Firmilian are wilfully wrong in the matter of fact. And once more, the definite praise which Vincentius awards to Stephen, is not for the precision with which he defined the truth upon this question; but the way in which he stated the important rule, that no novelty was to be admitted, but that tradition was to be observed. I ought to add, that the work of Vincentius does not owe its value to the precise historical correctness of the examples which he adduces. The reader will do well to refer to sect. vi. of the Commonitorium of Vincentius.

and by heretics *who used the words of the divine institution and in the true sense*, should be received into the Church by chrism and imposition of hands, after due penance, and a renunciation of their errors : but that the baptism of those heretics who *used not the words of the institution*, or who *so used them as to deny the Trinity*, should be repeated. Rome at present teaches, that the baptism even of Jews, infidels, and heretics, in cases of necessity, is valid: though I suppose she does not involve in her anathema against those who deny the validity of the baptism of heretics, those who repudiate the baptism of Jews and infidels; since these last cannot intend to do what the Church does, seeing they know it not, though the heretic may be supposed to know it, as he who shuns the good, must in some sense know it to avoid it. But according to the Romish doctrine of intention, is there no difficulty in this question from the necessary absence of intention from such baptism? When one insinuates such things against a Church which professes to follow catholicity and antiquity, it is quite necessary to avoid the suspicion of a little polemical romancing: I have therefore transcribed the declarations to which I refer below.[1]

Now that Stephen, much more that the Church in her final decree, symbolised with modern Rome in this matter, none but a Romanist will hold, and the Romanist will never prove. But setting aside the allusion to this latter controversy, Stephen holding that the baptism of all heretics and schismatics should be allowed; Cyprian pointedly denying this position in terms

[1] "Extremus ordo illorum est qui, cogente necessitate, sine solemnibus cæremoniis baptizari possunt ; quo in numero sunt omnes, etiam de populo, sive mares sive feminæ, quamcumque illi sectam profiteantur : nam et judæis quoque et infidelibus et hæreticis, cum necessitas cogit hoc munus permissum est ; si tamen id efficere propositum eis fuerit, quod Ecclesia Catholica in eo administrationis genere efficit." *Cat. Conc. Trid. De Bap.* xxii. "Si quis dixerit, Baptismum qui etiam datus ab hæreticis in nomine Patris, et Filii, et Spiritus Sancti, cum intentione faciendi quod facit ecclesia, non esse verum Baptismum, anathema sit." *Conc. Trid. Sess.* vii. *can.* iv. *de bapt.* "Si quis dixerit, in ministris, dum sacramenta conficiunt, et conferunt, non requiri intentionem saltem faciendi quod. facit ecclesia, anathema sit." *Conc. Trid. Sess.* vii. *can.* xi. *de sac. in gen.*

equally general; which was most nearly right? and which was most excusable in his error, if the nearest to the truth was in error at all? By the Church the question was certainly determined in a way which *seemed* most to favour the opinion of Stephen: was it so in effect, and in the principles which it involved? Let us take another view of the final decision of the Church, that we may not forget the exact character of that which is to be the standard by which the other two are to be measured.

That a distinction was to be made between heretics and schismatics: and that the baptism of the latter was to be admitted as *valid*, though by no means as *lawful;* as carrying with it a *springing* efficacy, so to speak, and as not therefore to be *repeated*, but to be *perfected* and *sanctified* by imposition of hands of a Catholic Bishop: and that the baptism of those heretics who were orthodox in respect of the Trinity, and used the words of Christ's institution, was to be accounted of in like manner: but that, on the other hand, the baptism of those heretics who denied the Trinity, and, without all manner of question, of those who baptised not in the name of the Trinity, was to be accounted no baptism at all; and that they who were converted from such heresies were to be received by baptism into the Church, as if they had been Jews or Pagans; —this is the decree of the Church Catholic: a decree less convenient in its application than that either of Cyprian or of Stephen; but one of higher authority, and by which therefore the decrees of both those Prelates must submit to be tested.

Now Stephen's *looks more like* this decree: Cyprian's, I am bold to say, *is more nearly consistent* with it. We must enter more deeply into the theory of the subject to appreciate the points of difference, or of accordance, in these several judgments.

We have first to note, that the Church is the depository and the steward of the Sacraments; in dispensing which the Bishop, or other ecclesiastic, is but her minister: and it rests with her to determine, with the authority which Christ hath given to her, but with the responsibility also which attends so high a charge, who shall baptise, and who not; whose baptism shall be valid, and whose legitimate; whose perfect, whose only perfectible, and whose utterly null. But there are limits which the Church could not pass, without becoming tainted with the heresy to which she should allow too much: which is indeed impossible; but we must so express ourselves at present, for the sake of elucidating our position. Or we may express the same thing in another way: there are some baptisms which it is morally impossible that the Church should allow; for if she allowed them, she would be sullied with error; and no such sulliage can ever cleave to her.

Now it admits a doubt, whether, if the Church had determined with Stephen, and had received the baptism of *all* heretics; as of the Marcionites, for instance, who blasphemed the Father, or of Paul of Samosata and his followers, who blasphemed the Son;—it admits a doubt, I say, whether she would not then have been tainted with such profane and sacrilegious errors. The Church, in fact, seems to me to have judged, that she could not do this without incurring such a stain: for while she showed that mercy and liberality was the rule of her proceeding, by extending her favour, so to speak, to converts from other heresies, and deeming their baptisms valid, though not legitimate; she showed equally clearly that some imperative claim rested on her to place bounds to her indulgence, before it had included those extreme profanations. Thus with becoming caution did she exert her dispensing power, as steward of the mysteries of God; showing favour where it could not be claimed from her as of right, but where it was the spontaneous motion of her love, yet not against right. But, on the other hand, was it not imperative on the Church to deny the like favour to the worst heretics; while it was but an act of her grace to allow it to the less profanely heterodox? Might she not, with perfect justice, have judged as Cyprian judged? Could she have judged as Stephen judged, without denying all the principles of authority, of sanctity, and of obedience, by which she was bound to regulate her conduct in this matter?

If I am right thus far, it follows that Cyprian was not wrong in this matter; for he did that in his own Church which it was competent for the whole Church to do: and he did it before the Church had determined otherwise; and while it was competent therefore for him, as Bishop, to do in his own diocese, whatever the Church might do in all Christendom. But Stephen was wrong; for he did that (before, indeed the Church had declared against him) which the Church could never do, because it was in itself wrong, and the Church does not err.

Or even admitting that Stephen's judgment was not incompatible with sound doctrine and custom; yet still, the Church in her highest authority being the steward of Baptism;—and until a General Council, the Bishop in each Diocese, or the Synod of Bishops in each Province, being the highest authority in the Church;—it was wholly unwarrantable in Stephen to attempt to obtrude his custom on any other Church, even as Dionysius, before quoted, expressly declares; and so the great St Basil taught, that in this matter their own custom was to be conceded to particular Churches; of course antecedently to a decree of the Church universal. The interference then of Stephen was unjustifiable and uncanonical, even supposing his opinion to have been sound.

And be it observed, that, to this day, one cause of complaint against Rome, is often *not* the error of her doctrine, even where we cannot wholly agree with her, so much as the uncatholic spirit of domination and overbearing dogmatism, by which she would bind her own doctrines and customs on other Churches, and on the consciences of men. For instance; though we deny, and dare not assent to, the doctrine of Transubstantiation, yet we should scarce be justified in condemning those who hold it, without breach of charity, and in Christian humility; but we have good right to complain, if that which cannot be proved by God's word, and was never believed or dreamt of in the Church for many ages, is made a test of our Catholicity, and a term of communion: and if we are either anathematised or burned for withholding our assent to such a dogma so brought in, we may well utter a sad or an indignant complaint.

So far for the *merits* of this great controversy. As for the comparative *skill* displayed on either side, it would not be just to Stephen to say, that he seems to have been beyond compare the weakest, whether he was right or wrong in principle, without observing, that we have but obscure hints of the course of argument which he pursued, and those hints collected from his adversaries. Of the *conduct* of the argument on both sides, we may observe, that both appealed to Scripture and to custom.[1] Custom, if it had been Catholic, could of course have told in favour of one only; but nothing can be clearer to one who reviews this history, than that there was no Catholic custom; and none other than Catholic custom was conclusive, at any rate beyond the bounds of particular Churches. Therefore, neither Stephen nor Cyprian did well, if he appealed to custom, *i. e.* the particular custom of his own Church, in order to obtrude any rule of discipline upon all other Churches. Now which was it, Stephen or Cyprian, that did this?

But it may be said, "If both sides, appealing to custom, yet erred one or both in their conclusions; is not this an example of the utter uncertainty of this method of judging, and of the uselessness in practice of the rule of Vincentius?" We answer, That no rule is of universally *easy* application, and that none can free us from the errors in its application, which may result either from the weakness or from the depravity of men. The error of Stephen (whether of weak-

[1] One or two expressions such as this, *Let no man prefer custom to truth*, appearing in some of the suffrages in the Council of Carthage, have been adduced to show, that Cyprian's own party perceived the most ancient custom to be against them: but this reasoning is really most unjust: expressions such as these are aimed at Stephen's claim of custom; and are not admissions in disparagement of their own authorities. The words of Firmilian will convey the spirit of such expressions. "Nos veritati et consuetudinem jungimus; et consuetudini Romanorum, consuetudinem sed veritatis, opponimus; ab initio hoc tenentes quod a Christo et ab Apostolis traditum est." We couple truth with custom, and oppose custom, the true custom, to the custom of the Romans: for we hold that which was handed down from the beginning by Christ and his Apostles. Page 149.

ness or of dishonesty I will not determine) was, that he took a particular for a general custom; and hence his arrogant attempt upon the liberties of all Churches. He argued rightly, but from wrong premises. Cyprian was right, so far as we are able to judge, both in his premises and in his conclusion; since, pretending only a particular custom, he left every Church at liberty to maintain its own rule. These cases then are not *exactly* in point. When we speak of Tradition, we mean Catholic Tradition, and our adversaries know that we mean that alone. Wherever there was *Catholic* tradition to be appealed to, it was triumphant in the days of Cyprian; and the question involved not *the principle of Traditions*, but the *fact of the catholicity of any particular Tradition*. Just as, for instance, every contested appeal to Scripture, involves not *the sufficiency of Scripture*, but *the fact on which side Scripture actually decides*. At all events, the enemies of Tradition ought for their own sakes to keep every such objection in the background, lest they should irritate us to retort the question in another form: "If you agree among yourselves in almost nothing but in your abhorrence of custom, are you not a standing example of the uncertainty of whatever rule you may please to follow?" Let me add (that the question may not be misapprehended), that it glances not at Scripture (which is neither uncertain nor insufficient), but at private judgment and individual interpretation. The very controversy before us exemplifies this remark.

I said, that both Stephen and Cyprian appealed to Scripture: and I say, too, that to Scripture every heresy that ever sprang from the ignorance, or folly, or pride, or presumption, or impiety of men, or from the darkest suggestions of the Devil, has appealed, and will appeal, we may be sure, to the end of time. And not unoften heretics have vindicated their claims to particular texts with such *a show* of reason, as to *seem* more nearly entitled to them than the Catholic Church. Thus, for instance, Theodoret tells us of the Novatians, of whom we have had occasion to say so much, that they set in array against the truth, the fourth, fifth, and sixth verses of the sixth chapter of Hebrews;[1] not understanding that the holy Apostle was then teaching the doctrine of Baptism, and not interdicting the medicines of repentance.[2] Now none can deny the apparent aptitude of this text to serve the cause of the Novatians; nor fail to perceive that theirs is even the most natural application of the text, though without all question a wrong one. What is the conclusion? This is certainly *a* conclusion (and let those who object to it provide another, for the phenomenon is of too constant recurrence, and of too stupendous effect to be passed over without use or comment), this is a conclusion: that no rule of applying Holy Scripture can defend the Church against every conceivable error, but one that goes to the Church itself, as the interpreter of Scripture.

In the particular case before us, Cyprian quoted Scripture with better effect than his opponents: as we have before shown that his judgment was the nearest to the truth; for though the letter of the texts which he cites scarcely bears out the whole of his reasoning, yet their spirit is quite in his favour; but Stephen, quoting St Paul's doctrine of *One Lord, one Faith, one Baptism*, clearly justified the retort, that by receiving the Baptism of heretics, he multiplied Baptisms, so as to make as many Baptisms *in* the Church, as there were heresies *out of* the Church.

The temper with which this controversy was carried on does not seem to me to throw unsullied light on either party: nor can I imagine how the Romish historian can venture to assert, that it was concluded by the consent of the whole Church, and without any rupture during its continuance; and moreover, that one of the final causes for which our Lord permitted this discussion, was, that posterity might learn from

---

[1] "It is impossible for those who were once enlightened, and have tasted of the heavenly gift, and were made partakers of the Holy Ghost, and have tasted the good word of God, and the powers of the world to come, if they shall fall away, to renew them again unto repentance: seeing they crucify to themselves the Son of God afresh, and put Him to an open shame."

[2] *Vide* Theodoret *in locum*, vol. iii. p. 579. *Ed. Halæ* 1771. 8vo.

the example of the contending parties what was the temper and the conduct which became men under such circumstances.[1] I believe, however, that none either will or can excuse Stephen personally, if the question is fairly proposed to them; and though Cyprian's humility and mildness have been commended: and though, as I have before remarked, he does in some respects deserve very high commendation; and though at any rate as compared with Stephen he was admirable in his temper, and in the whole management of the controversy, yet if I were Cyprian's panegyrist, instead of his historian, I should be disposed to pass very lightly over this page of his history. Controversy, especially personal controversy, is not a favourable field for the growth of the Christian virtues.

If there are any questions agitated in the present day upon which the history of this controversy can throw any light, they are those, I suppose, which are pending between the Church Catholic, and all manifest heretics and schismatics, as to the validity of all or any of the rites administered by their *soi-disants* pastors. But it must be borne in mind, that since a self-imposed, or invalidly conferred office is as nothing, the

---

[1] These are such bold misrepresentations of polemical history, that I must quote the very passage to which I refer, lest I should seem to be inventing myself. "Tandem disserendo perveniunt ad celeberrimam illam de baptismo controversiam, in qua non parva hæreticorum aut schismaticorum manus universæ Ecclesiæ bellum indixit, sed insignes ecclesiæ, Africa, Cappadocia, Silicia et finitimæ provinciæ de re longe gravissima cum aliis ecclesiis decertarunt. Etsi autem in ipso dissentionis incendio luctuosa rerum facies extitit; tamen ex commodis, quæ in Ecclesiam ex hac controversia fluxerunt, facile perspicitur eam Christo providente et dispensante natam fuisse, non solum ut res tanti momenti conflato et conspiranti omnium consensu aliquando firmaretur, sed etiam ut haberent posteri quid in ejusmodi dissentioribus imitarentur. Nam baptismi hæreticorum defensores fraternæ caritatis fœdus non ruperunt cum iis, a quibus maximam sacramentis injuriam fieri videbant; isti autem et cum iis quos ne baptismo quidem initiatos putabant, et cum iis qui baptismum morientibus infantibus denegare, et Eucharistiam non baptizatis porrigere videbantur, communicare non dubitarunt." *Vita Sancti Cypriani, Opera Ben. Ed.* p. cviii.

ministers of such sectaries, except in the instances comparatively few in which they have been in their own persons seceders from the Church, and betrayers of her orders, are *simply laymen;* or rather *less than laymen*, notwithstanding their assumed titles. The controversy now therefore is very different from what it was in Cyprian's days, when every schism and heresy maintained a succession of ministers, validly, though not canonically, ordained. Though the sectaries of that age lived in heresy and in schism, as unthinkingly as any do now, yet were they in respect of a valid ministry in a very different position; and they at least assumed, whether justly or no, a higher position.

Upon the subject of Lay-baptism, to which this branch of the controversy in part resolves itself, I would refer to Bingham's very learned scholastical treatise on that question. Bingham has exhausted the subject, so far as the collection of authorities is concerned.

## CHAPTER XVII.

Valerian instigated by Macrianus to Persecute the Church.—Death of Stephen :—And election of Sixtus.—St Cyprian summoned before the Proconsul :—His Confession :—His Banishment :—His Vision.—Dionysius of Alexandria also Banished.—Cyprian recalled to Carthage by Galerius Maximus.—He retires for a short time when summoned to Utica.—He returns to Carthage, and is brought before the Proconsul.—His Examination,—Sentence,—and Death.

THE external peace of the Church, which left opportunity for these internal discords, was disturbed, before they were well hushed. Valerian had been hitherto most friendly to the Christians, many of whom had been admitted even within the precincts of the palace : but now, at the instigation of his minister Macrianus, a man equally superstitious in his paganism and barbarous in its support, Valerian became a persecutor, and issued decrees to the several parts of his empire, for the suppression of Christianity.

The first edict of Valerian savoured almost as much of his own lenience, as of the ferocity of Macrianus, by which it was extorted; for the assembling of the Christians in their churches and cemeteries, and not the mere profession of the Christian faith, was necessary to bring them within the meaning of the imperial Edict; and the laity were suffered to depart unpunished even from their assemblies, and no greater pain than banishment was inflicted on the Bishops and Priests who presided in the religious assemblies of the Christians. All that we certainly know of the results of the first Edict of Valerian, accords with this representation of its comparative mildness. We should therefore for the present admit very cautiously supposed proofs of the martyrdom of any Christian however eminent; and we need not hesitate to express a conviction, that Stephen, Bishop of Rome, who died on the second of August, anno 557, long before any appearance of additional severity in the decrees of Valerian, and of the manner of whose death we have no authentic accounts, died a natural death, and not by decollation, as has been pretended.

On the twenty-fourth of the same month, Sixtus was elected to fill the Chair of Stephen;[1] and in the following month (September, 557) the imperial Edict reached Carthage, where Paternus was Proconsul; and Cyprian, as the most prominent in character and office among the Christians, was the first to be summoned before the heathen tribunal.[2] Of what passed on that occasion, we have a circumstantial record in the acts of St Cyprian, Bishop and Martyr.

"The most sacred Emperors, Valerianus and Gallienus, have honoured me with their commands," said Paternus, " to exact of those, who worship not the Gods of Rome, a due recognition of the Roman rites. I would examine you therefore concerning your name and profession:[3] what is your

[1] Were it not that St Augustine, who was most favourably situated for acquiring a knowledge of the subject, and whose argument greatly requires it, is wholly silent on the subject of a reconciliation between the Roman and Carthaginian Churches; and were it not that all ecclesiastical historians are equally silent on the same subject, I should be inclined to suppose, that, under the Pontificate of Sixtus, full peace, though not perfect agreement of opinion, was restored between the Churches of Rome and Africa: for now we find the communication with Cyprian, which had been forcibly interrupted by Stephen, restored, apparently, to its previous friendly terms; and Pontius, the panegyrist of Cyprian, gives to Sixtus the very significant character of a "*good and pacific Prelate.*" To Pontius, who viewed everything and every person only as an accessory to the one object of his veneration, this marked praise could scarce seem due to any, who had not fully acknowledged the communion, and justly appreciated the conduct, of St Cyprian. Nothing, however, can more strongly indicate the absolute want of all *evidence* of this desired reconciliation, than the way in which St Augustine speaks of it as in itself likely, though he ventures not even to insinuate a proof that it was effected.

[2] *Ep.* lxviii. p. 161.

[3] "*Exquisivi ergo de nomine tuo.*" The answer of Cyprian shows that

answer?" "*I am a Christian,*" said Cyprian, "*and a Bishop. I know no other Gods but that One only and true God, who made heaven and earth, the sea and all that therein is. Him do we Christians serve: Him night and day do we supplicate for ourselves, for all men, and for the preservation of the Emperors themselves.*" Paternus asked; "Do you persist in this determination?" Cyprian replied; "*A good determination, taken up in the knowledge of God, is unchangeable.*" "Are you ready, then," said the Proconsul, "according to the Edict of Valerian and Gallienus, to be exiled to the City of Curubis?" "*I am ready,*" said Cyprian.

Then the Proconsul, having thus received the profession of Cyprian, and appointed the place of his banishment, endeavoured to extort from him the names of others who were obnoxious to the same sentence. "My commission extends," said he, "not only to the Bishops, but also to the Presbyters of your party: I ask you then, who are the Presbyters in the city?" The Bishop replied, "*Your laws have well provided against the abuse of informers; in obedience to them I refuse to betray my brethren: they may be found, however, in their own places.*" "But I will know who they are now, and in this place," said Paternus. Cyprian said, "*It is equally contrary to the discipline of their order, and to the spirit of your laws, that they should expose themselves unforced: yet they may be found by you, if you do but seek them out.*" Paternus said, "They shall be found out; for I have commanded that none shall hold assemblies anywhere, nor enter your cemeteries; and if any venture to disobey this wholesome provision, they shall suffer death." Cyprian replied: "*Obey the orders which you have received.*"[1]

Thus as a good Bishop, worthy of his pre-eminence, did Cyprian take the lead in that confession which was required something more than his *name* was included in the question *de nomine*. Perhaps if we had ventured to descend to a phrase, it might be rendered, "*your denomination.*"

[1] The personal history of Cyprian is now entirely derived from the acts of his martyrdom, and from his life by Pontius, and this notice will preclude the necessity of more minute references.

of his flock; sounding the trumpet with no uncertain sound, to call the soldiers of the faith to the combat; and receiving in his own person the first assaults of the enemy, while he marshalled his willing followers in the rear.[1]

There was nothing of gratuitous severity in the sentence of Cyprian, nor in the manner in which it was executed. Curubis,[2] to which place he was banished, was agreeable and healthy in its situation; and the house which was allotted to him was deficient in no comfort which an exiled Bishop could desire. His friends too, among whom was Pontius, his deacon and his future panegyrist, were permitted to accompany him; and his fame having preceded him to the place of exile, the people received him with respect, and continued, so long as he remained there, to treat him with affection. Such comforts had God mercifully provided for his faithful servant, just fresh from his confession, and hastening rapidly to his martyrdom: though, as Pontius piously remarks, it was impossible that exile, to whatsoever place, could be punishment to such an one as Cyprian; or that he could be alone, whose God was with him at all times, and under all circumstances.

And if Cyprian was happy in the place of his banishment, not less happy was Curubis in its illustrious guest. Cyprian was less injured, than Curubis was benefitted by the sentence of Paternus: for whithersoever the confessor was sent, He for whose sake he was an exile accompanied him. For Christ, who said, *Lo, I am with you always, even to the end of the world*, received him as a member of his own body, whithersoever the fury of the enemy drove him. Oh, the blindness of a heathen persecutor! If thou wouldest find a place which shall be a place of exile to a Christian, find one if thou canst from whence Christ can first be banished![3] If thou wouldest

---

[1] *Ep.* lxxviii. The Martyrs to Cyprian.

[2] "A free and maritime city of Zeugitania, in a pleasant situation, a fertile territory, and at the distance of about forty miles from Carthage." Gibbon's *Decline and Fall*, ch. xvi.

[3] Vid. Augustini *Sermo*, cccix. *In Natali Cypriani Martyris*, vol. viii. p. 1247.

not that the Christian faith should be propagated, drive not
the confessors from their homes, for they are heralds of
Christ's kingdom whithersoever they go! [1]

The exiled confessor arrived at Curubis on the fourteenth
of September; and on the first night of his residence there
he saw one of those visions of which he often speaks. I shall
follow Pontius in putting the relation into the mouth of
Cyprian himself.

"I was not yet perfectly asleep, when there appeared to
me a youth of gigantic stature, who seemed to lead me away
to the prætorium, and to place me at last before the judgment-
seat of the Proconsul. He, so soon as he beheld me, began
to write my sentence, which I did not see, upon his tables;
but he did not put to me any of the usual interrogatories.
An attendant, however, who stood behind, looking on him
as he wrote, read the whole sentence; and since he was not
able to speak in that presence, he made me acquainted by
signs of what was written. For with outstretched arm and
open hand, he imitated the stroke of the executioner, so that I
understood, as well as if I had seen the words, that the
sentence was recorded for my death. I began therefore to
pray earnestly for a short respite, though it were but for a day,
that I might arrange my affairs; and after I had often repeated this petition, the judge again began to write on his
tables. I knew not what he wrote, yet I judged from the
mildness of his aspect that he had been moved by my just
request: and the young man, who had before made me acquainted with the sentence, now informed me, by the same
method of signs, that my petition for a day's respite was
granted. Although I had not actually read the sentence, I
received this intimation of delay with a joyful heart; yet still
I trembled so much with the fear that I had mistaken the
interpretation of the latter sign, that my heart beat more
quickly for a long time."

This vision of St Cyprian was interpreted by the event,
when a year after, a day being taken for a year in the pre-

[1] See Acts viii. 4.

figurative indication of his vision, he was beheaded in pursuance of the sentence of the Proconsul Galerius Maximus.

Paternus, the Proconsul at Carthage, seems to have acted upon his determination of searching for the Presbyters, according to the imperial edict; for we find intimations of their being brought to confession, before the renewed and more severe provisions for the persecution were promulgated. At any rate in Numidia the Bishops of the Church were treated with less clemency than Cyprian had experienced. They were beaten with clubs, and their faith not being subdued by this brutality, they were fettered, and sent in separate companies to the mines. This we learn from Cyprian's letter of congratulation to them on their sufferings and constancy; in which he modestly postpones his own confession to theirs, and acknowledging the comparative ease of his banishment, speaks of his communion with them in suffering being rather that of a Christian fellowship and love than of actual endurance. They in their turn confess the dignity with which the priority of his confession in point of time, as well as the eminence of his character and station, invested his exile for the cause of Christ. The answers of the confessors to Cyprian are from three separate places, which is the only intimation that we have of the separation of those who were still one in faith, in sufferings, and in religious fellowship. Nothing can be more remarkable than the total absence of all querulous allusions to their sufferings in these letters of the persecuted confessors. If the tale of the sufferings had been left to be gathered from their own Epistles, written in the bitterest of their afflictions, and after some had even fallen a victim to the rigour of the punishment, we should have had no horrors to relate, so greatly do the consolations and high hopes of their condition outweigh in their own expressions the pains and the terrors of their situation: and so entirely do their Christian humility and love obliterate every trace of pride and selfishness from the record of their feelings, that we should almost suppose that the sufferings of every other person whom they mention were greater and more meritorious than theirs.

In other parts of the world the Christian name was followed with like persecution. We shall here mention the sufferings of those only of whom we have already had occasion to speak. At Alexandria, Dionysius was summoned before Æmilius the Prefect, with Maximus a Priest, Faustus, Eusebius, and Chæremon, Deacons, and a Roman Christian, then at Alexandria. These persons were his companions in a noble confession, and also in his banishment to the confines of Lybia. The place of his exile was less pleasant than that to which Cyprian had been sent just before; but, like Cyprian, Dionysius carried with him a blessing, which consoled him in his banishment, and abounded also to the benefit of those among whom his lot was cast. "God," says he, "has opened to us in this place a way for the preaching of His word. At first we were received with execrations, and pelted with stones; but afterwards many Pagans renounced their idolatry, and they are now enrolled among the faithful." Eventually this illustrious Prelate and his companions were still farther separated; but wherever the place of their banishment was appointed, and however it was changed, still the same blessings followed their step; for God was with them.[1]

At Rome, Sixtus and four deacons with him,[2] who were engaged in celebrating divine worship in a cemetery, were seized and put to death.[3] This was on the sixth of August; and

[1] See Euseb. vii., xi.  [2] *Ep.* lxxxii. p. 165.
[3] Gibbon, in the sixteenth chapter of his "Decline and Fall," desiring to extenuate the dangers which beset the Christian name under the heathen emperors, remarks, "The experience of the life of Cyprian is sufficient to prove, that our fancy has exaggerated the perilous situation of a Christian Bishop; and that the dangers to which he was exposed were less imminent than those which temporal ambition is always prepared to encounter in the pursuit of honours. Four Roman Emperors, with their families, their favourites, and their adherents, perished by the sword in the space of ten years, during which the Bishop of Carthage guided by his authority and eloquence the counsels of the African Church." Gibbon knew, but he thought perhaps that his less learned readers knew not, or would not remember, that during the same space, *four Roman Bishops* also had perished for the faith, or, if we allow the reports of Stephen's martyrdom,

was among the first effects of a far severer edict which Valerian had just issued. Of these events at Rome we are informed by a letter of Cyprian to Successus, his brother in the Episcopate, and we are thus called back to the few remaining personal acts of Cyprian.

Cyprian had been eleven months in his exile at Curubis, and in the interval Galerius Maximus had succeeded Aspasius Paternus in the Proconsulate. The new Proconsul recalled Cyprian from his banishment, though not for any purposes of mercy; but rather, in all probability, that he might be more entirely within his power. He was allowed, however, to reside in "his gardens;" of which we have before spoken, as the place where he probably wrote his Epistle to Donatus, and as a part of the possessions which he sold, at his conversion, for the benefit of the poorer brethren: this residence was now restored to him by the providence of God; and though he would again, had he followed his own inclination, have converted it into alms, he was deterred from his charitable purpose by the fear of exciting popular jealousy.[1]

The interest with which every breath of news from Rome would be received by the Christians, situated as they now were, may be well imagined. Cyprian took effectual measures to receive authentic information, and in the letter to Successus, to which we before alluded, he conveys the following intelligence: that Valerian[2] had directed his rescript to the Senate, in which it was decreed, that Bishops, Priests, and Deacons should be condemned by a summary process; but that Senators, and other men of noble rank, should be deprived of their dignity, and should forfeit their goods; and that if they still persisted in the Christian faith, having already forfeited the privilege of rank, they too should be capitally

*five*. The comparison if fairly made will not answer Gibbon's purpose, even though he could persuade us to cast out of the reckoning this very important consideration; that the ambitious competitor for the purple meets a soldier's death as one of the probable consequences of his career; while violence must turn aside from its appointed course to meet the Christian Bishop, whose profession is peace.

[1] Pontius.  [2] He was then in his Persian expedition.

punished. That the possessions of matrons should be forfeited, and themselves banished; and that any of the officers of the royal household who either then professed, or had professed before, the name of Christ, should suffer fine and confiscation, and be sent in chains to the imperial possessions.

To this rescript Valerian had subjoined the form of his letters to the several governors of provinces, directing them in their proceedings against the Church. The arrival of these imperial instructions at Carthage he daily expected; and, with the intrepid faith of one who knew in whom he believed, even desired. With the example of Sixtus before him, with his knowledge that the heathen officers were determined to carry out their instructions to the utmost, he lived in constant expectation of martyrdom; and only intent on meeting death in a proper manner, his conversation turned more entirely than ever on divine things, and he desired that his end, if it might be, should find him discoursing concerning God.

He had yet, however, more than a month's respite: for Galerius Maximus retiring for a while to Utica, there received the imperial mandates. He sent presently an officer to bring Cyprian to Utica, but the holy Bishop determined on suffering in that place where his blood would most effectually witness to the truths which his lips had spoken; and where his death might most benefit the flock which he had faithfully guarded during his life. He retired therefore from Carthage, not to avoid his end, but intending to return so soon as the Proconsul should proceed thither in person. From this his retirement he wrote his last letter to the Clergy and people of his flock, explaining to them the motive which actuated him in the present instance, and exhorting them, as circumstances might demand, to maintain a like prudent courage and constancy. "Do you, my dearest brethren, according to the divine rules which you have ever heard from me, possess your souls in quietness and peace; neither exciting any tumult among the brethren, nor exposing yourselves voluntarily to the Gentiles. But when you are apprehended and delivered up, then speak: and the Lord himself shall speak in you;

who would rather that we should confess His name with constancy, than profess it rashly. We will consult together, the Lord directing us, as to the course which I myself ought to pursue, when I shall be called to my confession before the Proconsul. And now, my dearest brethren, may the Lord graciously keep you and preserve you in His Church, of His abundant mercy."[1]

It fares ill with the reputation of the wisest and best men, when those who cannot appreciate their wisdom, and have no sympathy with their goodness, are their self-constituted judges. Cyprian has on this occasion, and on account of his former retirement, been accused of cowardice; though, had he acted otherwise than he did, he might have been justly accused of rashness and folly. If the Christians, excited into an irrepressible enthusiasm, courted martyrdom too earnestly, they were wrong; and though they may well be forgiven, the very laws of the Christian Church were their accusers: if they yielded even to the most excruciating tortures, they were punished as apostates then, and now they are despised as cowards: but if with Cyprian, consulting the peace of the community, and the good of the Church;—if with Cyprian, obeying the spirit and the very letter of the divine precepts; —if with Cyprian, pursuing a course which they were never ashamed to vindicate and to recommend to others, and in which their own conscience acquitted them of cowardice, as decidedly as the world acquitted them of rashness;—if thus, with Cyprian, they retired from the violence of persecution while they might do so with honour, to present themselves again to its fiercest assaults when it was required of them for the good of the Church, surely they ought to escape every censure and every sneer.

And the event shows, that Cyprian was not more deficient in courage than in wisdom; for no sooner did the Proconsul return to Carthage, than Cyprian also came back to his Gardens, and there awaited the summons to confession and death. Nor was his expectation long delayed; for on the

[1] *Ep.* lxxxiii. p. 166.

thirteenth of September, two officers of the court suddenly came to demand his appearance before Maximus, at a place called Sextus, about six miles from Carthage, where Maximus was residing for his health. These officers placed him between them[1] in a chariot, and thus conveyed him, under guard, to the Proconsul, who remanded him for final examination till the next day.

The report soon spread through Carthage, that Thascius was apprehended, and crowds assembled to witness the spectacle; melancholy even to the Gentiles, for the honour in which Cyprian was held, but glorious to the Christians on

[1] St Augustine (Sermo cccix. vol. viii. p. 1248,) finds a parallel here between Cyprian and our blessed Lord crucified between two thieves; " Christus namque inter duos latrones ligno suspensus, ad exemplum patientiæ præbebatur; Cyprianus autem inter duos apparitores, ad passionem cum portatus Christi vestigia sequebatur." Such a parallel will seem too bold to some persons; but the truth is, that we cannot judge of such things, without entering into the spirit of those who write them. As a portion of a laboured and merely rhetorical eulogium on St Cyprian, uttered by one who used sacred things as if they were so far only valuable as they added a splendour to his composition, such a passage would be even impious: but from the lips of one who was instinctively alive to every sacred association, and valued it for its own sake; coming warm from the heart of one who believed with St Paul, that the sufferings of the saints filled up in their bodies what was behind of the sufferings of Christ, and who knew that to live in Christ was to take up our cross and follow Him;—from such an one, and such was St Augustine, it is the expression of a chastened piety, and ought to excite no emotion of disgust.

In writing these remarks, I have had in view the objections which some have made against the implied parallel between our blessed Lord and Saviour in His sufferings, and the Royal Martyr King Charles, of whom our Church worthily boasts, in his misfortunes and martyrdom, which seems to be recognised in the Church service for the thirtieth of January. Judging the Church which has appointed that service by the same rules which I have suggested for judging St Augustine, (and surely this is not claiming too much,) the reason will not condemn, and the heart will certainly applaud. If the reader would see an example of that sort of parallel between the Saviour and the Saint (so called) which I have before denounced as impious, he may refer to the British Critic, No. xlix. p. 178, for an extract from a Sermon at the dedication of a chapel to Ignatius Loyola, in the Cathedral of Bologna.

account of the devoted constancy of the Martyr.  During his short respite, Cyprian was guarded, but with no unnecessary rigour, in the house of an officer of the court, and the visits of his friends were freely permitted; while the crowds of persons without, testified their respect and affection by watching the whole night in the street; thus keeping, as it were, the vigil of their Bishop's glorious nativity.  Nor was the composure of Cyprian so disturbed, either by his own situation, or by the expression of sympathy by his people, as to prevent his taking such charge of them as his circumstances permitted; for he gave especial orders for the protection of the women, who were thus exposed, by their affectionate solicitude for him, to the fatigue and dangers of a night-watch.

At length the glorious day of his martyrdom dawned, and he was conveyed to the residence of the Proconsul, still accompanied by his affectionate children in the faith. On his way he had to traverse the Stadium; a happy circumstance, observes Pontius, and as it would seem providential, that he who was to receive his crown, should pass over the place of conflict on his way to it. When he arrived at the Prætorium, the Proconsul had not yet taken his seat on the tribunal; he was permitted therefore to retire to a less public place, and there, hot and tired with his journey, he reclined upon a seat which had been accidentally left covered with a linen cloth; so that in the very article of his passion, he was not without some insignia of his sacred function.[1]  One of the guard, who had formerly been a Christian, offered him a change of vestments, purposing to keep the garments of the Martyr as a valuable relic; but Cyprian rejected the proffered luxury, observing on the folly of too solicitous a use of remedies for those evils which can last but for a day.

At length Galerius Maximus assumed his place in the judgment-hall, and Cyprian being brought before him, he said,

---

[1] The remark is that of Pontius.  "Sedile autem erat fortuito linteo tectum, ut et sub ictu passionis episcopatus, honore frueretur." This may, perhaps, be but a puerile conceit of Pontius; but it is valuable as a record of the use of clerical vestments and distinctions in that age.

"Art thou Thascius Cyprian?" Cyprian answered, "*I am.*" "Art thou he," said Maximus, "who hath borne the highest offices of their religion, among the Christians?" "*Yes,*" answered the Bishop. "The most sacred Emperors have commanded that you offer sacrifice," said the Proconsul. "*I will not offer sacrifice,*" replied Cyprian. "Be persuaded," said the Proconsul, "for your own sake." Cyprian replied, "*Do thou as thou hast received orders: for me, in so just a cause, no persuasion can move me.*"

Maximus, having consulted with his assessors, pronounced the following sentence with much emotion. "Thou hast long lived in impiety and hast made thyself the centre of a band of pestilent conspirators; thou hast acted as an enemy to the gods and to the sacred laws of Rome: neither the pious and most august princes Valerianus and Gallienus, nor the most noble Cæsar Valerian, have been able to recall you to a dutiful adherence to their religion. Since then thou art convicted as the author and instigator of so many iniquities, thou shalt become an example to those whom thou hast seduced: the authority of the law shall be vindicated by thy blood." After these words he pronounced the sentence from his tablet, "LET THASCIUS CYPRIAN BE BEHEADED."

"*Thanks be to God!*" said Cyprian: and the crowd of Christians who surrounded him exclaimed, "Let us die with him!"

The holy martyr was then led away, followed by a great concourse of people, to an open field near the place where he had received his sentence; and having put off the rest of his garments, and committed them to the Deacons, he first prostrated himself in prayer to God, and then stood in his inner vestments prepared for the fatal stroke. The executioner, who stood trembling at the office he had to perform, was animated by his encouragement. He tied the bandage over his eyes with his own hands; and that he might owe that office to friends which he could not himself perform, Julian a Presbyter, and a Subdeacon of the same name, bound his hands. To the executioner he appropriated a gift of twenty-five pieces of gold: the Christians, whose avarice was not mercenary, sought no other memorials than handkerchiefs dyed with the blood of their Bishop. The body was for a while exposed to the gaze of the heathen; but having been removed by night by the brethren, it was buried in the Mappalian Way. Two Churches afterwards marked the spots which had been consecrated by his death and by his burial.[1] The anniversary of his death was long observed; and five sermons of St Augustine, preached on this festival, still remain as memorials of the martyr Cyprian.

Thus died Thascius Cæcilius Cyprian, with a courage too common in those days to excite our surprise, but of such intrinsic merit as to demand our admiration. He was the first Bishop of Carthage who had attained to the crown of martyrdom; and he was truly worthy of this high distinction. Few men have more forcibly arrested the affections of their associates; few have more powerfully influenced the opinions of others; none have been more honoured by posterity. The wish which broke from the tumultuous assembly at his condemnation, *To die with him*, was uttered afterwards coolly and solemnly by his Deacon Pontius: but his widowed Church rather lamented her own misfortune than his; and soon learned to glory in his crown more than she lamented her own loss. His name was long a household word with the Church which he had governed, and even the heathen paid to his memory the tribute of respect.

Neither Carthage nor Africa set bounds to his influence or to his fame. Prudentius says of him,

> Disserit, eloquitur, tractat, docet, instruit, prophetat,
> Nec Libiæ populos tantum regit; exit usque in ortum
> Solis, et usque obitum: Gallos fovet, imbuit Britannos,
> Præsidet Hesperiæ, Christum serit ultimis Hiberis.

And to this day, whenever any party can claim the support of

---

[1] One of these Churches was the scene of an affecting incident in the early life of St Augustine. See his Confessions, V. viii. with the note p. 75, of the Oxford translation.

Cyprian's authority, the claim is made with a confidence which sufficiently determines its value.

But perhaps the most marked indication of the deserved respect in which the name of Cyprian is held, is its place in the Roman Calendar: not because this is itself a proof of peculiar sanctity, but because it is extorted in the present instance by the voice of the Church, antecedent to the corruptions of Rome, and because here whatever is specifically Romish, has been forced to yield to that which is truly Catholic. The works of Cyprian are a strong protest against the arrogant pretensions of the Bishop and Church of Rome: his theology, like that of every primitive Bishop was opposed to the present system: circumstances even placed him in direct collision with Rome; his whole energies were exerted for a long while in opposition to the dogma of a Pope and his Clergy; and he died under what would now be called excommunication by Rome, though then indeed his position had no such character. And yet St Cyprian, though such an one as would now be anathematised without compunction and without mercy by his Holiness of Rome, is worshipped by the Churches of his obedience as a saint: for his title to be enrolled among the saints was already determined by the general voice of Christendom; and Rome, when she departed from his theology, and deserted all his favourite principles, could not afford to repudiate his name.

THE END.

In compliance with current copyright law, Heckman-ICI/PA produced this replacement volume on acid free paper to replace the irreparably deteriorated original.

2006

www.ingramcontent.com/pod-product-compliance
Lightning Source LLC
Chambersburg PA
CBHW031338230426
43670CB00006B/373